SPORT, ACTIVE LEISURE
AND YOUTH CULTURES

Editors:

Jayne Caudwell
and Peter Bramham

LSA

LSA Publication No. 86

Sport, Active Leisure and Youth Cultures

First published in 2005 by
Leisure Studies Association
The Chelsea School
University of Brighton
Eastbourne BN20 7SP (UK)

A catalogue record for this book
is available from the British Library.

ISBN: 0 906337 97 6

Layout, cover and typesetting by Myrene L. McFee

Cover photograph:
Grateful thanks are expressed to Marcus Österberg
for permission to adapt his original photograph.

Printed in the UK by
Antony Rowe Ltd, Eastbourne

Contents

Cover art:
Grateful thanks are expressed to Marcus Österberg
for permission to adapt his original photograph.

EDITORS' INTRODUCTION: SPORT, ACTIVE LEISURE AND YOUTH CULTURES

One starting point for making sense of young people and leisure, given frequent expressions of concern by governments and public, is to revisit the ideas of Stanley Cohen, writing in the early 1970s, and in particular his concepts of moral panics and folk devils. Drawing on American symbolic interactionists, and in particular labeling perspectives on deviance, he highlighted the role of mass media in defining and stigmatizing categories of youth. In this context, there is public orchestration of moral outrage and social reaction against troublesome and disorderly youth.

In later work, Cohen and Young (1981) map out the complex and select-ive processes involved as journalists manufacture 'news' and newsworthy stories. News narratives simplify, trivialise, personalise and dramatise young people's leisure so that stories become morality tales where the good are rewarded, the weak are saved and evil is duly exposed and punished. As a result, young people provide a rich reservoir of potential stories for the general public to take interest in and tales for media to circulate. So mass media always have this proclivity to define youth as a problem, as a new generation of 'folk devils' who live unhealthy lifestyles – they eat fast foods, they drink alcohol, they smoke, they take recreational drugs, they have unprotected sex, and stay fixed on television, the internet and video games. Consequently, young people are often accused of slipping into a life of excess which appears at an ever younger age, as current newspapers bemoan the fact that 9–12 year olds have started to adopt consumption patterns previously attributed to and associated with 'teenagers': 'tweenies' now are mini adults with mobile phones, bank accounts and a penchant for shopping. Further, when it comes to adopting healthy adult lifestyles, most young people resist physical activity such as playing sport, working out through fitness and exercise regimes, cycling to school, or even taking part in any kind of outdoor recreational activities and adventure.

Mass media have a crucial role in setting political agendas that define youth behaviour as throwing up (metaphorically and literally) problems which cry out for policy solutions. Heated debates about underage alcohol abuse amongst teenagers and 'binge drinking' amongst young adults, particularly students, provide clear examples of current media outrage, precisely at a time when government in the UK seeks to liberalise licensing laws. It seems that lessons from nation states elsewhere, such as Ireland, are not just ignored but rather cast as myopic or irrelevant. The real costs and benefits of twenty-four hour licensing on health and public disorder seem distorted or suppressed by powerful interests from the brewing and entertainment industries, eagerly supported by local chambers of commerce, local government and even police authorities. The government knows best, insofar as it can point to the need to liberalise drinking times and simultaneously showcase legislative measures to deal with particular problems should they arise. Consequently, in 1998 the New Labour government first introduced Anti-Social Behaviour Orders (ASBOs), the legislation gives police powers to disperse youths in groups and deal with troublesome behaviours in residential neighbourhoods, inner-city communities and city-centres.

One would expect social scientists and leisure scholars to cast a critical light over claims from both government and mass media about the changing nature of youth, physical activity and their leisure lifestyles. Firstly, social scientific research should, at the very least, be able to contextualise issues and moral panics that absorb the mass media, so as to provide historical commentary and social analysis of contemporary youth and leisure networks. Secondly, one would expect detailed empirical research and data to ground generalised claims about modern youth leisure lifestyles and highlight the diversity of youth experiences and identities in what postmodernists claim as 'new times'. Thirdly, one expects some semblance of value freedom in recognising the need to engage with a diversity of ideological traditions and policy positions in youth policy and practices.

It is with these issues in mind that readers should approach this collection of papers, all originally presented at the July 2004 Leisure Studies Association Conference "Active Leisure and Young People", at Leeds Metropolitan University. The conference identified several major themes: Policy and Provision; Engagement and Participation; Alienation and Subculture; Health; Risk; Environment; and finally Consumption. Companion volumes (Flintoff,

Long and Hylton, 2005; Hylton, Long and Flintoff, 2005) focus on papers concerned with participation and evaluation, and policy issues. This collection explores legislation and risk-taking behaviour, examines the social construction of gendered and sexualised youth identities and reviews the problematic nature of youth and youth cultures.

The first part of the volume contains papers that share two common themes of adventure and risk-taking behaviour amongst youth. Ulrich Beck's writings have argued coherently that risk and uncertainty are central components and permanent features of everyday life in contemporary society. Public policy has only a tenuous grasp of the complex processes in natural and social worlds, as decision makers rarely understand the impacts and consequences of policies and plans. Legal processes become more complex, giving rise to what some commentators refer to as a 'blame culture' with individuals and organisations living in the shadow of the ever-present threat of litigation.

In the first contribution, **Brian Simpson** starts with the UN Convention on the Rights of a Child that includes a right to leisure, play and participation. He then proceeds to trace their possible expression in two recent documents – one by the Children's Play Council (2004) and the other, the DCMS Review, *Serious about Play*. However, adults often define children's play as anti-social behaviour and, for example, demand that skateboarding in cities should be contained, regulated and subject to adult supervision, with safety paramount. Inspired by the work of Bach (1993), Simpson argues that children's play generates spontaneous informal sporting-like activities and children should have a legal right to flexible risk-taking spaces and be actively involved in deciding access, design and location. Drawing on Fusty (2000) he argues that city spaces are increasingly commodified, privatised and corporatised, yet those engaged in play — e.g. buskers, skaters and street theatre artists — refuse to disappear from the urban scene.

John Hunter-Jones' paper starts with the observation that school trips require teacher and parent volunteering and the risk of injury is ever present. He raises the issue of how UK teachers and schools are responding to potential liability and discusses the Cabinet Office's (2004) assessment of the impact of a compensation culture given that UK schools in 2004 paid out £200 million in compensation. He then briefly outlines elements of criminal and civil law and the legal concept of 'duty of care'. Trips and resultant prosecutions relate historically to the Health and Safety at Work Act (1974) and its demand that reasonable and practical steps are taken to avoid risks. He provides commentary on some important cases which caught the attention of national media, and the chapter concludes with a survey, limited by low response rate, of schools in the Manchester and Cheshire area.

In the next paper, **Arnold Grossman** draws on his own substantial research, entitled 'The Q & A Project', into lesbian, gay and bi-sexual youth in New York, to explore their risk-taking behaviour as it relates to substance abuse. He and colleagues recruited a large sample of LGB youth (ss=528) who were party to three separate interviews over a two-year period (June 1999 to December 2001). The importance of the study is not only its sample size but also the battery of psychological research instruments deployed in health questionnaires around indices of mental health, anxiety, self-identity and self-loathing. The paper focuses specifically on interview and questionnaire responses in relation to recreational substance use – alcohol consumption, marijuana and 'party drug' use, while regression analysis on the test scores was used to relate drug use to stress, trauma, depression, social problems, attention problems and rule-breaking behaviour. Interestingly, the measured variables accounted for a third of variance in substance use. In discussion towards the end of the chapter, Grossman argues that adolescence is a period of experimentation and LGB youth have the pressing identity problem of whether to pass as 'normal' or to 'come out'. In keeping with Goffman's groundbreaking analysis in Stigma (1968), LGB youth face unique stressors in relation to homonegativity and fears of disclosure.

Risk and adventure tourism provide the experiential context of **Shelagh Ferguson and Sarah Todd**'s paper on bungee jumping in Queenstown, New Zealand. But as the title of the paper 'Cool Consumption' implies, her primary focus is on consumer behaviour and the ways in which young people define and value 'cool' and being seen as 'cool'. Coolness is characterized by a lack of display of strong emotions yet functions both as a strong motivator and as an expression of distinctive style. The paper proceeds with an overview of conventional wisdom about consumer choice, branding, status and conspicuous consumption. However, Ferguson suggests an informed sociological approach would be more fruitful, one that recognises the distinctive cultural characteristics of 'generation Y' (15-30 year olds), paying close attention to the importance of subcultural tastes and to ways in which young people refer to consumption networks. At the end of the chapter, preliminary findings are summarised of interviews with almost 100 bungee jumpers, reflecting on being 'cool' as they share experiences and provide narratives for both friendship and family networks, usually within a couple of hours of completing the eight-second jump, which costs £100 for the experience, photographs and a video.

Part Two explores the importance of gendered and sexualised identities to young people's leisure. In the first paper, the definitive management of gender identity is the focus of **Ruth Jeanes'** ethnographic research into a small group of girls aged 10–11 years. She explores "what they perceive 'gender' to mean, what they see as being stereotypical gender assumptions, and how they fit within the gender discourses they describe". Inspired by postmodern arguments, Jeanes explores the girls' multiple conceptions of femininity and how playing a sport such as football [what Bryson (1990) defines as one of the flagships of hegemonic masculinity] can be reconciled with notions of femininity. The paper explores the extreme categories of 'tomboy' and 'girlie girl' from interview data and focus groups, prompted by magazine images and a story of a girl footballer. What follows are rich conversations about girls' experiences, including this extraordinary exchange between the researcher and a primary schoolgirl:

> Ruth: "Why is it not important for girls to play football?"
> Anna: "Because it is not in their social stereotypes, their feminine
> list they should be doing in modern contemporary culture [giggle]."

Jeanes lucidly concludes that three major themes of gender identity construction are body shape, image and behaviour, as girls draw upon a variety of available discourses at different times, negotiating football and a feminine identity.

Ian Macdonald also interrogates gender identity in his analysis of representations of the skateboarding body. He maps the shifts in representation of the skateboarder as an "alternative" active body to the commodification of the skater's body and the production of a desirable male masculine body. He is critical of the disciplinary gaze that casts the skater's body as in need of surveillance and discipline, and illustrates how a similar gaze now functions to fetishise the male "Sk8ter Boi" and articulate him as desirable. Drawing on the works of Pierre Bourdieu, Judith Butler and Michel Foucault, Macdonald highlights the ways skaters' bodies are produced and how this production relies on exclusion. For example female skateboarders, the "Skate Betty", struggle for viability and Macdonald evidences how female bodies are produced within the regime of hegemonic masculinity. The paper contributes to and extends existing work on skateboarding (cf. Beal, 1995). Macdonald makes this point in his conclusions:

> While previous research on skateboarding culture has focused on
> its qualities of resistance, this analysis into the construction of gender

identity has shown that the skating body has undergone a process of cultural normalisation and has, to an extent, been removed from its marginal position and been repackaged as part of 'normal' culture.

Ian Wellard's paper resonates with the key themes as he continues to attend to social construction of gendered identities and its relation to sexuality. He focuses on the crucial significance of gendered performances in sport. His respondents are not primary schoolboys but a range of adult men who are encouraged by his research to reflect upon their experiences of childhood sport and physical activity. The men interviewed belong to both mainstream and gay tennis clubs and many describe their experiences of bodily shame, of being less active, less able to participate in comparison to 'real' men. In Wellard's own words:

> A significant aspect of their interpretation of the body was formed in conjunction with readings of gender and sexuality where femininity and gayness were equated with weakness and passivity.

Hegemonic masculinity in sport, or what Wellard has termed exclusive masculinity, is sustained by distinctive bodily performances with the usual outcomes as heterosexual males and their values occupy centre stage in competitiveness, aggression, assertiveness and power. Other forms of masculinities and femininities valued and expressed by others are thereby subordinated and marginalised. Wellard argues that to perform successfully in sport demands the capability to display hegemonic masculinity. Consequently, many young people, both boys and girls, are and will be excluded from sport because of their inability and or resistance to "perform masculinity" in the expected manner.

If one was searching for some recent icons of hegemonic masculinity within UK popular culture one would probably need look no further than men's magazines such as *Nuts* and *Zoo*. **Fiona Jordan and Scott Fleming**'s final paper in this section focuses on making sense of and comparing TV reviews in both magazines. One could only imagine what the tabloid press would say of such an intellectual project by leisure scholars — even more about their reflexive account of their concerns as a feminist woman and an anti-sexist man about buying and (even worse) being seen buying their research materials! But it would be their loss, as the authors offer a brief history of the market for men's magazines drawing on a Mintel Report (2002), a commentary on the crisis in masculinity and the emergence of 'new laddism' in the early 1990s, and literature exploring interrelationships between leisure, sport and media. As regards the construction of gender identities, their content analysis reveals the dominance of "an homogenous, youthful, hegemonic, predominantly white, heterosexual masculinity" in the representations the magazines mediate.

The final section of this volume brings together different interests of three staff working at Leeds Metropolitan University, the host of the conference in July 2004. Although exploring different theoretical questions, all three contributions more or less engage with the problematic of community and shared historical collective experience. This is clearly the case with **Karl Spracklen**'s empirical research, and his long-term interest in rugby league draws upon A. K. Cohen's cultural anthropology and the changing significance of symbolic boundaries. His paper examines the role of the sport in representing northern working-class masculinity and more recent changes due to rugby league development activity, growing rates of participation and issues of sports equity. Having outlined the policy context of Active Sports, the chapter draws upon statistics collected by the London Active Partnership on gender and ethnicity of participants and so provides some comparative data with an earlier research project completed by Leeds Metropolitan University for the Commission of Racial Equality. Spracklen then highlights the continued under-representation of ethnic minorities, particularly Asians, in the game, the virulent persistence of stereotyping of black players and different participation rates between the traditional northern game and those in the development area in London.

The north-south divide plays a central role in **Jack Fawbert**'s telling analysis of contemporary football fandom. Revisiting Phil Cohen's seminal arguments about youth and change in working–class communities, Fawbert challenges the postmodern argument about youth cultures as neo-tribalism, as chosen fragile communal shelters against increased risk and uncertainty. Fawbert's data come from an email survey of 82 Northern Hammers, West Ham United football supporters who now find themselves living in the north. Belonging to a 'proletarian traditionalism' of the East End of London is now no longer possible for a variety of reasons, mostly those of spatial displacement, but as a 'cockney diaspora' travelling to home and away matches, the fans magically recover their roots and communal identity through supporting their football team.

Following Fawbert's case study, **Peter Bramham**'s paper makes a general demand for historically informed social analysis. To attempt to understand young people and successive youth cultures requires that they be placed within age cohorts grounded in their distinctive collective experiences. In broad-brush fashion, Bramham focuses on the "grasshoppers" of the 1960s generation, historically exceptional in their continuing quest for 'liminal' experiences and persistently youthful attitudes. These post-war 'baby boomers' growing up in the 1960s provide sharp contrast with their parents' "ant-like" generation, facing austerity in the 1930s and 1940s, yet dutifully going on to fund social reconstruction and comprehensive state welfarism. Different yet again is the cohort of "butterflies" growing up in the 1980s and 1990s as children of the Thatcher's years, in an era of privatism and individualism while adopting appropriate social values and a commodified culture to match that ethos. In developing each of these three cohorts, Bramham emphasizes the links between youth cultures and their formative socio-historical contexts. He shows that to understand the leisure lifestyles of each generation, it is essential to understand the economic, political, social and cultural formations experienced, since these shape every generation: each cohort lives in the present but must make a future out of resources inherited from the previous parental generation.

The contributions in this volume discuss and analyse youth cultures as they are experienced within sport and active leisure contexts, providing accounts that help illuminate the intricacies and complexities of 'youth' by exploring the ways young people take part in sport and leisure activity. The volume brings together a range of approaches to understanding young people's experiences, and contributors introduce the reader to a variety of contexts, ranging from playgrounds and sports clubs to magazines and fandom. The focus on young people in the media and the emerging concerns as they appear within policy documentation and legislation are open to academic scrutiny.

The papers presented here both document contemporary issues and highlight the importance of a social and cultural analysis of sport and leisure activity. Along with those in the companion volumes [Flintoff, A., Long, J. & Hylton, K. (eds) (2005) *Youth sport and active leisure: Theory, policy and practice*; Hylton, K., Long, J. & Flintoff, A. (eds) (2005) *Evaluating sport and active leisure for young people*] they contribute to a much wider debate.

Peter Bramham
Leeds Metropolitan University

Jayne Caudwell
University of Brighton

References

Bach, L. (1993) 'Sports without facilities: The use of urban space by informal sports', *International Review for Sociology of Sport* Vol. 28, Nos. 2 & 3: pp. 281–295.

Beal, B. (1995) 'Disqualifying the Official: An exploration of social resistance through the subculture of skateboarding', *Sociology of Sport Journal* 12: pp. 252–267.

Bryson, L. (1990) 'Challenges to male hegemony in sport', in Messner, M. and Sabo, D. (eds) *Sport, men and the gender order: Critical feminist perspectives*. Champaign, Illinois: Human Kinetics.

Cabinet Office (2004) *Better regulation task force. Better routes to redress*. London www.brtf.gov.uk.

Cohen, S. and Young, J. (1981) *The manufacture of news*. Harmondsworth: Penguin Books.

Cohen, Stanley (1972) *Moral panics and folk devils*. Harmondsworth: Penguin Books.

Department for Culture Media and Sport (2004) *Getting serious about play: A review of children's play* (March). London: HMSO.

Flintoff, A., Long, J. & Hylton, K. (eds) (2005) *Youth sport and active leisure: Theory, policy and practice* (LSA Publication No. 87). Eastbourne, Leisure Studies Association.

Flusty, S. (2000) 'Thrashing Downtown: Play as resistance to the spatial and representational regulation of Los Angeles', *Cities* Vol. 17, No. 2: pp. 149–158.

Goffman, E. (1968) *Stigma: Notes on the management of spoiled identity*. Harmondsworth: Penguin Books.

Hylton, K., Long, J. & Flintoff, A. (eds) (2005) *Evaluating sport and active leisure for young people* (LSA Publication No. 88). Eastbourne, Leisure Studies Association.

Long, J. Tongue, N. Spracklen, K. and Carrington, B. (1995) *What's the difference?* Leeds, LMU/CRE.

Mintel (2002) *Men's Magazines–UK*. London: Mintel.

About the Contributors

Anthony R. D'Augelli, Ph.D. is Professor of Human Development at The Pennsylvania State University and Professor-in-Charge of the Human Development and Family Studies baccalaureate program. He is the Principal Investigator of a National Institute of Mental Health grant about victimization and mental health among lesbian, gay, and bisexual youth. He is the coeditor of three volumes reviewing psychological research on sexual orientation: Lesbian, Gay, and Bisexual Identities over the Lifespan, Lesbian, Gay and Bisexual Identities in Families, and Lesbian, Gay, and Bisexual Identities and Adolescence, all published by Oxford University Press.

Peter Bramham is an experienced lecturer and researcher who has spent over 30 years in academic life in several Higher Education institutions in the UK. He has published work in conjunction with colleagues in the UK and across Europe and makes conference contributions in the broad 'leisure and sport policy' area. In 2004, he was appointed as a Reader in School of Leisure and Sport Management, Carnegie Faculty of Sport and Education at Leeds Metropolitan University. His research interests include research into Leisure and Sport Policy, History and Social Theory; Globalisation, Leisure, Sport and the City; and Gender Relations and Physical Activity.

Jayne Caudwell lectures at the University of Brighton, Chelsea School, in sport and leisure cultures. She has completed research on women who play football and is particularly interested in issues surrounding gender and sexuality. Her work draws on feminist theories of gender, as well as theories of sexuality and includes a focus on lesbian, gay, bisexual, transgender (LGBT) and queer.

Jack Fawbert worked in construction for many years as a carpenter and joiner before graduating as a mature student with an Honours degree in Economics and Sociology in 1985. Whilst subsequently working as a lecturer in Further Education for many years he gained an MA in Sociology and a Certificate in Education. He then taught Sociology for Anglia Polytechnic University on their Regional Student Scheme before moving to Leeds Metropolitan University as a Senior Lecturer in Sociology in 1998. He now has a Postgraduate Certificate in Research Methodology and will shortly be submitting his PhD thesis. He has recently taken up a new post as a Senior Lecturer in Sociology at De Montfort University. He has previously had articles published in Sociology Review and Social Science Teacher as well as contributing to a previous Leisure Studies Association publication.

Shelagh Ferguson is a Senior Teaching Fellow in the Department of Marketing at Otago University. Shelagh is a recent addition to the Department. Arriving three years ago from the UK, to work on her PhD in the area of consumer behaviour and adventure tourism. She has since developed research interests in consumer communities and subcultures, narration and videography. Her research crosses several disciplines and her current research on "Cool" is relevant to the fields of consumer behaviour and tourism and as well as leisure studies.

Scott Fleming is with the School of Sport and Leisure at the University of Gloucestershire, and is the current Chair of the Leisure Studies Association. He has conducted research concerned with 'race' and ethnicity, sport and leisure cultures, and corporate governance. He is the co-editor of *Ethics, Sport and Leisure: Crises and Critiques* (with Alan Tomlinson, 1997), and also of LSA volumes entitled *Policy and Politics in Sport, Physical Education and Leisure* (with Margaret Talbot and Alan Tomlinson, 1995); *Masculinities: Leisure Identities, Cultures and Consumption* (with John Horne, 2000); and *New Leisure Environments: Media, Technology and Sport* (with Ian Jones, 2002).

Arnold H. Grossman, Ph.D., ACSW, LMSW, is Professor of Applied Psychology in The Steinhardt School of Education at New York University (NYU). He is Co-Investigator of a National Institute Mental of Health grant about victimization and mental health among lesbian, gay and bisexual youth and Principal Investigator of a NYU funded research grant about transgender youth. His scholarship and teaching focus on people who experience stigmatization, marginalization, and social exclusions. He is the recent author of chapters focused on lesbian, gay, bisexual and transgender youth and on physical and mental health of lesbian, gay, and bisexual older adults.

John Hunter-Jones is the course director and a lecturer on the Management and Leisure Degree at the University of Manchester. His teaching is focused on legal studies for the leisure and teaching professions, in particular matters relating to the health and safety of children. He is currently undertaking a Ph.D researching the validity and effectiveness of the current law in providing a legal framework for school trips.

Ruth Jeanes is a PhD student and research associate at the Institute of Youth Sport, Loughborough University. Her doctoral research is concerned with examining the influence football has on young girls gender identities, particularly looking at how playing football can affect gender stereotypes. She is also interested in ways of conducting research with young people and developing interactive methods and new approaches to collect data with children.

Fiona Jordan is a Principal Lecturer in Leisure and Tourism in the School of Sport and Leisure at the University of Gloucestershire. She has research interests in the gendered production and consumption of leisure and tourism and in exploring the linkages between teaching and research. Fiona is a member of the LSA Executive, the Leisure Editor for the Journal of Hospitality, Leisure, Sport and Tourism Education and sits on the Steering Group of the Higher Education Academy Subject Network for Hospitality, Leisure, Sport and Tourism.

Ian Macdonald recently completed his postgraduate studies at the University of Surrey, Roehampton. He is currently working as a Lecturer in Sport at Bromley College, and a youth project co-ordinator at Canterbury City Council. His interest in this subject has been initiated by a combination of his postgraduate studies and experience of working on a number of community based youth projects.

Brian Simpson is a Senior Lecturer in the Law Department at Keele University where he is director of the LLM in Child Law. His work focuses on the autonomy rights of children in various contexts: media (Children and Television (London, Continuum, 2004)), cyberspace and urban space. In addition to his legal background he has post-graduate qualifications in urban planning. In this area he has written on the participation of children in urban planning and design and his interest in the extent to which young people's play is accommodated within cities furthers his cross-disciplinary perspective on children's rights.

Karl Spracklen is a Senior Lecturer in Socio-Cultural Aspects of Sport and Leisure at Leeds Metropolitan University. Previously to this, he worked as a National Development Manager for Sporting Equals, a project funded by the Commission for Racial Equality and Sport England to promote racism in sport. He is an advisor on racial equality to UK Sport and the English Golf Union.

Sarah Todd is Associate Professor in the Department of Marketing at Otago University, New Zealand. Sarah has been with the Department since 1989. Sarah is a founding member of the Department's Consumer Research Group, which has undertaken several major studies into New Zealand consumers' lifestyles and values, with the most recent being New Zealand beyond 2000. She is also a member of the Tourism Research Group and is currently researching children's consumption behaviour and their understanding of advertising. Additionally, Sarah has strong interests in the Japanese language and culture.

Ian Wellard is based in the Centre for Physical Education Research, Canterbury Christ Church University College, where he is a Senior Research Fellow in the Sociology of Sport. He is currently involved in a number projects related to physical education, the body and gender. Ian was previously based in the Sociology department of the Open University where he completed a PhD investigation into body practices, masculinities, and sport.

I

ADVENTURE AND
RISK-TAKING BEHAVOUR

CITIES AS PLAYGROUNDS: ACTIVE LEISURE FOR CHILDREN AS A HUMAN RIGHT

Brian Simpson
Keele University

> … play becomes a stark refusal to disappear beneath the imperatives of spatial regulation that favours select target markets. In this refusal to disappear is an insistence on a right to claim, and remake, portions of the city. And in playing, this right is not merely asserted. It is acted upon in creative and highly visible ways. (Flusty, 2000: p. 156)

The child's right to play is enshrined in article 31 of the United Nations Convention on the Rights of the Child. That article recognises the right together with an obligation on nation states to ensure that the right is recognised:

1. States Parties recognize the right of the child to rest and leisure, to engage in play and recreational activities appropriate to the age of the child and to participate freely in cultural life and the arts.
2. States Parties shall respect and promote the right of the child to participate fully in cultural and artistic life and shall encourage the provision of appropriate and equal opportunities for cultural, artistic, recreational and leisure activity.

Other parts of the Convention also bear on matters to do with the right of children to play. For example, article 3 states that "in all actions concerning children whether undertaken by public or private social welfare institutions, courts of law, administrative authorities or legislative bodies, the best interests of the child shall be a primary consideration". Article 12 demands that children should be provided with the opportunity to express their views on all matters which affect them, and article 23 states that children with disabilities are to be provided with a "full and decent life" and "in conditions which ensure dignity, promote self-reliance and facilitate the child's active participation in the community". When blended together, such rights provide a context within which the right of the children to play must be analysed and given effect.

Of course, such statements of rights are often praised as good intent with little real impact on the lives of children. The Convention should not be looked at in this way. While the Convention is sometimes presented as if it were a statement of moral aspirations, it must be understood that this is a legal document which creates legal rights for children recognised in international law. It is true that the Convention does not automatically create legal rights which can be enforced in domestic law, but the Convention itself creates an expectation that its principles will be brought into the domestic law of each country which ratifies it.

The result is that the Convention is becoming more and more integrated into our legal system. For example, the Working Together guidance which assists local authorities and other agencies to understand their obligations under the Children Act 1989 states that '[the guidance] reflects the principles contained within the United Nations Convention on the Rights of the Child' (Department of Health, 1999: p. viii). The Government's response to the Climbié Inquiry report also recommended the establishment of a National Agency for Children and Families to, inter alia, 'advise on the implementation of the UN Convention on the Rights of the Child'(Department of Health, 2003: p. 29). The Children Bill currently before (UK) Parliament creates a Children's Commissioner who must have regard to the United Nations Convention on the Rights of the Child when determining what constitutes the rights and interests of children when performing functions under the legislation [Children Bill 2004, cl. 2(8)]. The Convention is also being increasingly turned to by the Courts to clarify the nature of the obligations the state is under in relation to children. (See for example, The Howard League for Penal Reform v Secretary of State for the Home Department, High Court, 29 November 2002; Fortin,1998: p. 49.)

In the United Kingdom there is also the effect of the incorporation of the European Convention on Human Rights into domestic law by the Human Rights Act 1998. While there is no specific mention of a child's right to play in the European Convention, article 8 (the right to respect for private and family life) and article 10 (freedom of expression) could be relevant in discussions of the child's right to play. The effect of the incorporation of the European Convention is also to make courts more adept at articulating the content of human rights generally, including the rights of children. We thus live in a time when human rights discourse — and children's rights discourse — is more central to law-making. A central part of this discourse is the inclusion of children in deciding matters which affect them. The right of children to participate in this manner has been described as one of the most 'remarkable' aspects of the United Nations Convention as it rests on the idea that children have the capacity for a degree of self-determination (Fortin, 1998: pp. 40–41). As children may shape their environment through play, this right to participate, as contained in article 12, is central to this present discussion.

The point is that the rights contained within the United Nations Convention on the Rights of the Child are becoming integrated into our legal system with the effect that they are beginning to have a real impact on the lives of children, their families and those responsible for matters which affect children. As these rights begin to be claimed by children and their advocates, it becomes increasingly important to examine the content of those rights and articulate their parameters.

The content of the 'right to play'

One challenge then, is in defining what a 'right to play' actually means if the United Nations Convention is going to have effect for children. The Children's Play Council has set out a list of policy objectives with respect to *The Objectives of Good Play Provision* which may be of assistance here. Those objectives include the following principles:

- All children and young people have the right to play freely and free of charge in their own neighbourhoods.
- Good mainstream play provision is accessible, welcoming and engaging for all children and young people including those who are disabled or have specific needs and wishes.
- Children and young people of different ages have different play interests and needs.
- Ensuring good play opportunities means more than providing fixed play equipment.
- The benefits to children and young people of good play provision are tangible. (Children's Play Council, *The Objectives of Good Play Provision*, February 2004)

The Council has also articulated its view of the characteristics of good play spaces and provision:

- A varied and interesting physical environment which inspires mystery and imagination
- Features and activities which stretch children's capabilities
- Opportunities to experience and handle natural elements
- Space and structures for physical activity
- Natural and manufactured materials
- Structures and features which stimulate the five senses
- A chance to experience changes in the natural and built environment
- Spaces and features which allow for different types of social interactions

(Children's Play Council, *The Objectives of Good Play Provision*, February 2004)

Continuing in this vein the Council's explanation of good play provision is stated to be one that 'extends the choice and control that children have over their play, the freedom they enjoy and the satisfaction they gain from it; recognises the child's need to test boundaries and responds positively to that need; manages the balance between the need to offer risk and the need to keep children safe from harm; maximises the range of play opportunities; fosters independence and self-esteem; fosters children's respect for others and offers opportunities for social interaction; fosters the child's well-being, healthy growth and development, knowledge and understanding, creativity and capacity to learn' (Children's Play Council, *The Objectives of Good Play Provision*, February 2004).

The recurring notion in this statement from the Children's Play Council is that children's play is about a lot more than the provision of a playground. Play is about such issues as engaging with the environment, social interaction, a balance between risk and safety, all serving to promote the independence of children and to challenge boundaries. Is then the right of the child to play, the right of the child to access play in these terms?

The United Kingdom government's review of play: from fear to safety

In March 2004 the Department for Culture, Media and Sport released its review of children's play: *Getting Serious About Play: a Review of Children's Play* (DCMS, 2004). At one level the review accepts the broad approach of the Children's Play Council about the nature of children's play. Thus it adopted, for the purposes of the review, a definition of 'play' as:

> … what children and young people do when they follow their own ideas and interests, in their own way and for their own reasons. (*Getting Serious About Play*: p. 6)

But at this point the review uses text in an interesting way. In various parts of the document, statements appear which draw on the expansive notion of play discussed above. However, these statements do not form part of the text of the actual review. For example, article 31 of the United Nations Convention on the Rights of the Child appears only as a side quote on one page of the report (p. 9) On another page the following appears, also as a side quote, in terms which echo article 12 of the United Nations Convention:

> We need to make our public spaces safe, inviting and inclusive for everyone — and the only way of doing that is working with young people to design places and spaces that meet their needs. (Tony Hawkhead, CE of Groundwork, UK cited in *Getting Serious About Play*: p. 17)

The review similarly lists the 'seven play objectives' — these have been formulated by the Children's Play Council and, as noted above, are deemed to be key features of good play provision. But again, this list is disconnected from the text. Indeed, the list only receives a brief mention as part of the discussion of play provision design (p. 20).

Although these various statements do appear in the review, by being placed 'outside' the text, they are consequently not actually discussed by the DCMS. Thus, there is no attempt to articulate what is actually meant by a child's right to play, even though article 31 'appears' in the review. Moreover, there is no acknowledgement of the Children's Play Council's other objectives with respect to the nature of children's play, even though reference is made to one set of seven principles. Indeed, there is almost complete silence on the full implications of Hawkhead's submission that children should be included in designing places and spaces. Does that mean that children might play almost anywhere and that as a consequence the community is under an obligation to ensure that urban design accommodates such activity? The DCMS review sidesteps such debates.

The only attempt to take up this point appears on page 10. Under the heading 'informal play locations' the DCMS recognises that play spaces do not simply mean playgrounds as commonly understood. It notes:

> Any effort to improve children's play opportunities must recognise
> as a fact of life that most play does not take place on sites formally
> designated as play spaces. When not playing at home, many children
> resort to local streets or any nearby open spaces and buildings from
> which they are not excluded. This is most important for children with
> little or no play space at home. Those responsible for promoting
> children's opportunities to play in safety must make sure that
> children on foot or on bikes have high priority on local streets. (*Getting
> Serious About Play*: p. 10)

This last sentence suggests a more pervasive theme in discussions about
children's play — the issue of safety. At this point concern with risk taking,
challenging interactions and testing boundaries, as contained within the
Children's Play Council's defined characteristics of good play spaces, begins
to be relegated to a more deep-seated fear for — and of — children.

While much of the DCMS review appears to be concerned with the safety
of children in their play, as we shall see, there is also a suggestion that children
may also be feared. This fits with recent concern about the problem of anti-
social behaviour amongst young people and legislative action to remove
'gangs' of young people from streets and other public spaces. Thus, in
continuing its discussion of informal play locations the review proceeds:

> The visible presence of children and young people making *harmless
> and inoffensive* use of public spaces is a sign of a healthy community.
> It is also vital to recognise that what to a planner or developer may
> appear to be an unused brownfield site may turn out to be a major
> informal play area, whose disappearance would deprive local
> children. Safeguarding the freedom and safety of children and young
> people must come high on the public agenda in both urban and rural
> areas. (*Getting Serious About Play*: p. 10) (my emphasis)

The use of public spaces for play has to be 'harmless and inoffensive' for it
to be considered acceptable. This is the crucial point where 'children's play'
meets with the problem of the 'anti-social behaviour' of young people. The
DCMS review focussed on the play needs of children between 0 and 16. It
is noteworthy that section 30 of the Anti-Social Behaviour Act 2003 applies
to persons under 16. It empowers a police officer to order the dispersal of
groups of two or more persons under 16 where 'any members of the public
have been intimidated, harassed, alarmed or distressed as a result of the
presence or behaviour of [that group] in public places in any locality in his

police area' and 'that anti-social behaviour is a significant and persistent problem in the relevant locality.' This might suggest that there is a tension between providing play spaces for children and dealing with the anti-social behaviour of young people. But such a tension is not fully discussed in the review.

Instead the DCMS review recognises the connection in other ways. It refers to a public opinion poll conducted in 2001 which indicated that adults ranked 'activities for young people' ahead of health, education and housing and almost level with crime reduction as the most requested improvement to local services (*Getting Serious About Play*: p. 11) This suggests a suspicion of young people and a sense that they need to be made to exercise — a far cry from the notion that play is something determined by young people themselves. The review notes:

> These priorities no doubt reflected the long-standing recognition that 'the devil makes work for idle hands'. Other surveys show that parents believe that today's children have fewer opportunities for play than they did themselves. They feel that children today spend too much time watching TV or playing on computers. They would like them to get more physical exercise. (*Getting Serious About Play*: p. 11)

All of this appears to place play as a device for parental and social control rather than as an activity which begins with the rights of the child to be challenged and to engage in rich and diverse interactive experiences. While there is a need for community and parental guidance in play, there is a clear sense here that play can be used to protect adults from those children who may 'intimidate or harass'. This tension raises another dilemma: when is play acceptable and when does it become anti-social behaviour? One only has to consider the negative attitudes which exist towards skateboarders, for example, to understand this point.

What this leads to is a myopic vision of 'acceptable' children's play as only that which is contained within narrow physical boundaries. This means children's play must be in locations which are capable of being policed easily or which are so far away from the rest of the community that unwelcome side effects, such as noise, do not bother others. In other words, children's play is delineated and defined in direct opposition to the play principles enunciated above — it must be formal, regulated and located in spaces designated for that purpose. This is necessary in order to achieve the proper control over the activities classed as children's play. There is in such a definition of children's play a close convergence with the other concern with children's play — the safety of children.

The child safety agenda

There is no doubt that fear of what might happen to children in public spaces is one of the most controlling devices which hangs over children today and one which is well represented in the literature (see Tandy, 1999) The review of children's play builds on that fear — even though it acknowledges that in the context of many sites of children's play this fear is without any strong foundation:

> ... surveys show that many parents are very concerned about the safety of their children and are reluctant to let them out of the house. They cite fears of strangers and traffic as their main concerns. Traffic is a big danger with an average of 112 child pedestrians killed and 3,300 seriously injured in each of the last five years. It is extremely rare for children to be harmed by a stranger in any public space — on average 8 have been killed in each of the last five years. Hardly any children are ever seriously harmed by a stranger in a park or playground. But, as the focus groups carried out for the review confirmed, parents' fears are real. So they must be addressed. Children and young people are also concerned about their safety. Surveys show that children's main safety fears are about bullying and traffic. Both children and parents are keen on adult supervision. (*Getting Serious About Play*: p. 11)

The DCMS review also noted 'blame culture' and fear of litigation on the part of those who provide play facilities. This resulted either in the closure of play areas or in the reduction of such facilities to the point where they become 'boring' and, perhaps ironically, lead to children seeking 'excitement elsewhere often at much greater danger to themselves and others' (*Getting Serious About Play*: p. 12) To its credit the review recognised that the lack of concern with play as a political priority has meant that not only narrow conceptions of what constitutes children's play space have prevailed but also that there has been a failure to develop play strategies (*Getting Serious About Play*: p. 12)

Nevertheless the DCMS review continued to present child safety as the overriding concern in play provision. This fits well with the view that children's play is more about child control rather than child liberation.

Presenting supervision of the child in the play space as of primary concern leads one inexorably to the conclusion that playgrounds (in the traditional and narrow sense) will be what will come out of this review, despite acknowledging the risk of 'boring' play. It may be that the details of design and content of such playgrounds will be contentious, but what is clearly not going to be embraced is the notion that informal play spaces — which by definition have other purposes — will be well regarded. This appears to be evident in the discussion of 'VITAL' — the acronym which is to be used to determine priorities for New Opportunities Funding (NOF), the £200 million made available to improve children's play opportunities. VITAL stands for "Value based, In the Right place, Top Quality, Appropriate and Long Term" (*Getting Serious About Play*: p. 19) These terms appear to suggest the funding of play spaces which are specific in location and dedicated to a single use as play space. This is particularly evident in the discussion of projects which are assessed to be 'in the right place.' The review describes such projects in the following terms:

> Research shows that location is probably the single most important factor in the success of a play project, especially an outdoor public space such as a play area. In the right location even a poorly designed facility can be well used. But a well-designed facility in the wrong location is likely to fail. Location will ultimately be a matter for local decisions, and may require compromise with different interest groups achieved through local consultation. NOF guidance should emphasize that children and young people should have a big say in the location of their play provision. (*Getting Serious About Play*: p. 20)

This discussion seems to assume that the play space will be a site dedicated for that purpose. The politics of government funding might also suggest that is the aim. After all, playgrounds can be opened by beaming mayors and MPs, while a retained brownfield site on which children play will hardly be one which many politicians will want to visit. Clearly, the main thrust of the review is suggestive of funding projects which can be labelled as 'playgrounds' or 'play spaces' for children. This is reflected in the recommendation that 80 per cent of NOF funding of children's play should be devoted to play spaces based on this criteria (*Getting Serious About Play*: p. 23).

The question is whether this approach is actually consistent with the rights of children. The objective that play should aim to do such things as facilitate the child's integration into the community, challenge the child, promote children's independence and open opportunities for social interaction may not be achieved if such play is confined to particular spaces. The bulk of the funding, recommended by this review, is to be spent in a manner which relies on establishing and maintaining areas designed specifically for play. Within those boundaries some good may occur, but in terms of broader objectives connected with the inclusion of children into society, such an approach does more to reinforce the lesser position of children than give children more of a stake in the community. This lack of appreciation of the importance of the independent rights of children to claim real space in society is even demonstrated by the DCM's approach to the inclusion of children in the process of planning and designing play spaces. While the review placed some stress on the need to ensure that children and young people are included in the planning and running of local play projects (*Getting Serious About Play*: p. 24), the report then proceeds to conclude that:

> *All* concerned in play projects should apply a simple but demanding test. They should be able honestly to give the answer yes to the question: 'would this be good enough for my children.' (*Getting Serious About Play*: p. 28) (my emphasis)

It would seem that in the final analysis, the Review assumes that play spaces will ultimately be designed by adults for children. If so, then it is the views of children as held by those adults which will ultimately determine the nature of those play spaces and also the extent to which they do pay regard to some of the objectives articulated by such organisations as the Children's Play Council.

But adults also have other pressures to which they respond in relation to children's play. The child safety agenda is not just about adult fears of children's vulnerabilities. This concern with safety also relates to the manner in which urban space is becoming corporatised. As Aitken explains:

> In the United Kingdom, commercial playgrounds are associated with already established family restaurants and pubs, where play equipment is packaged and themed under names such as Alphabet Zoo, Jungle Bungle and Wacky Warehouse. Youngsters eat, learn, play games and tumble around while their caregivers relax in the knowledge that their children are safe from the perils of the street. Susan Davis (1997) argues that these enterprises are a shameless commodification of children's lives, designed and promoted on the basis of fear:
>
> [These] sites are offered as ways of getting customers out of

the house, ways to create a 'street' of activity in hyper-commercial space. That all this conviviality is based on a carefully cultivated market is more than ironic at a time when, in less touristic neighborhoods, minority youth are actively prevented from congregating. (Aitken, 2001: pp. 152–53, citing Davis)

This represents a darker side of debates on children's play — a side completely ignored by the DCMS's review — that of the manner in which the creation of play spaces relates to the increasing segregation of society based on inequalities of wealth and power. Childress has made the point:

As capital works harder to wring every last cent out of an owned space, there are fewer commercial leftovers. Increasing numbers of places are more finished, more corporately and distantly owned, and thus more protected and less negotiable. Broadening of insurance restrictions as an instrument of capital conservation brings about increasing limitations on street play such as skateboarding. These pressures are increasing: there is no reason to expect these pressures to spontaneously diminish for any reason. As property becomes more expensive and more protected, we can expect it to be increasingly difficult to be a teenager in American public space... (Childress, 2004: p. 203)

The manner in which the creation of play spaces for children connects with the needs of capital suggests that any discussion of children's play will inevitably confront important questions of how space is allocated. Indeed, even the notion that separate children's play areas have to be formally created can be understood as a mechanism for relegating children to less valuable locations (such as the out of town siting of skateboard or kart racing venues) or, in some cases, their location at the heart of corporate locations, with all the elements of control and surveillance which that implies.

The manipulation of concerns with child safety, and in the case of older children fear of children, to facilitate the removal of children from public spaces is another 'dark side' to debates about children's play. This concern with the safety of children and the argument that many urban spaces are unsafe for children not only conflicts with the reality — even this was recognised by the review — but also with any acceptance that, for many children, such public spaces represent important spaces within which they develop their social networks and identities (Matthews, Limb & Taylor, 2000: p. 76).

This indicates that debates and discussions of the child's right to play take on even greater importance. It is to this notion of the child having legal rights that we can turn to claim some space for children, based in need rather than driven by the imperatives of global corporations. The content of that right and how it might be understood become of central concern. How do we then frame and reconstruct the child's right to play in terms beyond that of the right to an adult-designed and controlled playground?

Alternatives: the city as playground

So far the suggestion is that children's play has become caught up in a number of other agendas. Control of anti-social children is a stated aim of play and one use to which play or recreational opportunities for children are put. Protection of children from a perceived threat from strangers is also a part of the discourse around children's play. Child safety certainly dominates many of the debates on play-space design. The manner in which social space is commodified and allocated creates the precise context within which many discussions of play takes place. Underpinning all of this, of course, are fundamental ideas about childhood and the nature of children. The fact that the DCMS review concludes that persons involved in play-space design are to ask whether it is good enough for their children reveals whose interests prevail, even when official discourse rests on the notion that children themselves should be central to decision making. The discourse on children's play explored above would suggest that there is a dominant paradigm of children's play which would relegate play to specified areas where 'children can be children.' In other words, children's play discourse segregates children from the 'adult world' in the same manner as other areas of social relations. This segregation rests on a view of the child as properly the subject of control and protection from 'harm' in a way which is at odds with other perspectives on children which would accord to them some autonomy and independent rights. It is to this latter view of children that some of the principles which underpin the objectives of play-space design articulated by the Children's Play Council speak. Thus my argument here is that a discourse of children's play which acknowledges those principles is required if we are to properly recognise the rights of children to play in the fullest sense.

This alternative paradigm which forms the foundation of this broader discourse of children's play can be detected to a limited extent in the DCMS review of children's play as discussed above. Though vague as to its criteria, the 'Playful Ideas Strand' is to receive 20 per cent of NOF funds. This strand will include support for projects which promote "playful elements in public spaces, museums and other cultural centres"(*Getting Serious About Play*: p. 26). The purpose of this funding strand is also to 'recognise success' in such areas as "improving a range of local policies, plans and strategies, such as those covering development and land use, green spaces, childcare, culture or transport" (*Getting Serious About Play*: p. 26). Part of this strand is also about encouraging "innovative ways to include disabled children and young people excluded from mainstream provision"(*Getting Serious About Play*: p. 26).

There is, though, a broader basis to this alternative paradigm upon which a discourse of children's play, which recognises the rights of children in a more comprehensive manner, might rest. Bach (1993) notes that many urban spaces are redefined by users as spaces which can be used for sport — in the widest sense of that term — although such spaces are not primarily designed for that purpose. He writes:

> Increasingly, everyday physical and recreational activities are being redefined as 'sport': everyone can engage in them, and spectators are not needed. Thus, riding your bicycle to work is considered a sportslike activity. The same redefinition process occurs when a group of senior citizens goes on a weekend hike, or when a group of youngsters engage in spontaneous games in open spaces between buildings, with rules often aligned to the requirements of the physical surroundings. While professional sports or top-level athletic activities make increasing demands for ever more highly specialized athletic facilities, such as indoor arenas for soccer or football stadiums, or golf-course driving ranges, everyday informal sports activities begin to invade and re-form urban spaces and facilities for shared use. As a result, such spaces are temporarily redefined as sports facilities: bike trails, yards, open spaces, empty lots, vacated factory buildings — all are utilized for informal or recreational sports activities. (Bach, 1993: p. 281)

This suggests that any urban space potentially could be redefined as a 'play space' by children and young people. Certainly, this much has been recognised by the review of children's play in its discussion of children colonising unused brownfield sites as informal play spaces. The usefulness of Bach's approach also can be explained in terms of the need for children to experience risk-taking and their desire to use their imaginations. An obvious example is the young people who skateboard in urban spaces, hardly designed for that specific purpose. But the use of roads, carparks, pavements and stairways to skate over will often be regarded as anti-social behaviour or inappropriate by others. Young people who use shopping centres to 'hang out' may not be seen as 'playing' by adults who consider such spaces as primarily commercial places. In other words, the use of urban spaces for play raises issues of who has the power to define the use to which such spaces may be put, as well as questions of how 'play' is to be defined, just as Bach raises the matter of how 'sport' should be defined.

Bach's ideas appear to have a clear application here as much of his argument revolves around the spontaneity of what he would describe as sporting activity. In the same way, much of children's play can be spontaneous. The DCMS review assumes that spaces for children's play demand that a certain amount of formality or organisation surrounds children's play. This might be understood as evolving from a culture that wishes to teach segregation of time and space. The work/play distinction also neatly fits with the idea that land use also can be segregated. The idea that commercial space might also be play space challenges powerful notions of who controls property and urban space. Even the DCMS review has to make the case for the use of school grounds for play after hours. It is remark-able that even a space which appears to have children at its heart has to surmount the notion that such space has to be transformed from educational use to play use. Given that, how difficult would it be to argue that a super-market carpark should be readily accepted as a play space when the shops themselves are closed?

Once it is accepted that the redefinition of urban spaces as play spaces can be a spontaneous act on the part of users, there will be problems awaiting those who wish to impose formal planning, legal and regulatory regimes over urban space. One can see how this also fits with child safety and child fear concerns. Informal and spontaneous redefinitions of urban space challenge the argument that play space must be designed with the safety and control of children in mind. What is unclear is whether such concerns are legitimate concerns which should govern the use of space for play, or whether such concerns serve to legitimate the power relations which lead to the segregation of land use for commercial and non-commercial functions (including play spaces).

At one level this raises a problem of planning and design. If urban spaces are to be permitted to be redefined by users as play spaces some of the time — for example, the shopping-centre car park — then what are the implications for the design of such spaces and their location? Does this mean that such spaces must be designed with multiple uses in mind? Does access have to be permitted at times when the commercial use has finished for the day? But most importantly, if these spaces are part of the urban fabric of play spaces, then do children have a right to access such spaces for their purposes? And how does one cope with the spontaneity of such use? How does one design spaces for uses which might not be realised until the point of use? Bach attempts to provide an answer:

> The concept of informal sports activities implies that people engage in such activities spontaneously; that is to say, such activities do not necessarily occur regularly, neither timewise nor spacewise. In general, the need for spontaneous activities is either assumed or accepted as a basic human need. However, spontaneous activities resist the controlling management of planning when it comes to assess such activities — their type, scope and locality — as activities potentially existing at this time or possibly arising in the future. Without doubt, field studies can be used to prove that informal activities occur; such evidence can also be used to justify the appropriation of land-use for such use. However, the planning of informal sports activities should or must remain 'supply-oriented.' Such planning derives the demand for areas and locations not directly from any actual demand: this would be 'demand-oriented planning.' Rather, the planning of informal sports activities as supply-oriented is justified by a socially accepted and presumed norm: Namely that cities are expected to provide, within their boundaries, areas which are temporally and spatially accessible in multiple and diverse ways, without stipulating that such spontaneous uses be clearly defined in kind and scope. (Bach, 1993: p. 285–87)

Seeing all urban space as potential play spaces meets the Children's Play Council's broad principles and objectives in a more comprehensive manner than the designation of spaces as 'play spaces'. The likely consequence of the latter is that most of such spaces will be heavily supervised and over-designed spaces which compromise risk and challenges to children for the sake of safety. But, as Bach suggests, the recognition of multiple uses raise other questions of practical design. In relation to assessing whether different urban spaces can support informal sport activity, he suggests a four step process. The first step is to eliminate all land which cannot support such activity because, for example, its primary use takes up all the time available or because of trespass restrictions (Bach, 1993: p. 287). The second step is to identify land which might be suitable for such activity. This requires consideration of matters such as the general useability of the land, access (both temporal and physical), and consent to use the land for other than its primary use (Bach, 1993: p. 287). The third step is first to conduct a more detailed evaluation of the suitability of the site in terms of "size, shape, surface condition and surface structure" (Bach, 1993: p. 287). The second phase of this third step is to assess the compatibility of its use as a site for informal sports activity with its primary land use and the surrounding use of land (Bach, 1993: p. 287). The final and fourth step is to assess "the possible impact of a specific site or space when used as an informal sports facility" (Bach, 1993: p. 287).

This fourth step leads to the selection of a site as a space for informal sports activity. This requires knowledge of the characteristics of the sites which can support informal sport activity and the types of use to which they might be put (Bach, 1993: p. 287 and Appendix C). In this context Bach suggests the need to distinguish between 'areal informal sports facilities' — which would include "lots, building spaces, or open spaces" and "linear informal sports facilities" — which would include"bike trails, hiking trails, and waterways" (Bach, 1993: p. 287). He assumes that some land will have a greater or lesser potential for informal sports activity (Bach, 1993: p. 287).

In terms of impact assessment, Bach makes the important point that impact is to be assessed in terms of the positive impact of including sites for informal sports activity in the community. Thus it is not a matter of simply considering impacts such as noise and effect on property values but also the benefits of increased sport activity and more opportunities for social interaction (Bach, 1993: p. 292 and Appendix E). The process of evaluating impacts must also be undertaken from the perspective of different interest groups (Bach, 1993: p. 292 and Appendix F).

The application of these ideas about assessing use of land for informal sports activities to the assessment of urban spaces for children's play can be seen as a logical extension. Children's play is recognised as being often informal and spontaneous, indeed, in principle, children's play should be encouraged to be so. But concerns with risk, safety and 'inappropriate' play often result in it being relegated to specific locations which mean a loss of spontaneity, social interaction and locations which do not meet the broader objectives of play. What Bach appears to provide is a process whereby the use of urban space might be assessed against criteria that take these broader objectives into account and which results in the encouragement of use of such spaces for activities beyond the day-time use, whilst also possibly encouraging design of such spaces which can accommodate such multiple uses. If this does result, then this will also go some way to assuaging some of the concerns with respect to the risks children may face when playing in 'inappropriate areas.'

Reconstructing the city through play: children as risk takers

If children are to claim a right to play on terms which equate with the broader principles already discussed, then Bach may provide a mechanism which demonstrates that it is possible to provide those play opportunities as a practical planning and design matter. Many rights, while acknowledged in principle, then fall down because it is not possible to give them practical effect. But is it unlikely that this alone will deliver the right of play to children in terms beyond the 'traditional' notion that this means designated play spaces. The problem is that the use of urban space, as argued by Bach, if applied to children's play, directly challenges entrenched views on city planning and on the role of play as well as conventional views on the proper place of children and the meaning of childhood.

Flusty argues that the ways in which buskers, skaters and street poets — that is, those engaged in play — refuse to disappear as public spaces in the city become more and more regulated and privatised — celebrates the manner in which they claim and 'remake' the city 'in highly creative and visible ways.' As he states, the 'near-criminalisation of street skaters' results in their becoming 'pavement commandos' and leads them to agitate for their right to 'skate free' (Flusty, 2000). This seems very close to Bach's conceptualisation that the need for 'spontaneous games in open spaces' leads to the invasion and re-forming of urban spaces and facilities for shared use. In other words, if spontaneous sport or play is an important part of the urban landscape, then this implies that the users of such spaces must have the power to redefine such space.

This point is also made by Borden in relation to skateboarding. For him, such play is a serious business because it is the way in which young people claim space:

Skateboarding is antagonistic towards the urban environment ('a skateboard is the one thing you can use as a weapon in the street that you don't get patted down for'). In redefining space for themselves, skateboarders take over space conceptually as well as physically and so strike at the heart of what everyone else understands by the city; they 'hammer the panic buttons of those uninterested in this pursuit of thrill and achievement'. (Borden, 2001: p. 247)

Children have the capacity to define urban space in sensible ways which more usefully accommodate their needs. In one case study where children were involved in the design of an urban space, the children did not suggest the inclusion of formal playgrounds, but instead focused on the city as a whole, including power supply, community spaces and transportation (Gallagher, 2004: p. 253, p. 259). In that study, reference was made to earlier studies on the connection between urban form and children's play. One finding was that:

> ... play in formal playgrounds was rarely seen in areas where children had virtually no other place to play. Overly prescribed spaces may have little appeal to children. There may not be enough room for their own exploration and creativity. (Gallagher, 2004: p. 258 citing Department of Environment, 1973; Hole and Miller, 1969)

This has profound implications for those concerned with the provision of play spaces for children. While many organisations advocate for 'children's right to play' it is not necessarily the case that this right is understood to imply that children have the right to define for themselves where and how they should play. In short, the 'child's right to play' is not usually taken to mean the child's right to reshape her or his environment.

Here rights become crucially important, because if the need for play space is regarded as part of the package of the rights of the child to play, then this redefinition of urban space transforms from 'a fine idea in principle' to something that children might realistically claim and have enforced in their interests. Rights are powerful and are means by which those without power may claim things (Donnison, 1989). But what is being challenged should not be underestimated when views about how urban space is defined are contested. Those who currently possess the power to shape and define the city have a vested interest in reading down the meaning of the child's right to play. This is, after all, about the value and use of urban space in an increasingly corporatised world.

In an attempt to achieve some kind of balance between competing interests, some legal commentators have argued for zoning strategies which maintain the social mix by arguing for 'zones of tolerance' on the basis that such approaches provide a place for all to engage in their preferred behaviour. For example, Ellickson (1996) has suggested that cities should be zoned into red, yellow and green zones. Red zones would occupy about 5% of downtown space and allow behaviour which might be considered inappropriate or deviant in other areas, such as prostitution and public drunkenness. Yellow zones would account for about 90% of downtown space and would be space where there would be toleration of 'the flamboyant and eccentric' but not to the extent that most people would choose not to enter. Finally, green zones would set aside the remaining 5% of city space for the frail, elderly, parents with children and the like (Ellickson, 1996: p. 1221).

While such schemes represent some attempt to preserve diversity in the city, they do also indicate the difficulties of defining the boundaries of acceptable behaviour. Given his aims, Ellickson also somewhat ironically relegates children to the margins. This is the problem with zoning strategies: it carries with it the potential to segregate and sanitise the city. The failure of attempts to establish such zones of tolerance in relation to street prostitution in many cities also indicates the various vested interests which confront proponents of such schemes and indicates the power relations which are challenged in proposing such a strategy.

The other difficulty in according to children a 'right to play' (which embraces more than the right to be segregated into 'well designed' play spaces or 'carefully located' skate parks) is that this might suggest that children actually have a right to experience risk-taking. For those adults who see children's rights as the right to be protected from harm, the idea that children should also be granted some autonomy and the power to define the use of urban spaces conflicts with their restricted notion of how the child is to be conceptualised. In this regard, the discourse on children's play cannot be disconnected from how children are located in political and popular discourse in contemporary society. While documents such as the United Nations Convention on the Rights of the Child may represent a discourse which contains some strands of thought based on the independent rights of the child, this conception of the child still struggles with a view which regards the child as the proper subject of surveillance, control and protection from harm rather than one which is prepared to acknowledge the need for the child to exercise independent judgement, with the accompanying danger that bad decisions will be made (see, e.g., Collins and Kearns, 2001).

The claim that children have a 'right to play' cannot thus be seen as a simple statement about the need for better and more interesting playgrounds. Rather it signifies a battleground upon which many conflicting notions about the rights, the role of law, the idea of childhood, the use of urban space and the purpose of play are still to be fought.

References

Aitken, S. (2001) *Geographies of young people: The morally contested spaces of identity*. London & New York: Routledge.

Anti-Social Behaviour Act 2003 (http://www.legislation.hmso. gov.uk/acts/acts2003/20030038.htm).

Bach, L. (1993) 'Sports without facilities: The use of urban space by informal sports', *International Review for Sociology of Sport* Vol. 28, Nos. 2 & 3, pp. 281–295.

Borden, I. (2001) *Skateboarding, space and the city: Architecture and the body*. Oxford: Berg.

Children Bill 2004 (http://www.publications.parliament.uk/pa/cm200304/cmbills/144/2004144.htm).

Children's Play Council (2004) Children's Play Council Policy Positions: *The Objectives of Good Play Provision* (http://www.ncb.org.uk/cpc/dcms.htm#object, visited 9 September, 2004).

Childress, H. (2004) 'Teenagers, territory and the appropriation of space', *Childhood* Vol. 11, No. 2: pp. 195–205.

Collins, C.A. & Kearns, R.A. (2001) 'Under curfew and under siege? Legal geographies of young people', *Geoforum* Vol. 32: pp. 389–403.

Davis, S. (1997) Space jam: family values in the entertainment city. Paper presented at the American Studies Annual Meeting, Washington, DC.

Department for Culture, Media and Sport (2004) *Getting serious about play: A review of children's play (www.culture.gove.uk)*.

Department of Environment (1973) *Children and play*. London: HMSO.

Department of Health, Home Office, Department for Education and Employment (1999) *Working together to safeguard children*. London, HMSO.

Department of Health, Home Office, Department for Education and Skills (2003) *Keeping Children Safe: The Government's response to The Victoria Climbié Inquiry Report and Joint Chief Inspectors' Report Safeguarding Children* (Cm 5861).

Donnison, D. (1989) 'Rethinking rights talk', in L.Orchard & R.Dare (eds) *Markets, morals and public policy*. Annandale: Federation Press.

Ellickson, R.C. (1996) 'Controlling chronic misconduct in city spaces: Of panhandlers, skid rows, and public space zoning', *Yale Law Journal* Vol. 105: pp. 1165–1248.

Flusty, S. (2000) 'Thrashing Downtown: Play as resistance to the spatial and representational regulation of Los Angeles', *Cities* Vo.l 17, No. 2, pp. 149–158.

Fortin, J. (1998) *Children's rights and the developing law*. London: Butterworths.

Gallagher, C.B. (2002) '"Our Town" children as advocates for change in the city', *Childhood* Vol. 11, No. 2: pp. 251–262.

Hole, V. and Miller, A. (1969) 'Children's play on housing estates', *Architects' Journal* Vol. 143: pp. 1529–36.

Howard League for Penal Reform v Secretary of State for the Home Department, High Court, 29 November 2002.

Human Rights Act 1998 (http://www.legislation.hmso.gov.uk/acts/acts1998/ 19980042.htm).

Matthews, H., Limb, M. and Taylor, M. (2000) 'The street as thirdspace', in S.L.Holloway and G.Valentine (eds) *Children's geographies: Playing, living, learning*. London and New York: Routledge.

Tandy, C.A. (1999) 'Children's diminishing play space: A study of inter-generational change in children's use of their neghbourhoods', *Australian Geographical Studies* Vol. 37, No. 2: pp. 154–164.

United Nations Convention on the Rights of the Child (http://www.unicef.org/ crc/crc.htm).

WHAT FUTURE FOR SCHOOL TRIPS IN A RISK AVERSE SOCIETY?

John Hunter-Jones
University of Manchester

Introduction

The school trip can be a valuable opportunity for many children to experience new forms of leisure and to develop social and recreational skills, including how to respond to challenging and even hazardous environments (DFES, 1998). Given this breadth and depth of experience, such trips can be the highlight of the school year. However, trips rely in their organisation and running on the enthusiasm and altruism of schoolteachers and other volunteers; without such involvement the trips would not take place.

Trips can take a considerable amount of time and skill to organise and the need to conform to current safety standards is all part of that commitment. The burden of taking responsibility for children, outside the school, on high-spirited and adventurous activities, where the risk of injury may be ever present, is an additional consideration (Ford *et al.*, 1999). Recent legislation and guidelines, coupled with a perception of a greater willingness of injured parties and public bodies to litigate against teachers, have added to the pressure on teachers to minimise the risks or face the consequences (Wainwright, 2003). The extent to which such actions have impacted upon teachers' willingness to undertake such trips remains largely unreported in academic research.

The aim of this paper is to consider whether the fear of litigation against teachers and schools may be having an impact on the organisation of school trips. The relevant law is considered and examples of recent litigation identified, the purpose of which is to identify society's expectations of teachers and schools in organising trips. There follows a discussion of research carried out with teachers in order to consider how they, and their schools, are responding to the legal concern with potential liability. The research involved the administration of a questionnaire to teachers in Cheshire and Manchester. The sample population was selected to reflect the diversity of schools within the compulsory education sector.

School trips and risk

The purpose of school trips can be as varied as the trips themselves. Cooper (1999), Kalinowski and Weiler (1992) and Smith and Jenner (1997) have all provided much needed research into the characteristics of this market. It is estimated by Wainwright (2002) that seven million British children go on field trips every year. There are positive outcomes: the links with the National Curricula; the development of skills in recreational activities; appreciation of other cultures; learning to manage risks; the development of life skills; helping to advance greater understanding and cohesion within the school community. Trips can also act as a stimulus for young people in developing interests in travel and outdoor activities that may well continue into their adult lives. Their role is acknowledged by the current Education Secretary, Charles Clarke:

> We have to ensure that children from all socio-economic backgrounds, the poorest as well as the wealthiest, have the same chances to go to an art gallery, hear a concert, travel abroad — whatever it might happen to be. Now that's a difficult and demanding issue, of course, and very hard to get right. But I believe it's an aspiration, to which we should be working, because the fact is academic attainment in itself is important, but so too is helping children to grow and succeed. Personally I am a strong supporter of being able to offer every child some residential experience during the course of the year (…) I can see it contributing to the self confidence, resilience, independence of children. So I am looking very closely, at the moment, at how we can extend these possibilities and ensure that those experiences are taken more widely. (Clarke, 2004: p. 1)

Yet, this area of a school's life is dependent upon the willingness of the teachers and their employers to organise and run the activities. In essence this is a voluntary activity, very often undertaken in the teacher's free time with no payment for such commitment. However, support and encouragement to engage in such an activity is not widespread. The advice from one of the largest teaching unions, the NASUWT, for instance is to actively discourage its members from looking at organising such an activity.

> …the Association strongly counsels members to give very careful consideration to any involvement in any non contractual activity such as a school journey or educational visit. Involvement could put you at risk in almost every aspect of the planning and running of an educational visit or journey…. (NASUWT, 2001: p. 5)

National newspapers that have responded to tragedies and litigation with eye-catching statements compound the situation:

> "Jailing of Teacher may spell the end for school trips." (Jenkins and Owens, 2003, *The Times*)
>
> "Scandal of kids on school trips." (Swift, 2002, *Daily Express*)
>
> "Blame culture could end trips." (Smithers, 2001, *The Guardian*)
>
> "Schools paid £200 million last year [2003] in compensation, up from £50 million five years ago." (Bamber, 2004, *Sunday Telegraph*)

The concern with a blame culture and its impact on the willingness of organisations to undertake activities is not limited to school trips. The Better Regulation Task Force, in its report Better Routes to Redress (Cabinet Office, 2004), considers the issue of the perception of a compensation culture and how this may be affecting the willingness of organisations to undertake activities: "The prospect of litigation for negligence may have positive effects in making organisations manage their risks better, but an exaggerated fear of litigation, regardless of fault can be debilitating. The fear of litigation can make organisations over cautious in their behaviour" (Cabinet Office, 2004: p. 3). It concluded that much of the fear is based on myth and that government, with other interested parties, needs to do more to tackle the perception of a compensation culture. Much of its concern is with the media, in its exaggeration of the situation, and with high profile campaigns by claim management companies encouraging people to seek compensation.

So what is the reality of organising school trips and the consequent legal duties of teachers? Is this an area where the perception of a blame culture is reflected in the judgements of the legal system?

Criminal and civil law

For over a hundred years, teachers' duty of care to children has been subject to scrutiny by the courts. In Williams v Eady (1893) the definition of that duty, *'In Loco Parentis'*, was established (Ford *et al.*, 1999). Since then there has been no change to the fundamental civil law governing teachers' duties to children. The criminal law, too, has seen little change in the last thirty years, since the introduction of the Health and Safety at Work Act (HSWA) 1974. Yet there appears to be a perception amongst many teachers of a society that is more willing to consider blaming them for school trip accidents and a judicial system that is more willing to find fault.

A feature of the law that governs school trips is that there is no distinction in its application between commercial and not-for-profit organisations. The courts do not consider the benefit to society of the activity or the altruism of the defendant. In consequence the courts should be applying the law to school trips in the same way that they would to a commercial tour operator undertaking the same activity.

There are two main divisions of the law, criminal and civil law. Criminal law is typically categorised by the state punishing a defendant for an offence, civil law by individuals claiming compensation from those at fault.

Criminal Law

The Health and Safety Executive (HSE), under the HSWA 1974 and its Regulations, carry out the great majority of prosecutions involving school accidents. The main focus of the Act is to prevent workplace injuries, in particular to employees. However, section 3 (1) states: "It shall be the duty of every employer to conduct his undertaking in such a way as to ensure, so far as is reasonably practicable, that persons not in his employment who may be affected thereby are not thereby exposed to risks to their health or safety." It is not an absolute offence in that the defendant can, in defence, argue that a measure was not reasonably practicable. So that control measures can be considered in the light of the costs involved and the nature of the risk.

In 1992, further to a European Directive, regulations were introduced to require employers to carry out "suitable and sufficient" risk assessments on their "undertakings". In 1999 the Management of Health and Safety at Work Regulations updated the law. The combination of these two pieces of legislation means that Health and Safety legislation can now have a long reach. A school that fails to check out a supplier's safety measures (e.g. an outdoor adventure centre) could be regarded as having fallen below acceptable 'conduct'.

Criminal prosecutions are typically against the employer, whether that is a Local Education Authority (LEA) or the school. The Act can also apply to an individual employee through section 7:

> It shall be the duty of every employee while at work — to take reasonable care for the health and safety of himself and of other persons who be affected by his acts or omissions at work.

The prosecution of individual teachers, though, is very rare. It is most common for prosecutions to follow an accident rather than after a general inspection. The HSE can also issue improvement and prohibition notices where they find fault and want to take action short of prosecution. The following cases provide circumstances that have lead to a successful prosecution.

In HSE v London Borough of Hounslow (1997) the local authority, as the employer, was fined £25,000 for one of its schools failing to assess adequately the safety measures at a Scout-run swimming pool, where an 11-year-old drowned during a school trip. The school had failed to check the centre staff's qualifications and the Scouts did not inform the school that there were no qualified lifeguards on site.

In HSE v Jewish Senior Boys' School (2003) the school was fined £3,500 for failing to give sufficient consideration to health and safety precautions with regards HSWA 1974 s.3 (1). A lone teacher, with the care of 15 children, on a hill-walking trip to North Wales, was injured and seven of the group became separated, resulting in one child sustaining a serious head injury. Insufficient thought had been given to evacuation procedures.

In HSE v Leeds City Council (2003) the local authority was fined £30,000 for the failure of a school to carry out a risk assessment of river walking activities. Two children, aged 13 and 14, died as a result of being swept away along Stainforth Beck in the Yorkshire Dales. The teacher leading the trip admitted, at an earlier inquest, that he had no knowledge of the guidance issued by the Department for Education and Skills (DFES).

Each of these cases demonstrates a need for schools to consider, in advance, the measures that are in place when there is a turn of events: a child in trouble; a group split on the hills; a dangerous river … whether the activity be under the supervision of their own staff or employees of another organisation.

In instances where death occurs the police can consider charging an individual with manslaughter. Such a charge can then result in the Crown Prosecution Service prosecuting the individual in the Crown Court. The prosecution would need to show, beyond reasonable doubt, that the defendant had been grossly negligent. This behaviour lies between negligence and recklessness, the latter resulting in a possible charge of murder.

Gross negligence is normally accompanied by evidence that the defendant had a warning of a risk and/or the victim was in clear danger and that this was ignored. The one case involving a teacher and a school trip is R v Ellis (2003). This case resulted in a Lancashire teacher being jailed for the death of a ten-year-old boy, Max Palmer, due to Ellis' gross negligence on a school trip. Ellis admitted the manslaughter of the boy, who drowned on a trip in the Lake District. Ellis had allowed the boy to jump into a turbulent mountain stream in spite of bad weather and the warnings of other teachers; he was sentenced to 12 months. He had failed to make an ongoing assessment of the adverse condition of the stream, had not taken sufficient safety measures and had not considered the greater risk to a ten year old in his assessment of the group (a group made up mainly of 12 and 13 year olds). The judge told Ellis that he had been "unbelievably negligent and foolhardy" and that had he not pleaded guilty a three-year sentence would have been imposed.

Although most would recognise that there was gross negligence in this case, many would also admit as teachers and parents that such lapses in judgement do take place in life and they could be seen as human failings rather than evidence of criminal activity. Fortunately, such lapses rarely result in injury and when they do prosecutions against parents and teachers rarely follow. Society is loath to prosecute unless the evidence is damning.

If it can be shown that the employer, through the action of senior management, was grossly negligent, then a charge of corporate manslaughter could be brought against senior management and the organisation itself. However, as the law stands, corporate manslaughter is rarely proven because of the difficulties in finding sufficient negligence of management in particular cases. An example of this, involving a leisure provider, was the successful prosecution of OLL Ltd in 1994 after the senior management of the company failed to respond to warnings about the safety culture in the company. As a consequence of the gross negligence of the company, four school children lost their lives in a canoeing accident in Lyme Bay.

Civil law

Civil law actions against schools are mostly based on the law of negligence. There is a need to establish:

1. a duty of care between the school and the pupil on the occasion of the accident;
2. a breach of that duty;
3. that the injury resulted from that breach in whole or in part (which could result in part damages (Nixon, 1999 p. 22–26).

The duty of care can vary, so that six-year-olds would be owed a higher duty of care than teenagers because of the formers' lower appreciation of risk. A trip to a foreign city may be regarded as more hazardous than a trip to a British equivalent because of the differences in culture and language. Farm trips require greater attention to hygiene than heritage attractions. Defining the standard of care is the principle of '*In Loco Parentis*', that is teachers are expected to take care of the welfare of children as would experienced parents looking after their own children. The breach of that duty establishes negligence and the focus of so many cases is whether the school could have done more, subject to it being reasonable to do so, and that the consequences of such failure should have been foreseeable to the school. The following cases illustrate the law in operation.

In Brown v Nelson and others (1970) the issue of the need for a site inspection prior to a trip was considered. A school had over a number of years sent its pupils to an Outward Bound School. A 16-year-old was injured because a cable had been negligently maintained; was the school also liable for not having inspected the premises and the equipment? Nield, J ruled that the school had taken reasonable steps in that it knew the premises, knew that they were apparently safe and were staffed by competent and careful persons. They had "a general duty to take reasonable steps for the safety of those under their charge and use such care as would be exercised by a reasonably careful parent" (Brown v Nelson and others, 1970). The case is helpful in that it recognises a need for schools to take reasonable steps to satisfy themselves about the safety culture of their suppliers. Questions about whether risk assessments have been carried out (relevant to the age/ experience of the pupils), that staff are appropriately qualified and trained, that equipment and premises are safe, that there is a safety policy and licence (if required) would all fall within such 'reasonable steps'. Carrying out an inspection of equipment would go beyond such a duty though a site visit, if a hazardous environment, could be regarded as a measure to help satisfy oneself as to the competence of the host organisation.

The original judgement in Chittock v Woodbridge School (2001) caused such concern that the NASUWT advised its members to cease non-contractual trips. In June 2002 the school successfully appealed though the case left many teachers unsure of how they stood in relation to such actions. In 1996 Simon Chittock, aged 17, was on a school skiing trip to Austria. He accompanied a party of junior pupils and, as an experienced skier, was permitted, with the agreement of his parents, to ski on piste unsupervised. There was little doubt that the trip was well organised and that the master in charge, Andrew Jackson, had followed good practice throughout the trip. A couple of incidents, involving Chittock skiing off piste, resulted in disciplinary action having to be taken. However, Jackson, preferring to treat him as an adult, did not withdraw his ski pass but rather issued warnings and sought assurances. Following these incidents, Chittock, skiing on piste, misjudged a manoeuvre, ignored warning signs, and was severely injured as a consequence. Chittock argued that, given his failure to behave on previous occasions, he should have had his pass removed and that his carelessness on piste reflected his history of ignoring warnings. In the High Court, Leveson J. held the school 50% liable for Chittock's injuries on the basis that there was a link between their failure to remove the pass and the accident that followed. The Court of Appeal held that there was neither a breach of duty in that it was a reasonable response not to remove the pass and, even if it were a breach, there was insufficient causation between such breach and the carelessness inherent in the accident. The Court of Appeal was willing to recognise that the teacher may be faced with a range of reasonable responses to an incident whereas the High Court were less willing to see the action as coming within that range. Both courts also emphasised the need to work within relevant guidelines.

In Porter v City of Bradford (1985), heard before the Court of Appeal, Stephenson LJ highlighted the difficulties involved in school trip actions:

> It is quite clear what the duty of an education authority and of the teachers is; the difficulty is to apply the law correctly to the facts of any particular case. In my judgement the facts of this particular case show that it is difficult to decide what the right answer is when applying to particular facts the well known principle that it is the duty of a schoolteacher to show the care towards pupils that

a prudent parent would show towards his or her own children. (Porter v City of Bradford, 1985)

The claimant, aged 16, was on a geology field trip. Another pupil had been reprimanded for rolling boulders down a hill without thought for the safety of others. After the teacher stopped the behaviour he then left the pupil. Unfortunately the pupil, out of the teacher's sight and hearing, then proceeded to start lobbing stones, one of which fractured the skull of the claimant. In this case both the High Court and Court of Appeal felt that the teacher's response was inadequate and that close supervision should have been applied rather than leaving it to chance whether his order continued to be obeyed.

In Dowling v London Borough of Barnet (2000) the local authority and Bowman's Open Farm admitted 95% liability and settled during the hearing. Dowling, a four-year-old boy, had contracted an e-coli infection on a farm visit, leaving him incapable of speech and without the use of arms and legs. Previous cases had occurred at the farm yet the local authority took no measures to protect the children.

Resumé of the case law

The case law, on examination, does not presume that accidents must be the fault of the teachers. The courts are looking to establish, in both civil and criminal cases, whether schools are in breach of their duty to the pupils. One can discern a pattern of trying to establish what the reasonable school/teacher would have done in a situation recognising that there may be a number of reasonable options open to them in handling safety on a school trip cf. Chittock v Woodbridge School (2002). The courts are looking for benchmarks in establishing that proper standards have been applied. This approach is common when looking at organised leisure activities, as exemplified by Smoldon v Whitworth (1996) whereby, in Colts' Rugby, referees are expected to protect young players by applying the appropriate rules of the Rugby Football Union. Very often guidelines can provide the benchmarks for those wishing to see whether proper standards have been applied.

School trip guidelines
Guidelines are there to help identify potential hazards and give the reader measures that can be taken to improve the safety of participants. Breach of

a recommendation is not, in itself, unlawful though it may be regarded as indicating fault. There has been an increase of guidelines in recent years and these have originated from a variety of sources. The courts take a dim view of teachers/schools that have failed to read or to adhere to such guidance. Table 1 lists the main sources of guidance that are available to teachers. The ease of access to these guides varies considerably depending on factors such as cost (many are free); whether held at a local level or available on the Internet; whether there is common knowledge as to their existence. Some of the guides are pamphlets whilst others are substantial.

DFES (1998) lists sixty organisations that may provide useful information to the leader of a school trip. Some bodies are only interested in a specific area, for instance Disability Sport England, so the relevance of these bodies may vary from case to case. However, teachers may find themselves being asked to explain which guidance they followed and if not why not.

The adherence to such guidance may present challenges to schools and teachers. The ratios of teachers to pupils, the prior training of staff,

Table 1: School Trip Guidelines

Producers of Guidance

The DFES has produced:
> Health and Safety of Pupils on Educational Visits (1998) (HSPEV)
> Standards for LEAs in Overseeing Educational Visits (2002)
> Standards for Adventure (2002)
> A Handbook for Group Leaders (2002)
> Group Safety at Water Margins (2002)
> Health and Safety Responsibilities and Powers (2001)

Local Education Authorities e.g. Cheshire County Council

Schools also produce guidance, in particular when a school is the employer.

Trade Unions, for instance NASUWT produce Educational Visits (NASUWT, 2001)

Safety Bodies, such as the Royal Society for the Prevention of Accidents (ROSPA).

Sports' governing bodies and Adventure Associations, for instance the English Ski Council and the British Schools Exploring Society.

undertaking risk assessments prior to the visit, appointing an Educational Visits Coordinator (EVC), organising parental consent forms, considering child protection issues, organising transport safety and emergency procedures, all have resource implications. However, it does make it clear in HSPEV that "group leaders are allowed sufficient time to organise visits properly" (DFES, 1998: p.4). Consequently, schools need to balance the responsibilities of teachers within the school and the time and cost involved in organising and running a trip. If a teacher is unable to follow the main themes of the guidance and something goes wrong that could have been avoided by adherence to such guidance, there is a risk that legal liability will be established.

The review of the law and guidelines provides the legal context under which schools and teachers are required to operate. Unfortunately, for teachers trying to interpret the law and judgements there is room for confusion and concern, especially when the main source of information is through the press. Informed examination of the law and guidance can help overcome this fog of news information. However, this assumes that teachers and their managers will have the time and the support to go down this route.

Research methodology

An empirical study was conducted in order to investigate whether the fear of litigation may impact upon the organisation of school trips. A questionnaire was designed to be administered to teachers. Drawing upon previous research a number of questions were investigated:
- what was the teachers' understanding of relevant law and guidelines?
- how have teachers responded to safety concerns particularly relating to their willingness to organise school trips?
- what changes had been made to the organisation and running of such trips?
- what support did schools provide to teachers wanting to undertake such work and what were the resource implications relating to this support?

A mixture of schools was chosen from South Cheshire and inner-city Manchester. Primary and Secondary schools were targeted; all were state schools with the exception of one independent school. Each school was contacted in the summer term of 2004 and was asked to suggest a member of staff who would be willing to distribute the questionnaires to colleagues in the school. In some schools this fell to the EVC, in others to a senior member of staff. In all 70 questionnaires were distributed but only seventeen were returned. One school returned one questionnaire with its teachers responding as one.

The questionnaire consisted of eleven questions: six of them were quantitative and the remainder allowed the teachers to express their views. It was envisaged that such a style would encourage participation without being prescriptive. The questions were selected on the basis of the concerns revealed in the review of literature. Prior to the administration of the questionnaire a pilot interview was carried out with a Manchester teacher in order to consider the validity of the questions.

Results and discussion

The response rate overall was low. Whilst only two of the schools failed to respond, citing other work commitments, most needed encouragement to return the questionnaires. One school commented that the best time of year to carry out the survey would be at the beginning of the year and not the end. In its way this was revealing as it demonstrated the day-to-day pressure on schools and teachers and the difficulty in carrying out this kind of research. This problem was compounded by the need to question potentially sensitive areas — in particular, issues relating to support and resourcing of school trips.

In order to encourage openness, schools were advised that their results would not be attributed. However, the concern remained that schools could see that their teachers' answers might imply that the school was authorising trips to go ahead without sufficient support for staff. This situation was not helped by the results coming back through the school contact, often a senior member of staff. It may be that a better route to the teachers might be via a trade union or professional association.

All the responses, except one, were from teachers with over 10 years experience. Thirteen of the respondents had experience with trips. Six had overseas experience, ten in the U.K; seven had residential experience and nine day trips. It was surprising that so few of the respondents had less than 10 years experience. If this reflects a trend in the organising of trips then the signs for the future are not good. There was a good spread of experience in terms of location and duration. Clearly, the longer and further afield the activity, the greater the demands on the teacher. It may well be that some forms of trip, for instance the residential, may be more vulnerable to risk aversion amongst teachers compared with day trips. However, the latter may be seen as an inefficient use of resources given the proportion of time spent on paperwork.

The first question explored the teacher's knowledge of the law governing school trips. This was considered in order to see how well teachers understood their duty of care on such trips. Only six respondents correctly identified the law of negligence and Health and Safety law. None of the remainder were able to identify the main law — either putting nothing down or identifying areas of marginal relevance for instance "under age drinking/ smoking" (respondent: 3–5 years experience); "law relating to travel agents" (respondent: 10+ years experience).

Respondents were then asked to name any school trip safety guidelines that they had consulted. The most common response (five) were their school's own guidelines; followed by the DFES website (three); Local Education Authorities (two); Trade Union Guidelines (one) and Adventure Activity Licensing Authority (one). The remainder (five) failed to identify any specific guidelines. It is of concern that no one identified HSPEV, which is free of charge and promoted heavily by the DFES. Of encouragement is that most teachers are aware of guidelines as a source of information.

When questioned on whether the need to follow regulations and guidelines had affected their willingness to run school trips, ten responded equally to 'considerably/to a degree' with only three saying 'not at all'. When asked whether such material had resulted in changes being made to school trips and, if so, what the nature of such changes were, six indicated that major changes had taken place whilst three that minor changes had been made. The nature of the changes included: risk assessments (five); paperwork related (seven); applying ratios (three); curtailing activities (one). A clear reaction to the guidelines is having to undertake additional paperwork, particularly if risk assessments come under that heading.

The respondents were asked how adverse publicity had affected their willingness to organise school trips. Six said 'considerably'; followed by five admitting 'to a degree'. Only three agreed with 'not at all'. Such findings suggest, even given the limited response, that many teachers are affected by their perception of the blame culture and the additional work needed by them in order to conform with the law through adherence to guidelines.

Respondents were asked about the support available from their employer. Of concern is that only three identified a trips coordinator: a low number considering all state schools are expected to have appointed such a person to give assistance to staff. Three said 'support through a checklist'; two felt there was 'plenty of help' and two said 'some help'. However, six were unable to identify any help. It would appear that there is a management issue here; the survey suggests that schools/LEAS are not committing sufficient resources to support their staff that are willing to undertake trips. Asked about any further thoughts that the teachers had on schools organising school trips, the responses suggest a pessimistic outlook. Two responded that trips will cease because of litigation; another responded with 'wary'; another that the trips competed with academic commitments; another that there will have to be a shift in the quality of leadership.

Conclusion

The work has sought to review the law and guidelines, and how courts have responded to litigation against schools and teachers. How teachers view these areas is an important factor in whether they will be prepared to undertake trips. The survey suggests that this decision is a fragile one and that schools, LEAs and Government need to recognise that 'support' in the form of more guidelines may not be the answer. Greater institutional concern that solely generates more guidelines and paperwork will inevitably mean a greater commitment of teachers' time for planning and executing school trips.

The primary research reported here sought to establish how teachers have been reacting to high profile litigation and their need to follow guidance. Essentially the study questioned their perception of the school trip, whether accurate or not, and how this translates into a willingness to get involved in an activity. There is little evidence that the law and its interpretation have radically changed in recent years. However, it may well be that there is a greater willingness of victims to seek compensation, no longer attributing the accident to 'fate'.

Overall the research provides a snapshot of the views of a small number of teachers drawn from the North West of England, most with over ten years experience in the profession undertaking school trips. The responses suggest a mixture of experiences. Clearly there are some teachers who are well informed about the law and what is expected of them, work in a school with an Educational Visits Coordinator or the equivalent and have the backing of their school in undertaking trips. However, the research does suggest that the concerns expressed by the Education Secretary about school trips are valid. There is caution about this area and, although that may have positive aspects, it could be damaging the experience of children, quite possibly from those schools that are poorly resourced. Some teachers may be put off organising trips; others may avoid potentially hazardous activities, for instance residential and adventure trips, whilst the concern with paperwork may cut out day trips because of the proportion of time spent on paperwork.

The review of the law and guidance, and teachers' knowledge of such, suggests that there is a gap that could be bridged by way of training and on-going advice for teachers wanting to undertake activities. It is surprising that a number of teachers did not identify an EVC within their school. The survey also suggests that teachers feel wary about their need to undertake extra work in order to conform with the law. The amount of support in giving teachers the time and resources to conform with the law may be vital in keeping school trips going.

In summary, the organisation of a school trip is subject to a balance of costs and benefits — some easily quantified, others not. These can be summarised as follows:

- Costs: financial; time in organising and running the trip — this could be in the teacher's free time; resources including adequate staffing, sufficient equipment, parental/pupil/school/LEA support;
- Benefits: Merit of the undertaking (e.g. does it support the National Curriculum?); anticipated satisfaction in the outcome.

If these factors come together such that the benefits outweigh the costs, then trips have the right environment to go ahead. In the commercial sector of tour operations the pursuit of profit drives the supply in the market; with school trips it is the altruism of the teachers and schools. If more pressure is put on the costs and/or there are reductions in the benefits then the future of trips may be affected. Ultimately though, whether school trips continue and in what form may well depend upon the willingness of government and the employers to give additional support to the teachers who want to undertake such activities.

References and bibliography

Bamber, D. (2004) 'School trips and charities hit by soaring insurance costs', *Sunday Telegraph* August 29: p. 12.

Cabinet Office (2004) Better Regulation Task Force. Better Routes to Redress (2004) London www.brtf.gov.uk (accessed 1 July 2004).

Clarke, C. (2004) Speech given to the NASUWT Annual Conference at Llandudno on 12 April 2004 www.dfes.gov.uk (accessed 1 July 2004).

Cooper, C (1999) 'The European school travel Market', *Travel and Tourism Analyst* No. 5: pp. 89–105.

DFES (Department for Education and Skills) (1998) *Health and Safety of Pupils on Educational Visits*. Sudbury: DFES Publications.

DFES (2002) *A Handbook for Group Leaders*. Sudbury: DFES Publications. DFES Publications Sudbury.

DFES (2002) *Group Safety at Water Margins*. Sudbury: DFES Publications.

DFES (2002) *Standards for LEAs in Overseeing Educational Visits*. Sudbury: DFES Publications.

DFES (2002) *Standards for Adventure*. Sudbury: DFES Publications.

Ford, J., Hughes, M. and Rubein, D. (1999) *Education law and practice*. London: Legal Action Group.

Jenkins, R. and Owen, G. (2003) 'Jailing of teacher may spell the end for school trips', *Times Newspapers*, London September 24: p. 1.

Kalinowski, K.M. and Weiler, B. (1992), 'Educational tourism' in Weiler, B. and Hall C.M. (eds) *Special interest tourism*. London, Belhaven Press, pp. 15–26.

NASUWT (2001) *Educational visits*. Birmingham : NASUWT.

Nixon, J. (1999) 'Teachers' legal liabilities and responsibilities', in Cole, M. (ed) *Professional issues for teachers and student teachers*. London: Fulton, pp. 22–37.

Smith, C. and Jenner, P. (1997) 'Educational tourism', *Travel and Tourism Analyst* No. 3: pp 60–75.

Smithers, R. (2001) 'Blame culture "could end trips"', August 2, 2001; www.EducationGuardian.co.uk (accessed 1 July 2004).

Swift, G. (2002) 'Scandal of kids on school trips', *Express Newspapers*, September 9.

Wainwright, M. (2002) 'Teachers' advice', *The Guardian*, May 28: p. 6.

Wainwright, M. (2003) 'School trips under threat', *Guardian Unlimited*, 24 September.

www.guardian.co.uk_news/story/0,3604,1048361,00.html. (accessed 1July 2004).

Cases

Brown v Nelson and others (1970) 69 LGR 20.

Chittock v Woodbridge School (2001) and (2002).

Dowling v London Borough of Barnet (2000).

H.S.E v Jewish Senior Boys' School (2003).

H.S.E v Leeds City Council (2003).

H.S.E v London Borough of Hounslow (1997).

Porter v City of Bradford (1985).

R v Ellis (2003).

Smoldon v Whitworth (1996). Times Law Reports Dec. 18, 1996.

Williams v Eady (1893) 10 TLR 41 CA.

COOL CONSUMPTION: HOW DO YOUNG PEOPLE USE ADVENTURE TOURISM?

Shelagh Ferguson and Sarah Todd
University of Otago, New Zealand

Introduction

While the use of the concept of 'status' has been widespread in the promotion of a variety of products and brands, our understanding of what 'status' actually means in contemporary consumption is rather limited. Status aspirations have been found to be primary motivators for a range of consumption experiences, but changes in consumer markets mean that our notion of what 'status' is may also require an update. This paper uses constructs widely discussed in the consumer behaviour literature to advance the idea that, for a new generation of consumers, consuming 'cool' has replaced the conventional perspective of consuming to gain status. Consequently, the meaning of 'cool' in terms of consumption is explored, and its relationship with 'status' as well as the social dimensions of consumption. The context for this paper is that of adventure tourism and preliminary findings are presented with regard to tourists in New Zealand and their use of bungee jumping to acquire 'cool'.

A new generation of consumers?

Before looking more closely at the relevant consumer behaviour literature, it is first important to define exactly this new generation of consumers . Generation Y (or the *millennials*) are described as even more sophisticated and media-wise than their Generation X predecessors (Coupland, 1991;

Howe and Strauss, 2000; Paul, 2001). Generally agreed to be born between the late 1970s and early 1990s, this is a generation defined by their high media literacy, high expectations of choice and strong image-consciousness (Martin, 2001; Neuborne and Kerwin, 1999; Paul, 2001; Quart, 2003). Perhaps paradoxically, they seek to define their individuality through discretionary consumption while also seeking to gain social approval and a sense of belonging. Individual identity is thus important within their relevant community, as is belonging to the young cognoscenti (Goodman and Roughcoff, 2003).

This essence of *difference* (from others or the mainstream) is a central part of identity for Generation Y (Nancarrow, Nancarrow and Page, 2002). Their concept of self is symbolised by their tangible consumption, by the labels that they wear, by the activities they pursue and by the music they like. These cut across the more traditional segmentation variables used to categorise consumers such as gender, ethnicity, social class or VALS ["Values and Lifestyle system" (Kamakura and Masson, 1991)]. Schouten and McAlexander (1995) argue that these subcultures of consumption offer far greater insight into the organising forces of society.

Just as Generation Y and their attitudes towards consumption appear somewhat contradictory, so too is 'cool' difficult to define. Historically, 'cool' has its roots in early American slavery, when imported Africans used a 'cool' face to protect themselves from the jibes and humiliation of their slave masters and the cruelty of the situation. 'Cool' was expressed as resistance to subjugation and humiliation. It was also used to protect their culture in this foreign environment and a language was formed that allowed the slaves to communicate excluding their masters (Pountain and Robins, 2000). A central theme in the phenomenon of cool is this lack of display of strong emotions — distinctly uncool!

The modern term 'cool' has a range of meanings dependent upon origin and locality. Australia, New Zealand and the UK use the term in a similar manner, whereas the USA generally use the term 'hip' in a similar context. This paper adopts the position of Pountain and Robbins (2000), whereby the term is used to represent a phenomenon that heavily influences human behaviour, does not define a person or a place but is dynamic and relational, with each generation defining it for themselves.

The notion of 'cool' in relation to consumption is not new. Nancarrow, Nancarrow and Page (2002) argue that 'cool' has provided a key underpinning in the understanding of popular culture for a significant time. However, consumer behaviour as a disciplinary field has not acknowledged 'cool' as a dominant determinant of consumption, despite acting in a similar way to the much studied concept of status. This paper posits that not only does 'cool' motivate the consumption of Generation Y much in the same way that status has been said to motivate consumption, but it is also a value derived from consumption. Thus, 'cool' is more than a motivation to consume: rather it comprises a myriad of interweaving motives and meanings that provide both a context for consumption and the compulsion to consume.

Why is Generation Y so influenced by 'cool' when making consumption choices? One essential element of 'cool' is its anti-establishment stance. This is evidenced by its mass adoption as an attitude in the 1960s, a time of rejection of traditional values, of adoption of free speech and civil rights and of opposition to nuclear weapons and the Vietnam War. Each successive generation has modified and re-invented 'cool' to match their generational characteristics. With Generation Y's distinctive characteristics including media literacy, expectation of choice, shared awareness of commodified symbolism (Frank, 1997) and access to communication technologies such as the Internet, this generation can easily share knowledge to stay ahead of the mainstream.

Key components of the phenomenon of 'cool' therefore include: an element of rebellion or defiance of authority; a close relationship with American popular culture (but not defined by it, as 'cool' has been found, built, developed, mutated and owned worldwide); the absence of a relationship to money (money may be a resource in the consumption of the symbols of 'cool' but this does not make consumers inherently 'cool', as the attitude runs more deeply). Teenagers have always been susceptible to the attraction of becoming and displaying 'cool'. During the 'rites of passage' period when the teenager is negotiating his/her self-identity, many actively reject replication of their parents' perceived identity. Hence the re-invention of 'cool' for each generation has always carried a theme of rebellion (Pountain and Robins, 2000; Thornton, 1995).

So who decides what is 'cool'? Is it the commodified media images of the MTV generation who consume everything from their Spring Break to the Osborne's reality of family life? Goodman and Roughcoff (2003) suggest that fashion, music, film, television, leisure and travel all fall into the category of important lifestyle consumption that can generate 'cool' for an individual. The understanding of what is 'cool' is facilitated by media saturation that serves a defining feature of Generation Y, as discussed earlier. Clearly there is not one single shared consciousness of 'cool' and there are distinctions specific to smaller symbolic communities, as discussed in depth by Hebdige (1979) in his study of punk rocker culture. Global media such as MTV, ESPN and FHM magazine have influenced the formation of the specific markers of 'cool'. Is it that, as Goodman and Roughcoff (2003) argue, the consumers of such images accept this as a representation of aspired life, deem it 'cool' and then replicate it, pushing the envelope even further each time and creating a giant feedback loop?

In what Featherstone (1991) called the 'paper chase effect', once the mainstream has adopted a trend then the 'cool' cognoscenti reject it and move on to the next consumption trend. For the industries targeting Generation Y, research into their consumption behaviour is labelled 'cool hunting', as they look for the next big trend to be adopted by 'trendsetters' and diffused to the rest of this market (Martin, 2001; Nancarrow, Nancarrow and Page, 2002). Thornton's (1995) study of dance music subculture revealed the importance of insider knowledge, knowing what is deemed 'cool' by nature of its authenticity (being real) and exclusivity and a rejection of the mass-produced or popular. This pattern of consumption echoes Bourdieu's (1984) concept of 'cultural capital' (or perhaps it should now be *subcultural* capital): knowledge that cultural intermediaries disseminate to others to secure their position as style leaders, and which signifies meaning to those in the 'know'.

Literature review

Status has long been regarded as a primary motivation to consume, with status acquisition also a post-consumption benefit. This primary role played by status is also evident in the discussion of related concepts such as con-spicuous consumption. The purchase, use, display and consumption of goods and services have frequently been described as a means of gaining social status (Solomon, 1992; Veblen, 1899), and originally seen as the domain of the wealthy. This structuralist perspective links status to society and social class, which in turn is defined by income and social stratification. Recent literature has also suggested that status has a role in lifestyle segmentation, a popular marketing concept in understanding group consumption behaviour. This refers back to Weber's (1948) original position on status as a group phenomenon that can be the basis for action and participation, in that such a group gives individuals their fundamental sense of identity (Todd & Lawson, 2003).

Solomon's (1999) proposition that status is in the eye of the beholder, thereby making it a uniquely individual concept, is strongly refuted in this paper because its importance is based on the perception of the consumption by significant others, and this two-way flow is central to its function. Nor should status be seen as a motivation for consumption that is confined to the wealthy elite. Belk (1988) noted that conspicuous consumption of status-orientated products and services exists even in the third world, a finding confirmed by Arnould (1985). Using an anthropological perspective, the latter explored the reasons why Niger natives wore the brand "addidas" and how they integrated and gave it meaning within their community.

Waters (1994) defines status as an outcome of a social construction process that assigns meaning to the desire for acquisition and/or display of valued objects calculated to increase social honour in a community. Holbrook (1999) positions status in his typology of consumer values as a form of value derived from consumption, in opposition to its more common reference as a motivation to consume. Holbrook identifies three key dimensions of consumer value: namely, extrinsic to intrinsic; self-orientated to other-oriented; and active to reactive. Within this framework, status is defined as the active manipulation of one's own consumption behaviour as an extrinsic means towards the other-oriented end of achieving a favourable response from someone else. This paper adopts the stance that 'cool' is the relevant value which should replace the position of status in Holbrook's framework when attempting to understand young consumers' consumption. That is, there is recognition of the value of 'cool' derived post-consumption and its other-oriented focus acknowledges the importance of consumption occurring within a context where a community's opinion is sought and valued.

While not the exclusive domain of the wealthy, the notion of status does appear to be more important to some consumption communities than others. Similarly, the status ascribed within a community may not have significance outside of that group. Schouten & McAlexander's (1995) work on Harley Davidson riders identified a wealth of meaning in the hierarchical and status driven communities of Harley Owners' Groups (HOG) Chapters. The structure and value of the ascribed status was known to all members but mystifying to anyone observing the community from the outside.

The term 'community' covers a broad range of groups of individuals from non-geographically bounded (Muniz and O'Guinn, 2001) to geo-graphically concentrated (Holt, 1995), from scattered (Boorstin, 1974) or even from the amorphous space of the Internet (Tambyah, 1996). It is not essential that the community share the consumption for it to be deemed 'cool', particularly with the ability for stories to be told and experiences to be shared relatively quickly via a range of communication technologies. For example, the consumption experience can happen in New Zealand, 12,000 miles from their home community in the UK but, once the consumer narrates the experience, s/he derives the value from their community or becomes 'cool' in their eyes.

Understanding such consumption communities arguably offers a greater insight into the organising forces of society than that secured by traditional segmentational tools (Schouten & McAlexander, 1995). The ascribed value that certain consumption has within these communities is specific to that community and this process of buying into such a value system differentiates the community from others. They can also actively reject group norms that govern other large sections of society (e.g. Thompson and Holt, 1996; Thornton, 1995). Post-modern influences drive communities to adopt distinctive cultures and status-goods express symbolic needs rather than yielding a 'one size fits all' approach. This process of defining and acquiring status within a specific group was well explored in the context of punk rockers by Hebdige (1979). He undertook an in-depth examination of young people's need to redefine and 'make their own' a set of cultural meanings that often rejected those of other mainstream communities, simply on the basis that they were mainstream!

For such communities, Levy (1959) argues that the acquisition of status through consumption is an extension of their social identity, whereby their consumption has symbolic meaning in these communities and is dynamic in nature. Each community collectively and individually negotiates that identity over time, and as such it can be seen as a work in progress. This individual negotiation of social identity through consumption is a form of self-construction, making ourselves the person we wish to be by using consumption to gain status within communities and by enhancing our construct of self within a community. The group identity is negotiated around expressive agreed symbols, and symbolic consumption is the key to the process.

The notion of consumption communities share similarities with the way in which subcultures have been viewed in the consumer behaviour literature, with groups based around the consumption of a range of activities from skydiving to dance music (e.g. Arnould and Price, 1993; Belk and Costa, 1998; Celsi, Rose and Leigh, 1993; Haslop, Hill and Schmidt, 1998; O'Guinn, 1991; Schouten and McAlexander, 1995; Thornton, 1995; Wheaton, 2003). Schouten and Mc Alexander (1995) define consumption subcultures as a distinctive subgroup of society that self-selects on the basis of a shared commitment to a particular product, brand or consumption activity. Other characteristics of such a subculture include: an identifiable, hierarchical social structure; a unique ethos or set of shared beliefs; distinctive values and unique jargon; particular rituals and modes of symbolic expression. Members of such a community have a dynamic relationship not just with the form of consumption but also with organisations providing the consumption experience and other consumers.

Muniz and O'Guinn (2001) focus on the related notion of a brand community, defined as a specialised, non-geographically bounded community, based on a structured set of relationships among users of a brand. Similar to cultures of consumption, these consumers have a relationship with the organisation providing the brand, the brand itself, the product in use and other customers. McAlexander, Schouten and Koening (2002) stress that this four-way dynamic relationship provides the context for these communities. This paper argues that, for members of Generation Y in particular, consumption has moved beyond the brand. Rather, consumption is manipulated to extract the desired meaning for the individual concerned, as opposed to consumption of the meaning imposed by the brand or corporation. Adopting such a perspective, it is easier to understand how a group of supposedly sophisticated and media literate consumers can still use consumption to create 'cool'.

To extend the theoretical basis for this paper, primary data collection was undertaken in adventure tourism. Specifically, bungee jumping in New Zealand was chosen as an appropriate context because of its commercial nature and the tendency of consumers to view it as a 'one-off' experience. Occasionally consumers may choose to jump more than once but research shows that it tends not to be repeated on a regular basis. Nor do consumers regard skill development as central to the activity. It is the domain of commercial licensed operators who charge approximately £100 per jump with video and photographs included in the package. There is no shortage of consumers for this eight-second experience, with one site processing over 50 jumpers per day, 365 days of the year.

The site chosen for this research was the Nevis High Wire Bungy near Queenstown in New Zealand. It is the second highest bungee jump in the world at 134 metres and is operated by A J Hackett, a well-regarded brand name in the adventure tourism world.

Method

The objectives for the primary research included investigating the audience for bungee jumpers' narratives of their experiences and the construction of such narratives. Additionally, consumers' perceptions of 'cool' were investigated together with the reactions they anticipated receiving from their audiences.

To complement previous work done from a psychological perspective, a sociological multi-method approach was adopted. The choice of methodology evolved during preliminary research and has been moulded by initial findings and reference to the relevant literature. This semi-inductive, iterative methodology matches both the perspective adopted and the exploratory nature of the research problem. An optimum research situation would be to follow each consumer back to his or her home communities and observe the narration of their experiences. Logistically this was impossible and would not capture the immediate post-consumption narration, when the consumer uses phone, text and e-mail to communicate with their relevant friendship networks and local communities. A methodological compromise was to approach participants very shortly after the completion of their bungee jump and discuss how they would construct their 'story' and what modifications would be made to their stories with regard to the audience. An additional area for discussion was how the imperative to narrate would develop or recede over time as they were physically separated from their home community. The participants were also asked to include the researcher on their mailing lists so that a copy of the narration would also be received in e-mail form. This provided a wider insight into the narrative and added greater depth to the stories told.

Over a period of two weeks, almost 100 informants were interviewed at A J Hackett's Nevis Bungy jump site. The participants were approached post-jump and requested to participate in a 'direct to camera' interview. Consent forms were completed and information sheets distributed as part of the researcher's University's requirements for ethical research. A very high consent rate was gained with less than ten refusals during the research period. Participants were asked to detail to whom they would first tell their stories and what they would say. This was then developed to explore how they would modify and emphasise certain elements of the story for different audiences and why that was deemed necessary. As an essential part of the narrative, participants were asked to describe how they viewed this particular consumption experience and how their friends would view them in relation to this consumption in terms of whether it was 'cool' or not. The video-recorded semi-structured interviews were then analysed with reference back to the literature to identify key emergent themes for development.

Emergent themes

The conceptual argument outlined in this paper was supported by initial research findings. It is clearly evident from these preliminary findings that this consumption is socially based rather than psychologically or internally focused. Every person interviewed intended to narrate their experience to someone from their home community within a couple of hours of consumption, either by phone, text or e-mail. Specific themes to emerge included:

1. *Definitions of 'cool'*

Participants were asked if they thought that their friends would think bungee jumping to be 'cool'. The participants came from a wide range of home countries including Mexico, Germany, Ireland, Spain, Brazil, United Kingdom and America. No-one queried the use of the word 'cool' in this context, suggesting that it is universally accepted as a descriptor of such an activity and understood by people within this consumption community from a range of cultural backgrounds.

2. *Status vs. 'cool'*

'Cool' is a broad term used not only to describe the activity (in this case bungee jumping) but also the attitude that the informant hopes to engender in their friends with regard to themselves, by participating in this activity. Hence the narrations of such experiences are central to the consumption. One informant commented:

> "Why else would you do these things, if not to tell your friends about them?"

When asked if their friends would think it was 'cool' that they had done the Nevis bungee jump, all agreed that they would and some informants went on to suggest that their friends would then think that they were 'cool' by association. An integral part of this 'being cool' was an element of envy. This was something that their friends would like to have done but have not achieved! Despite his jokey manner, one informant summarised

> "Of course they will think I am 'cool', they will want to be me!"

No one referred to status in their discussions. When it was raised they immediately reverted to the term 'cool' in their narration, thus reinforcing that 'cool' is a concept that young people use comfortably with reference to bungee jumping. 'Status', on the other hand, was often queried — "what do you mean by status?" — and replaced by 'cool' when recounting their stories and their community's reaction.

3.   Community influences

Immediate family were often indicated as the first group that would have the stories recounted to them. However, when further questioned, one informant noted that,

> "My family probably will not understand what a bungee jump is, I will have to explain it to them but all my friends will know. My parents will think I am crazy but my friends will think I am cool."

This was mirrored by several other similar quotes, indicating a clear difference in the consumer's mind as to whom they were telling the story to and what the purpose was of the recounting. Some respondents readily revealed that they would be 'sexing up' the version of their experience that they told to their friends back home so they would be more impressed. Most accounts included factual markers such as specific height (134m) and stressing that it was the second highest bungee in the world.

A central feature of 'cool' identified in the literature, namely that it is reinvented for each generation, is also identifiable. The previous generation's definition of 'cool' is actively rejected in favor of a shared, separate, exclusive understanding. Of course this consumer's parents will think he is crazy because they do not share his construction of 'cool' that his friends do. His friends, as part of Generation Y, will share his construction of 'cool'.

Conclusions and directions for further research

These findings support the contention that consuming 'cool' has replaced the conventional notion of consuming to gain status for Generation Y. 'Cool' as a phenomenon demonstrably had meaning for all informants and they used the term frequently and easily in their narrations. Informants differentiated between their audiences, in terms of who would think the consumption 'cool' and who would think it crazy. This supports the suggestion that each generation re-invents 'cool' and shares an understanding of the nature of that phenomenon.

At this stage, the analysis is preliminary. It is intended that a technique such as pattern matching (Campbell, 1975) will be used to further explore the emergent themes. Excerpts of the video taped interviews will also be shown to other members of Generation Y to ascertain their responses to the narratives, together with whether they would ascribe 'cool' to the narrators.

References

Arnould, E. and L. L. Price (1993) 'River magic: Extraordinary experience and the extended service encounter', *Journal of Consumer Research* 20: pp. 24–45.

Belk, R. and J. A. Costa (1998) 'The Mountain Man myth: A contemporary consuming fantasy', *Journal of Consumer Research* Vol. 25, No. 3: pp. 218–241.

Belk, R. W. (1988) 'Third world consumer culture, marketing and development' in . E. Kumuc and A. F. Firat. Greenwich (eds) *Research in Marketing, Supplement 4: Marketing and Development : Toward Broader Dimensions (Research in MarketingSupplement)*. CT: JAI: pp. 103–127.

Boorstin, D. J. (1974) *The Americans: The democratic experience.* New York: Vintage.

Bourdieu, P. (1984) *Distinction: A social critique of judgement of taste* [trans. R. Nice]. London: Routledge.

Campbell, D. T. (1975) '"Degrees of freedom" and the case study', *Comparitive Political Studies* Vol. 8, No. 2: pp. 178–193.

Celsi, R. L., R. L. Rose and T. W. Leigh (1993) 'An exploration of high risk leisure consumption through skydiving', *Journal of Consumer Research* Vol. 20, No. 1: pp. 1–23.

Coupland, D. (1991) *Generation X*. London: Abacus.

Frank, T. (1997) *The conquest of cool*. Chicago: University of Chicago Press.

Featherstone, M. (1991) *Consumer culture and postmodernism*. London: Sage.

Goodman, B. and D. Roughcoff (2003) *Merchants of cool*. [video]

Haslop, C., H. Hill and R. A. Schmidt (1998) 'The gay lifestyle — spaces for a subculture of consumption', *Marketing Intelligence and Planning* Vol. 16, No. 5: pp. 318–326.

Hebdige, D. (1979) *Subculture: The meaning of style*. London, Routledge.

Holt, D. B. (1995) 'How consumers consume: A typology of consumptive practices', *Journal of Consumer Research* Vol. 22, No. 1: pp. 1–25.

Howe, N. and W. Strauss (2000) *Millennials rising: The next great generation.* New York, Random House Inc.

Kamakura, W. A. and Masson, J. A. (1991) 'Value segmentation: A model for the measurement of values and value systems', *Journal of Consumer Research* 18 (September): pp 208–218.

Levy, S. J. (1959) 'Symbols for sale', *Harvard Business Review* 37 (July–August): pp. 117–124.

Martin, C. A. (2001) *Managing Generation Y*. Amherst. MA, HRD Press.

McAlexander, J. H., J. W. Schouten and h. F. Koening (2002) 'Building brand community', *Journal of Marketing* No. 38 (January): pp. 1–19.

Muniz, A. and T. O'Guinn (2001) 'Brand communities', *Journal of Consumer Research* 27 (March): pp. 412–32.

Nancarrow, C., P. Nancarrow and J. Page (2002) 'An analysis of the concept of cool and its marketing implications', *Journal of Consumer Behaviour* Vol. 1, No. 4: pp. 311–322.

Neuborne, E. and K. Kerwin (1999) 'Generation Y', *Business Week* Vol. 2, No. 15: p. 99.

O'Guinn, T. (1991) 'Touching greatness: The Central Midwest Barry Manilow Fan Club', in R. W. Belk *Highways and buyways: Naturalistic research from the consumer behaviour odyssey*. Provo, UT, Association for Consumer Research, pp. 102–11.

Paul, P. (2001) 'Getting inside Gen Y', *American Demographics* Vol. 23, No. 9: pp. 42–49.

Pountain, D. and D. Robins (2000) *Cool rules*. London: Reaktion.

Quart, A. (2003) *Branded: The buying and selling of teenagers*. Cambridge MA: Perseus Publishing.

Schouten, J. and J. McAlexander (1995) 'Subcultures of consumption: An ethnography of the new bikers', *Journal of Consumer Research* Vol. 22, No. 1: p. 43.

Solomon, M. R. (1992) *Consumer behavior*. New Jersey: Prentice-Hall.

Tambyah, S. K. (1996) 'Life on the Net: The reconstruction of self and community', *Advances in Consumer Research* 23: pp. 172–77.

Thompson, C. J. and D. B. Holt (1996) 'Communities and consumption: Research on consumer strategies for constructing communal relationships in a postmodern world', *Advances in Consumer Research* 23: pp. 204–205.

Thornton, S. (1995) *Club cultures: Music, media and subcultural capital*. Cambridge: Polity.

Veblen, T. (1899) *The theory of the leisure class*. New York: Macmillan.

Wheaton, B. (2003) 'A subculture of commitment', in R. E. Rinehart and S. Sydnor (eds) *To the extreme: Alternative sports, inside and out*. Albany: State University of New York.

RECREATIONAL SUBSTANCE USE AMONG LESBIAN, GAY, AND BISEXUAL YOUTH: FREQUENCY AND PREDICTORS

Arnold H. Grossman
New York University

Anthony R. D'Augelli
The Pennsylvania State University

Introduction

Although lesbian, gay, and bisexual (LGB) people have become an increasingly visible subculture of many Western societies, they remain an invisible component of others. In either situation, their existence is stigmatized, and they are alienated from societies' mainstream culture because their sexuality continues to be considered immoral and abhorrent to many. As D'Augelli (1998) indicated, the hostile environment may lead to sexual orientation victimization; and, this may be especially true with regard to LGB youth. Compared to LGB adults, LGB youth are more likely to be victimized, and the consequences of the victimization may have psychological consequences that are more severe. Additionally, being a member of a minority group that is not recognized as a legitimated minority not only leads to experiences of discrimination and violence, but also results in feelings of marginalization that can have a direct impact on one's mental health. Some studies have linked being a member of minority group and the association with "minority stress" to mental health problems, including substance use (DiPlacido, 1998; Savin-Williams, 1994).

Researchers have found recreational substance use among LGB youth to be high (Garofalo, et al., 1998; Remafedi, 1987, 1994; Rosario, Rotheram-Borus, et al., 1992; Rosario, Hunter & Gwadz, 1997). These studies, using convenience samples ranging from 29 to 239 participants, found high current substance use and lifetime substance use among LGB youth. At least 75%

of the youth reported using alcohol, and the rates for marijuana use ranged from 42% to 76%. In each case, these rates were substantially higher than the national averages at the time the studies were conducted. Crack/cocaine use among the samples ranged from 21% to 33% and injecting drugs/heroin ranged from 0% to 22%.

Using survey data from the 1995 Youth Risk Behavior Surveillance Systems (YRBSS) collected in Massachusetts and Vermont (as these two states ask questions related to sexual orientation), Bontempo and D'Augelli (2002) found LGB youth reported higher levels of substance use than their heterosexual peers. In addition, the LGB youth reporting high levels of at-school victimization were seen to have even higher levels of substance use. With the exception of alcohol consumption (which was approximately the same for LGB and heterosexual males and females), Bontempo and D'Augelli found that gay and bisexual males and heterosexual males reported higher levels of marijuana/cocaine use and other street drugs than females. A study using 1993 YRBSS data from Massachusetts presented findings with a more vivid description (Faulkner & Cranston, 1998). Same-sex sexually-oriented students were nine times more likely than heterosexual students to report using alcohol on each of the 30 days preceding the survey, and they were six times more likely to report having used cocaine. They were also five times more likely to report having used other illegal drugs 20 or more times in their lives. They were almost seven times more likely to report ever having injected an illegal drug. Findings from a community-based study (Lock & Steiner, 1999) of 106 LGB and 224 "unsure" youth are dissimilar from those presented above. They found that these youth were not at greater risk for substance abuse than their peers.

Only a few studies have examined substance use among LGB youth by gender. Among a sample of LGB youth, Rosario, Hunter, and Gwadz (1997) found higher lifetime substance use of alcohol, marijuana, cocaine/ crack and heroin/injecting among females than males. While Rotheram-Borus, Reid, Marelich, and Srinvasan (1999) found higher lifetime use of alcohol among males than females, but no differences in lifetime use of marijuana and crack/cocaine between males and females. Russell, Driscoll, and Truong (2002), examining trajectories of substance use and abuse over a one-year period among youth, found differences between males and females who reported same-sex and both-sex attractions and those with other-sex attractions. Females with same-sex attractions showed increases in cigarette smoking relative to those with other-sex attractions over time. At the first assessment, females were more likely to have gotten drunk and to have used marijuana and other drugs. Consequently, there are limited and inconsistent findings related to recreational substance use by gender among LGB youth.

Although the studies indicated that the rates of recreational substance use are high among LGB youth, there is little documentation emanating from research studies regarding predictors of substance use among this group. Rotheram-Borus, Rosario, *et al.* (1994) and Jordan (2000) suggested that the increased substance use may be indicative of high stress that LGB youth experience due to their sexual orientation, or it may reflect the bar culture that has been a main entry point into the adult LGB community, or that the use of alcohol and drugs is necessary to be part of the gay and lesbian subculture. Savin-Williams (1994) suggested LGB youth may be involved with recreational substance use for many of the same reasons as heterosexual youths (e.g., peer pressure, hedonism), as well as reasons specific to their sexual identity (e.g., to fog an increasing awareness that they are not heterosexual). D'Augelli (2004) indicated LGB youth face unique stressors and circumstances that might contribute to higher use of tobacco and other drug use. He pointed out that more LGB youth are "coming out" at earlier ages than previous cohorts during the years in which they are still in school and mostly living at home. Despite more accepting public attitudes about homosexuality, the stigma related to same-sex attractions remains powerful, frequently making verbal and physical victimization common experiences of LGB youth. Another common stressor is the lack of family support; and fear of rejection by families can create intense distress. D'Augelli also cited the psychological challenges of a different adolescent development trajectory, social isolation and distress, leading some LGB youth to alcohol and drug use.

To contribute to the limited literature about LGB youth and substance use, to bring clarity to some of the inconsistencies in the current literature, and to investigate the predictors of recreational substance use among LGB youth, the authors recruited a large sample of LGB youth with approximately the same percentages of females and males. The specific purposes of the study were to determine: a) the current frequency of recreational substance use among LGB youth, b) whether or not the frequency of recreational substance use differed by gender, and c) if there are emotional and behavioural problems that predict recreational substance use among this group. Comparisons with studies of heterosexual adolescents were made to examine if the frequency of usage is higher among LGB youth, and if similar predictors of substance have been found. On the basis of past research, we expected LGB youth would use recreational substances at a higher frequency than their peers, and the frequency of use would not differ by gender. We also anticipated that emotional and behaviour problems would predict high rates of recreational substance use among this group.

Method

Design and procedures

A research design method using a questionnaire and a structured interview was employed. In addition to obtaining demographic information, the questionnaire also asked the youth to indicate their experiences with alcohol and drugs. A battery of standard measures asked the youth to evaluate aspects of their mental and emotional health; and a face-to-face interview invited the youth to provide information related to their sexual orientation and its developmental milestones.

LGB youth between the ages of 15 and 19 were recruited from three non-profit social and recreational agencies serving lesbian, gay, bisexual, transgender and questioning youth in New York City and two of its suburbs. Consequently, this is a biased sample of LGB youth as they were recruited from agencies that are supportive of their sexual identity. The study, called "The Q & A Project," was designed to examine the impact of sexual orientation victimization on mental health among LGB youth over time. After the youth completed a questionnaire, they were then interviewed by a master's-level clinician of the same gender. The overall panel study was designed to interview youth three times over a period of two years. Youth were offered $30 to participate in the first interview, which averaged from two to three hours. The study currently being described uses data obtained from the first interviews of the larger study and focuses on questions regarding the youths' experiences with alcohol and other recreational drugs. Data collection for this aspect of the study took place from June 1999 to December 2001. Because seeking parental consent from LGB youth could put them at risk of exposure of their sexual orientation and could lead to verbal or physical harm, parental consent was not obtained. However, a youth advocate was present at each site to answer questions youth might have about the project or to discuss concerns about their participation in the study. In addition, data collected from participants is protected by a federal certificate of confidentiality. The study's protocols were approved by New York University's and The Pennsylvania State University's institutional review boards.

Assessment instrument

The questionnaire, which required approximately one hour to complete, contained a battery of mental health measures with strong psychometric properties, and the interview included questions designed for this study. Only the components of the questionnaire and interview relevant to the current analyses are described here.

Participants were asked to identify their current sexual orientation by selecting one of seven options: (a) totally gay or lesbian; (b) almost totally gay or lesbian; (c) bisexual, but mostly gay or lesbian; (d) bisexual, equally gay/lesbian and heterosexual; (e) bisexual, mostly heterosexual; (f) heterosexual; or (g) uncertain or questioning. (Note: those few individuals that identified as mostly heterosexual or totally heterosexual did not continue completing the questionnaire or participate in the interview.) Demographic information related to age, race, ethnicity, socio-economic status, and place of residence was also sought. The participants were also asked about sexual orientation developmental milestones (e.g., age of first becoming aware of their sexual orientation and age of first disclosure to someone else) as well as the disclosure of their sexual orientation (i.e., their "outness") at school.

We measured personal homonegativity, or negative views of one's sexual orientation, with a version of the Revised Homosexuality Attitude Inventory (RHAI; Shidlo, 1994), which consisted of seven items (e.g., "Whenever I think a lot about being LGB, I feel critical about myself"); the coefficient alpha was .76. The RHAI items were answered using a four-point scale from "strongly disagree" to "strongly agree." Gay-related fears (i.e., how much does the youth hide being LGB because he or she fears the situation such as being called names, being teased or being verbally harassed or physically hurt) were assessed using an eight-item index developed by the second author and used in a previous study of LGB youth. This fear index had a coefficient alpha of .83. Respondents rated each situation on a four-point scale ranging from "not at all" to "extremely" (Hershberger, Pilkington, & D'Augelli, 1997).

The Perceived Stress Scale (Cohen, Karmack, & Mermelstein, 1983) was used to assess participants' level of perceived stress during the last month. It is a 14–item scale (e.g., "How often have you felt that you were on top of things?"), and had a coefficient alpha of .79. Respondents answered on a five-point scale ranging from "never" to "very often." The Beck Depression Inventory (BDI-II; Beck, Steer, & Brown, 1996), consisting of 21 items, was used to measure depression, and its coefficient alpha was .90. Participants were asked to rate characteristics such as "sadness," "loss of pleasure," and "loss of energy" on four-point scales with each scale's number being followed by a descriptive statement (e.g., "I feel sad much of the time," "I feel sad all of the time"). Traumatic stress symptoms were ascertained using a 40–item measure, the Trauma Symptom Checklist (TSC-40; Briere & Runtz, 1989). The TSC-40 asks respondents to rate various symptoms (e.g., "nightmares," "uncontrollable crying") on a four-point scale from "never" to "often." This scale had an alpha coefficient of .96. We used the Brief Symptom Inventory (BSI; Derogatis, 1993) to assess mental health problems. It asks about the occurrence of 53 symptoms (e.g., "suddenly scared for no reason") in the past week on a five-point scale ranging from "not at all" to "extremely." The BSI produces a summary score, the Global Severity Index (GSI), which is an overall indicator of mental health problems. The alpha coefficient for the Global Severity Index was .94.

The Youth Self-Report (YSR; Achenbach & Rescorla, 2001) consists of problem scales that form continuous measures of eight dimensions of psychological functioning. The eight scales of the YSR are formed from scores on 112 items, each of which is rated on a three-point scale, e.g., "I have a hot temper": 0 if "not true," 1 if "somewhat or sometimes true," or 2 if "very true or often true" in the past six months. By summing the individual items of each scale, measures are obtained for eight different syndromes. The eight syndromes and their empirically-based published alpha coefficients are: withdrawn (.71), somatic complaints (.80), anxious/depressed (.84), social problems (.74), thought problems (.78), attention problems (.79), rule-breaking behaviour (.81), and aggressive behaviour (.86) (SAMHSA, 1999).

Recreational substance use was assessed by asking the youth about use during the last year. Youth were asked if they used alcohol, marijuana (pot), cocaine (coke), crack, uppers or amphetamines (speed, crystal meth, ice), narcotics (codeine, heroin, black tar), drugs you shoot with needles, drugs that you sniff other than cocaine (poppers, amyl nitrate, butyl nitrate, airplane glue, Rush), downers or sedatives/tranquilizers (valium, "ludes," Phenobarbital, "roofies"), and LSD or other hallucinogens (mushrooms, angel dust, PCP, peyote, MDA, Ecstasy, "special K"). Responses were rated on a six-point scale: 0 = "Never," 1 = 'Once a Month," 2 = "2–3 Times a Month," 3 = "Once a Week," 4 = "2+ Times a Week," and 5 = "Everyday." An index of recreational substance use was computed by averaging the items, and it had a coefficient alpha of .73.

Participants

The sample consisted of 528 self-identified LGB youth, 274 (52%) were males and 254 (48%) females. They ranged in age from 15 to 19 years, with a mean age of 17 (SD = 1.28). The majority (52%) identified as lesbian or gay, and 48% as bisexual. There were no significant gender differences by age or sexual identity. Of the participants, 45% (n = 234) were of Hispanic/Latino background, and 55% (n = 293) were not. Of the Hispanic/Latino youth, 86% (n = 201) were White and 11% (n = 26) were Black. Of the non-Hispanic youth, 43% (n = 126) were White, 36% (n = 105) Black, 4% (n = 13) were Asian, and two youth were American Indian/Alaskan Native.

Nearly a fourth (24%, n =125) of the youth lived in suburban areas of New York, another 71% (n =373) lived in New York City, and 5% (n = 26) lived in small cities or towns. Two youth reported living in a rural area. The large majority of the youth (70%, n = 369) reported living with their parents or stepparents, 9% (n = 47) lived with other family members, and 8% (n =42) lived with foster parents or in residential group homes. A few youth reported living with friends (5%, n = 25), living alone (2%, n = 10), living with roommates other than friends (2%, n = 10), or described their living situation as "other" (2%, n = 10). Only 1% (n = 8) lived with a girlfriend or boyfriend; and less than 1% (n = 2) lived with schoolmates in campus housing or reported being homeless (n = 4).

Youths' socioeconomic status was calculated using the occupations of their parents or the occupation of one, if only one was present. Each adult's occupation was first categorized using Entwisle and Astone's (1994) system for rating adolescents' socioeconomic status. To simplify the presentation of data, the 16 categories in their system were collapsed into 6. Of the sample, 416 youth provided adequate information about parents' occupations to allow categorization. If two parents' occupations were available (n = 155), they were averaged; if one (n = 261), only that score was used. Of the 416 youth who provided sufficient information, 4% (n = 17) of parents were in the "Executive" category (e.g., real estate manager, financial manger), 16% (n = 66) were in the "Professional" category (e.g., lawyer, teacher), 15% (n = 62) were in the "Sales Occupations" category (e.g., car salesperson, advertising salesperson), 22% (n = 90) were in the "Technical/Administrative Support" category (e.g., computer programmer, secretary), 24% (n = 101) were in the "Service Occupations" category (e.g., bartender, nursing assistant), and 19% (n = 80) were in the "Manual Labor" category (e.g., mechanic, sewing machine operator). Female participants reported significantly higher SES ratings than males (Females: $M = 3.16$, $SD = 1.47$; Males: $M = 2.78$, $SD = 1.45$; t [414] = 2.66, $p < .01$; $d = .26$, small effect size).

About three-quarters of the youth (73%, $n = 387$; 208 males, 179 females) said they felt "different" from other youth when they were growing up. They experienced this at about 8 years of age. Sixty percent of the males and 52% of the females said someone had suggested they were "different." Sixty percent of the youth indicated that they had been called a "sissy" or "tomboy"; the first time this occurred was around age 8 for both males and females. The LGB youth in the study first became aware of their same-sex attraction at about age 12, with males becoming aware about age 12 and females at age 13. However, there was no significant difference between males and females regarding the age they identified themselves as LGB, which occurred approximately at age 14. Both males and females first disclosed their sexual orientation at about age 15. About 65% of the youth told a female and 32% told a male. The person first told about the youths' sexual orientation was most often a female friend (35%, $n = 185$); a male youth was the first person told by 18% ($n = 93$) of the youth. Mothers were told first by only 8% ($n = 39$) of the youth, and fathers were told first by only four youth (1%). The large majority of the participants had disclosed their sexual orientation in the school setting. Half (50%) said they were "out" to everyone at school, 26% to some or most people, and 14% to a few or no one. (Ten percent indicated that they did not attend school in the last year.)

Results

Descriptive statistics indicated that 67% of the LGB youth used one or more recreational drugs in the last year; 72% of the lesbian and gay youth and 63% of the bisexual youth. Sixty percent of the youth used alcohol, 44% marijuana, 7% cocaine, 1% crack, 7% stimulants (including amphetamines), 4% narcotics, 2% injection drugs, 6% inhalants, 5% sedatives, and 14% hallucinogens (Table 1). In order to provide a more concise picture of recreational drug use during the past year, these categories were collapsed into three major categories: alcohol use, marijuana use, and "party drug" use (i.e., cocaine, amphetamines, narcotics, inhalants, sedatives, hallucinogens).

Of the 60% of the youth who reported alcohol use in the last year, 57% were males and 64% were females. Twenty percent of the alcohol users reported weekly use of alcohol, and there were no gender differences among them.

Of the 44% of the youth who reported marijuana use in the last year, 41% were males and 47% were females. Fifty-one percent of the marijuana users reported weekly use, and there were no gender differences among them. Eighteen percent of the youth reported using at least one "party drug" in the last year, 18% were males and 17% were females. Forty-four percent of the party drug users reported weekly use of party drugs, and there were no gender differences among them. Ninety percent of the party drug users used alcohol, and 89% party drug users also used marijuana. Consequently, party drug users tended to be poly drug users.

Based on the literature, preliminary regression models were created to examine the degree to which the variables assessed did or did not contribute to the variance of substance use. Variables included in the preliminary models were those related to homonegativity, gay-related fears, mental health symptoms, perceived stress, traumatic stress symptoms, and psychological functioning. Those variables not giving information that was distinct were removed, setting the stage for the final test. A final regression model (using simultaneous entry) that explained the largest percent of the variance was maintained, and the results were significant using the Bonferoni adjustment. The regression model was found to be significant, $p < .001$, when recreational substance use was regressed on scores of indices related to stress, trauma, depression, social problems, attention problems, and rule-breaking behaviour. The set of variables accounted for 31% of the variance (adjusted $R^2 = .30$), $F [6,512] = 38.56$, $p < .001$). Further analyses by gender were not conducted as there were no significant differences regarding the use of any drug by gender (Table 1).

Research limitations

Several limitations of the study are noteworthy. First, the sample is not representative of all LGB youth, having been drawn from several agencies which provide social and recreational services for self-identified LGB, transgender, and questioning youth in the New York City area. Those youth who are involved in these agencies, which are supportive of various sexual and gender identities, may be precocious in their sexual orientation development, coming out to their peers and parents at earlier ages than other youth. Without representative national samples of LGB youth which provide data comparable to that gathered in this study, results from convenience samples (such as this one) are still needed, despite their limitations (Savin-Williams, 2001). Second, these data were cross-sectional, and without

Table 1   *Use of Drugs in Last Year by Lesbian, Gay, and Bisexual*
Youths (%)

Drug	Never	Once a Month	2–3 Times a Month	Once a Week	2–3 Times a Week	Daily	M vs. F
Alcohol	39.8	29.0	18.6	4.6	5.5	2.5	$\chi^2 = 7.08$
Marijuana	55.7	15.2	6.7	4.2	10.3	8.0	$\chi^2 = 7.38$
Cocaine	93.0	3.8	1.1	.8	1.1	.2	$\chi^2 = 8.06$
Crack	98.9	.4	.4	.4	0	0	$\chi^2 = 1.87$
Uppers/ stimulants	93.0	3.2	1.7	1.1	.6	.4	$\chi^2 = 3.67$
Narcotics/ heroin	96.4	1.9	.9	0	.2	.6	$\chi^2 = 3.49$
Injection drugs	98.7	.8	.4	.2	0	0	$\chi^2 = .95$
Sniffed drugs/ inhalants	93.7	3.0	.8	1.5	.6	.4	$\chi^2 = 2.69$
Downers/ sedatives	95.6	2.3	.8	.2	.6	.6	$\chi^2 = 4.51$
Hallucino- gens (inc. Ecstasy, K)	86.3	6.8	1.7	2.3	2.3	.6	$\chi^2 = 6.18$

longitudinal data they only indicate relationships among the variables. Only longitudinal data can resolve causal directionality; consequently, recreational substance use may have preceded some of the predictors identified in this study. Finally, the data reporting recreational substance use gathered for this study is self-reported data. To what degree it accurately reports the youths' actual usage is unknown.

Discussion

Adolescence is a developmental period in which youth are challenged to achieve individuation and emotional independence from their parents, to seek a sense of belonging with their peers, and to discover their sexual identity. It is a period in which they tend to live in the "here and now," perceive themselves to be invulnerable, and engage in risk-taking behaviours. It is also a time in which they initiate adult sexual behaviours and use of alcohol and other drugs.

LGB youth face additional challenges, specifically dealing with the fact they find themselves more sexually attracted to people of their own sex than the opposite sex, and coping with derogatory terms applied to people with such feelings. They have to decide whether to hide these feelings and "pass" as heterosexual, or to disclose them and cope with sexual orientation prejudice (i.e., homophobia) and possible verbal and physical victimization. Consequently, LGB youth not only deal with the generic life stressors accompanying adolescence, but also cope with those stressors unique to their same-sex sexual orientation, same-sex behaviour, or self-identification as lesbian, gay or bisexual (Savin-Williams & Ream, 2003). These include internalized homophobic feelings, e.g., homonegativity, and fears about the consequences of disclosure, e.g., losing a job or friends, or being verbally or physically harassed at school or at home. One possible way to ease this path is the recreational use of alcohol and other drugs.

Recreational substance use in adolescence is seen differently than it is in adulthood. Sussman, Dent and Galaif (1997) discussed this difference in four ways. While regular substance use by adults may or may not be considered abuse, it might be considered abuse in the teen years because of its potential to interfere with developmental growth and adjustment tasks. High-risk situations also differ between adolescents and adults; for example, adolescents may use drugs in situations in which they are not responsible for the caretaking of others. On the other hand, adolescents tend to exhibit less physical dependence and fewer physical problems related to use than adults. Adolescents, however, may suffer more serious social consequences, e.g., problems at school, truncated development, and statutory difficulties. For example, it is considered benign for adults to have a cocktail or two after work or at a party, while it is seen differently when youth has a couple of drinks after a hard day at school or drink recreationally with friends. While the adult circumstance is considered "mainstream" by societal norms, the youth situation is viewed as "bad," and a risk for abuse (Capuzzi & Gross, 1996).

The Monitoring the Future Study, which tracks illicit drug use among 8th, 10th, and 12th grade students in the United States, started in 1975. It found that 31% of high school seniors reported using an illicit drug in the previous month of that year. The figure climbed to 39% in 1978 and 1979, but declined to 14% in 1992. Illicit drug use increased to 26% in 2001 and dropped to 24%

in 2003 (National Survey Results on Drug Use from the Monitoring the Future Study, 2004). Over the years, studies of LGB youth have consistently found the percentages of substance use to be higher than these national averages of adolescents (Cochran & Mays, 1996; D'Augelli & Hershberger., 1993; Davies, et al., 1992; Grossman & Kerner, 1998; Rosario, et al., 1997; Rotheram-Borus, et al., 1994; SAMSHA, 1999). Comparing the findings of the current Q & A study to those of 12th graders (students with the same mean age of 17) of the 2000 Monitoring the Future Study (Johnston, O'Malley & Bachman, 2001) indicated that the LGB youth reported higher rates of the use of some drugs over the past year, i.e., marijuana and cocaine, and lower rates of use of other drugs, i.e., alcohol, hallucinogens, stimulants, and narcotics/heroin. Both indicated approximately equal use of inhalants, sedatives injection drugs, and crack (Table 2). However, as the Monitoring of the Future study noted, self-reports of drug use among high school seniors may under-estimate drug use of that age because high school dropouts and truants are not included, and these groups may have more involvement with drugs than those who stay in school (University of Michigan, 2001). Previous studies

Table 2   *Use of Drugs in Last Year by Lesbian, Gay, and Bisexual Youth and by Heterosexual Youth (%)*

Drug Used	Q & A Study (LGB Youth) N = 528, 15–19 years, Period of Use: 1999–2001, 12th Graders	Monitoring the Future (Heterosexual Youth) M = 17, N = 13,300, Period of Use: 2000
Alcohol	60%	73%
Marijuana	44%	37%
Hallucinogens (including ecstasy)	14%	16%
Cocaine	7%	5%
Stimulants	7%	10%
Inhalants	6%	6%
Sedatives	5%	6%
Narcotics/heroin	4%	7%
Injection drugs	2%	1%
Crack	1%	2%

have documented truancy and dropping out of school as significant problems among LGB youth because of harassment and other forms of victimization (see Savin-Williams, 1994).

Predictors of recreational substance use among heterosexual adolescents were identified in a special report issued by the U.S. Substance Abuse and Mental Health Services Administration (SAMSHA, 1999). Using data from 1994–1996 National Household Survey on Drug Abuse supplemented by data collected utilizing the Youth Self-Report among a subset of the sample the study found that the likelihood of substance use among adolescents (12–17 years) was associated with the severity of emotional and behavioural problems across age and gender groups. This association was found to exist when emotional and behavioural problems were examined in relation to alcohol use, marijuana use and illicit drug use (including cocaine, crack, inhalants, hallucinogens, heroin, or abused prescription drugs). Additionally, alcohol and illicit drug dependence was found to be more than four times more likely among adolescents with serious emotional problems and seven times more likely among adolescents with serious behavioural problems than among adolescents with lower levels of these problems. The findings strongly suggest that emotional and behavioural problems represent significant risk factors for adolescent substance use.

Findings from the current study predicting substance use among LGB youth are similar to those found among heterosexual youth. Not only were emotional and social problems associated with recreational substance use, i.e., stress, trauma, depression, social problems, attention problems, and rule-breaking problems, but also the latter three dimensions of the YSR were the same dimensions of psychological functioning that were most strongly associated with substance use among heterosexual youth. On the other hand, the Global Severity Index (GSI) of the Brief Symptom Inventory, which measures mental health symptoms, did not significantly contribute to the variance of substance use. Surprisingly, the scores of the two measurers associated with adopting an LGB identity, namely homonegativity and gay-related fears, were not associated with recreational substance use. Other stressors that have been found to be associated with environmental reactions to same-sex sexual orientation (e.g., victimization, discrimination and harassment) may have been more appropriate measures, as they have been linked to psychological distress among LGB youth (D'Augelli, 1998; Savin-Williams & Ream, 2003). Additional research is needed to further explicate the risk relation between emotional and behavioural problems and recreational substance use among LGB youth. Such information can play a key role in designing programs aimed at prevention and treatment of recreational substance use and abuse among LGB youth.

Summary

LGB youth are among the groups of youth who use recreational substances as an active leisure activity. Overall, past studies indicated that youth who report an LGB identity or engage in same-sex behaviours are at greater risk for substance use than their peers. Various reasons have been suggested to explain this phenomenon, including society's negative societal attitudes about same-sex behaviours, peer pressure, association with other problem behaviours, affiliation with the gay and lesbian subculture, coping with their same sex feelings and behaviour, and to alleviating the anxiety they feel when in a gay and lesbian environment or situation (Jordan, 2000).

In response to the specific purposes of this study, we found that there was a high frequency of recreational substance use among LGB youth, with two-thirds (67%) using at least one recreational substance in the past year. In contrast to previous studies, the percentages of LGB youth who used one or more recreational substances in the last year were higher for some drugs, but lower for others. Overall, their percentage of use was not significantly higher than their peers with other-sex attractions. Additionally, we found no significant differences in the percentages between lesbian and bisexual females and gay and bisexual males in their use of specific recreational substances. With regard to predictors of recreational substance abuse among LGB youth, we found that emotional and behaviour problems that predict recreational substance use among youth with other-sex (versus same-sex and both sex) attractions also predicted the use among self-identified LGB youth: stress, trauma, depression, social problems, attention problems, and rule-breaking behaviour. Clearly a clustering of problematic behaviours that appears to be supported in the literature for heterosexual youth (Jordan, 2000).

Jordan (2002) suggested two paths to prevention. The first approach is to increase the visibility of LGB youth, which can alter the sociopolitical climate in schools, neighbourhoods, and communities, and thereby increase the acceptance of these youth. This will also increase information about them for all youth, educating about the realities of LGB life and dispelling the myths. The second approach is to offer age-appropriate groups to provide socialization opportunities for LGB youth, while at the same time providing occasions to enhance social support and develop social skills. Additionally these programs may offer avenues for addressing the victimization of LGB youth and reducing the stimuli for recreational substance use. With regard to intervention, D'Augelli (1996) suggested seven critical areas in mental health treatment of LGB youth that can be useful with LGB youth whose use of substances exceeds recreational use. They include stress management connected with an LGB identity; peer relationship disruptions; the decision to disclose to family and the consequences of disclosure; emotional reactions to development close relationships; being isolated from gay-affirming situations; sexual orientation victimization, including discrimination, harassment, and violence; and anxieties about sexuality, especially HIV/ AIDS. Additionally, evaluation research is needed to determine the effectiveness of various interventions, as their effectiveness may be related to variations in youths' social class, ethnicity, religious and spiritual beliefs.

Recreational professionals play important roles in the lives of all adolescents, including LGB youth. Not only should they promote positive youth development by focusing on creating environments that focus on achievement, positive peer role models, close ties to caring adults, and other forms of resiliency; but they should also provide visibility and support for LGB youth and work to reduce bullying and other forms of victimization. Recreational professionals can also detect emotional problems when they first begin and intervene in ways that limit exploratory substance use from becoming chronic substance abuse.

Acknowledgments

The authors acknowledge the youth who participated in this study, the project staff and interviewers, and the chief executive officers and staff members of the research sites. This study is part of a larger project supported by a grant from the (U.S.) National Institute of Mental Health (MH58155).

References

Achenbach, T.M., & Rescorla, L.A. (2001) *Manual for the ASEBA School-Age Forms & Profiles*. Burlington, VT: University of Vermont, Research Center for Children, Youth and Families. University of Vermont Department of Psychiatry.

Beck, A.T., Steer, R.A., & Brown, G.K, (1996) *BDI-II: Beck Depression Inventory (2nd ed)*. San Antonio: The Psychological Corporation.

Briere, J., & Runtz, M. (1989) 'The Trauma Symptom Checklist (TSC-33): Early data on a new scale', *Journal of Interpersonal Violence*, Vol. 4: pp. 151–163.

Bontempo, D.E., & D'Augelli, A.R. (2002) 'Effects of at-school victimization and sexual orientation on lesbian, gay, or bisexual youths' health risk behavior', *Journal of Adolescent Health*, Vol. 30: pp. 364–374.

Capuzzi, D., & Gross, D.R. (eds). (1996) *Youth at risk: A prevention resources for counselors, teachers, and parents (2nd ed.)*. Alexandria, VA: American Counseling Association.

Cohen, S., Karmack, T., & Mermelstein, R. (1983) 'A global measure of perceived stress', *Journal of Health and Social Behavior*, Vo. 24: pp. 385–396.

Cochran, S.D., & Mays, V.M. (1996) 'Prevalence of HIV-related sexual risk behaviors among 18 to 24 year old lesbian and bisexual women', *Women's Health*, Vol. 2, No. 1/2: pp: 75–89.

D'Augelli, A.R. (1996) 'Lesbian, gay, and bisexual development during adolescence and youth adulthood,' in R.P. Cabaj & T.S. Stein (eds) *Textbook of homosexuality and mental disorders*. Washington, DC: American Psychiatric Press, pp. 267–288.

D'Augelli, A.R. (1998) 'Developmental implications of victimization of lesbian, gay, and bisexual youths', in G. Herek (ed) *Stigma and sexual orientation: Understanding prejudice against lesbians, gay men, and bisexuals*. Thousand Oaks, CA: Sage, pp. 187–210.

D'Augelli, A.R. (2004) 'High tobacco use among lesbian gay, and bisexual youth', *Archives of Pediatric and Adolescent Medicine*, Vol. 158: pp. 309–310.

D'Augelli, A.R., & Hershberger, S.L. (1993) 'Lesbian, gay, and bisexual youth in community settings: Personal challenges and mental health problems', *American Journal of Community Psychology*, Vo. 21: pp. 421–448.

Davies, P.M., Weatherburn, P., Hunt, A.J., Hickson, F.C.I., McManus, T.J., & Coxon, A.P.M. (1992) 'The sexual behavior of young gay men in England and Wales', *AIDS Care*, Vol. 4, No. 3: pp. 259–272.

Derogatis, L.R. (1993) *The Brief Symptom Inventory: Administration, scoring, and procedures manual*. Minneapolis: National Computer Systems.

DiPlacido, J. (1998) 'Minority stress among lesbians, gay men, and bisexuals: A consequence of heterosexism, homophobia and stigmatization,' in G. Herek (ed) *Stigma and sexual orientation: Understanding prejudice against lesbians, gay men, and bisexuals*. Thousand Oaks, CA: Sage, pp. 138–159.

Entwisle, D.R., & Astone, N.M. (1994) 'Some practical guidelines for measuring youths' race/ethnicity and socioeconomic status', *Child Development*, Vol. 65: pp. 1521–1540.

Faulkner, A.H., & Cranston, K. (1998) 'Correlates of same-sex sexual behavior in a random sample of Massachusetts high school students', *American Journal of Public Health,* Vol. 88, No. 2: pp. 262–266.

Garofalo, R., Wolf, R.C., Kessel, S., Palfrey, J., & DuRant, R.H. (1998) 'The association between health risk behaviors and sexual orientation among a school-based sample of adolescents', *Pediatrics,* Vol. 101: pp. 895–902.

Grossman, A.H., & Kerner, M.S. (1998) 'Self-esteem and supportiveness as predictors of emotional distress in gay male and lesbian youth', *Journal of Homosexuality,* Vol. 35, No. 2: pp. 25–39.

Hershberger, S.L., Pilkington, N.W., & D'Augelli, A.R. (1997) 'Predictors of suicide attempts among gay, lesbian, and bisexual youth', *Journal of Adolescent Research,* Vol. 12: pp. 477–497.

Johnston, L.D., O'Malley, P.M., & Bachman, J.G. (2001) *Monitoring the Future national results on adolescent drug use: Overview of key findings, 2000.* (NIH Publication No. 01–4923). Bethesda, MD: National Institute of Drug Abuse.

Jordan, K.M. (2000) 'Substance abuse among gay, lesbian, bisexual, transgender and questioning adolescents,' *School Psychology Review,* Vol. 29, No. 2, pp. 201–206.

Lock, J., & Steiner, H. (1999) 'Gay, lesbian, and bisexual youth risks for emotional, physical and social problems: Results from a community-based survey,' *Journal of the American Academy of Child and Adolescent Psychiatry,* Vol. 38, pp. 297–304. *National Survey Results on Drug Use from the Monitoring the Future Studies, 1975–2003.* Retrieved August 12, 2004, from http://monitoringthefuture.org/pubs.htm

Remafedi, G. (1987) 'Adolescent homosexuality: Psychosocial and medical implications. *Pediatrics,* Vol. 79: pp. 331–337.

Remafedi, G. (1994) 'Predictors of unprotected intercourse among gay and bisexual youth: Knowledge, beliefs, and behavior', *Pediatrics,* Vol. 94: pp: 163–168.

Rosario, M., Hunter, J., & Gwadz, M. (1997) 'Exploration of substance use among lesbian, gay, and bisexual youth: Prevalence and correlates', *Journal of Adolescence Research,* Vol. 12: pp. 454–476.

Rosario, M., Rotheram-Borus, M.J., & Reid H. (1992) *Personal resources, gay-related stress, and multiple problem behaviors among gay and bisexual male adolescents.* Unpublished manuscript, Columbia University.

Rotheram-Borus, M.J., Reid, H., Marelich, W.D., & Srinvasan, S. (1999) 'Risk for HIV among homosexual, bisexual, and heterosexual male and female youth', *Archives of Sexual Behavior,* Vol. 28: pp. 159–177.

Rotheram-Borus, M.J., Rosario, M., Meyer-Bahlburg, H.F.L., Kooperman, C., Dopkins, S.C., & Davies, M. (1994) 'Sexual and substance use acts of gay and bisexual male adolescents in New York City', *The Journal of Sex Research,* Vol. 31: pp, 47–57.

Russell, S.T., Driscoll, A.K., & Truong, N. (2002) 'Adolescent same-sex romantic attractions and relationships: Implications for substance use and abuse,' *American Journal of Public Health,* Vol. 92, No. 2, pp. 198–202.

Savin-Williams, R.C. (1994) 'Verbal and physical abuse as stressors in the lives of lesbian, gay male, and bisexual youths: Associations with school problems, running away, substance abuse, prostitutions, and suicide', *Journal of Counseling and Clinical Psychology,* Vol. 62, No. 2: pp. 261–269.

Savin-Williams, R.C. (2001) 'Suicide attempts among sexual minority youth: Population and measurement issues', *Journal of Consulting and Clinical Psychology,* Vol. 69: pp. 983–991.

Savin-Williams, R.C., & Ream, G.L. (2003) 'Suicide attempts among sexual-minority male youth', *Journal of Clinical Child and Adolescent Psychology,* Vol. 32: pp. 509–522.

SAMHSA [Substance Abuse and Mental Health Services Administration] (1999) *The relationship between mental health and substance abuse among adolescents.* Rockville, MD: SAMSHSA Office of Applied Studies, U.S. Department of Health and Human Services.

Shidlo, A. (1994) 'Internalized homophobia: Conceptual and empirical issues in Measurement', in B. Greene & G.M. Herek (eds) *Lesbian and gay psychology: Theory, research, and clinical applications.* Thousand Oaks, CA: Sage, pp. 176–205.

Sussman, S., Dent, C.W., & Galaif (1997). 'The correlates of substance abuse and dependence among adolescents at high risk for drug abuse,' *Journal of Substance Abuse,* Vol. 9, pp. 241–255.

University of Michigan (2001) *Monitoring the Future national results on adolescent drug use: Overview of key findings 2000.* Retrieved November 29, 2001. http://www.ojp.usdoj.gov/bsjs/dcf/du.html.

Youth Risk Behavior Surveillance System (YRBSS; 2001). http:// apps.nccd.cdc.gov/YRBSS/ListV.

II

GENDERED AND
SEXUALISED IDENTITIES

GIRLS, FOOTBALL PARTICIPATION AND GENDER IDENTITY

Ruth Jeanes
Loughborough University

Introduction

Football is generally viewed as a male-orientated sport with very strong links to masculinity and male identity (Mean, 2001). Despite this, women and girl's football has witnessed a conspicuous expansion over the last three years. In April 2002 the Football Association announced that it was the largest participation sport for women and girls, ahead of more traditional 'feminine' sports such as netball or hockey. This expansion can be seen as significantly challenging the conventional reproduction of dominant male discourses and conformist, restrictive notions of femininity (Mean, 2001). The challenge female participation presents is influential in questioning what constitutes femininity and masculinity in modern culture. However it is unclear whether involvement has the potential to significantly change dominant gender beliefs and resulting behaviour.

This paper examines the impact playing football can have on girls' gender beliefs and ideals. A small group of girls (13 in total) aged between 10–11 have contributed their understanding of what they perceive 'gender' to mean; what they see as being stereotypical gender assumptions; and how they feel they fit within the gender discourses they describe. Football is discussed with the girls to understand how they feel participation in the sport might challenge or reinforce the dominant beliefs discussed. Their own participation is also examined to understand how playing may affect the construction of their gender identities and to see how it can influence where they view themselves within feminine/masculine binaries.

Girls and gender construction

Social learning theory has been used extensively to explain the polarised gender beliefs that children develop. More recently, such theories have begun to be criticised as limited because they cannot account for changes within the gendering process. As a result many feminists have turned to a more flexible understanding of gender relations, often using postmodernist theory. This allows the possibility that children do not passively take up gender roles in a uniform way. Instead, they actively construct their own position, sometimes resisting the dominant discourses presented to them.

Francis (1998) and Davies (2003) both offer an interpretation of how children develop gendered beliefs in their studies of primary school age boys and girls. Children were found to construct gender as visually and behaviourally different. Clothes were seen as important indicators of gender identity as was 'correct' gender behaviour. Similarly, in Davies' (2003) research children were found to learn the discursive practices of their culture and had the ability to position themselves as male or female from an early age. Not doing this was seen as failing. This created a very constraining framework for children to develop their identity. It was not a straightforward matter of choice for a child. Gender choices and shaping of gender identity depended on access to particular discourses they wished to adopt to make their 'choice'. Davies explains these as not simply an "external constraint, they [discourses] provide the conceptual framework, the psychic patterns, the emotions through which individuals position themselves in relation to the social world" (p. 13). The 'correct' gender identity was not achieved without a struggle by the child and was an ongoing process to continually reinforce them within the discourse they chose to adopt.

The children clearly defined masculinity and femininity as opposites. This construction of gender led to power being associated with masculinity. In mixed sex settings, such as the school, discourses of gender were found to empower the boys and dis-empower the girls (Francis, 1998: p. 137). Girls could gain access to this power but it involved a complicated negotiation of the male/female binary. Davies (2003) demonstrated that girls want to be powerful in the same way as boys could be, but they had to find dominant males who were willing to give them access to the power discourses. These boys therefore risk compromising their dominance (p.160). Such structures were not easily challenged.

Children draw on gender discourses from an early age to establish a gender identity. Primarily they use the dominant opposite discourses of masculinity and femininity as the foundation for this. These are neither unitary nor static, and can be interpreted and 'acted' out in different ways by different children. Equally, children constantly adopt different personas according to the situation. They can challenge the dominant discourses and disregard them completely at times. The structures keeping gender discourses in place are powerful making such challenges a difficult process for the individual child. Such a challenge also risks being viewed as unacceptable by peers and adults within their social sphere.

Football and gender identity

In Britain football is a source of national pride and a very visible celebration of male culture. The men's game continues to dominate the mass media and is presented as an essential component of hegemonic masculinity.

Renold (1997), Skelton (2000), and Swain (2000) have theorised how playing football both formally and informally in the primary school setting contributes to the development of boys' masculine identity. Football in these studies is shown to be an essential part of boys' development. It plays a significant role in defining what it is to be a real man or a boy. The research also illustrates how football has no real part to play in moulding girls' gender identities, who instead define their femininity by not playing football. Girls who do play football have to negotiate a complex set of norms, and move between the competing discourses of football and femininity. Whether they accept the feminine norms or reject them, they still have to contend with the 'rules' of femininity.

The research illustrates the power of football to retain its masculine status and the ability of boys and men to restrict girls' access to it, reinforcing the masculine discourse as inaccessible to girls. However, as demonstrated, children do not automatically take up the dominant discourse most appropriate for them but can select parts of the discourses available or challenge and contest certain aspects.

The study

The research set out to examine gender identity and the influence of football. It focused on four main areas.
- The girls' understanding of gender and femininity.
- Girls' perceptions of football and how gender affects these beliefs.

- How girls construct their own gender identity.
- The impact of football on girls' gender identity construction.

I have used aspects from postmodern theory to guide this research. I wanted to use a theory that would help me in understanding why and how the girls developed certain beliefs and how football fitted within these beliefs. I also wanted to incorporate feminist theory into the research process so that the analysis of how gender affects the girls' values and reasoning is central to the process. The deconstruction of subject and identity encouraged in the thinking of Derrida (1982) and his followers has enabled me to de-layer with the girls their notions of femininity and how this influences their everyday lives. Through this we have also been able to deconstruct 'football' and see how the girls feel participation in the sport can fit in with their notions of femininity. This is despite football always being positioned as opposite to the dominant discourses of 'being a girl', which tell us that women and girls playing football is not acceptable.

A post modernist approach has allowed me to examine with the girls the concept of multiple identities, moving away from the assumption that there is one single fixed notion of femininity. Instead there is the possibility of drawing on a multitude of gender identities and the discourses associated with these (Foucault, 1979). Some of these reflect traditional notions of femininity and others move away from this and sometimes sit within traditional masculine discourses. By using postmodernist thinking I have been able to explore how the girls position themselves as many different types of 'girl'. These can be fluid and changing according to the situation.

The research was conducted using a methodology guided by feminist and childhood studies methodological principles. I used an ethnographic approach and worked with a single school. This allowed me to develop a very strong and ongoing relationship with the girls involved. I agreed with the school that I would gain access through running an after school girls football club. The girls who attended the club were invited to take part in the research as well but it was not compulsory for them to do so; they could come to the club without being involved with the research. In total 13 girls attended. Three Asian girls attended, one black African–Caribbean girl and the remainder were white. The case study was conducted in a private primary school so the majority of girls were from a fairly wealthy upper middle class background.

Working with the girls as their coach as well as a researcher was very beneficial. It allowed me to build up a real trust and rapport with the girls.

I was able to get fairly close to emulating the interested 'adult friend' model that Fine and Sandstrom (1988) advocate. Although they did see me as an authority figure at times, due to being their coach and having to organise them and direct them through this, they were far more relaxed and informal around me than with their teachers or other visitors to the school. Cox and Thompson (2000) have used a similar technique successfully with adults to integrate themselves as coaches and players into football teams they were researching.

Data was initially gathered during the football coaching sessions with the help of an assistant doing the practical work. I would take small groups to the side and chat to them for five to ten minutes. Once I got to know the girls and their friendship groups I asked them if we could meet at lunchtimes. I would see different girls each day in small friendship groups. I had a rough outline for each meeting but was very flexible and open to what the girls wanted to do, how to structure the sessions and what methods were used. Keeping the research child-centred and allowing the girls to feel in control at all times in the research process was of paramount importance. The methods used were crucial in assisting with this. I primarily used interviews and focus groups with pairs or 4 or 5 of the girls. In conjunction with this I introduced the girls to a number of participatory techniques using photographs and stories to help them with communicating and generally to make the research process more interesting. The data was recorded using mini disc players to tape the girls' conversations. Added to this were my own observational field notes and the images they produced. This paper focuses on data collected from subsequent interviews and focus groups that had been prompted using magazine images and a story about a girl footballer. The girls were given a range of magazines and asked to cut out images of women they liked and disliked and we then discussed why.

Thomas and O' Kane (2000) maintain that drawing pictures and writing stories is often more appealing to children because they are concrete and tactile ways to express themselves rather than being verbal and abstract. Neither of these methods substituted verbal communication between the girls and me. Instead they acted as prompts to improve and focus the conversation we had and help the girls to describe the complex issues they were discussing. It also appeared to make the process much more interesting for them. The decision to use this approach was not made immediately but was developed over time and through interaction with the girls. A more traditional interview approach was adopted but was found to produce very stilted discussion with the girls.

Girls and femininity

Central to the research process has been an understanding of what the girls mean by the terms masculinity and femininity. There were many contra- dictions in the girls' conversations. Initially their conversations depicted femininity as a dualistic with very rigid frameworks for how a girl should behave. They could either be hyper feminine or non feminine. Once discuss- ing their own identities this binary was rejected and it was evident they slipped between a number of identities and did not sit rigidly within the feminine dualism they had created. At times they would talk about male and female freedom to behave in any way they wish. In other discussions they would place rigid frameworks on what they believed were inappropriate ways of acting. Looks and behaviour were considered a key aspect of defining a feminine identity. The girls often articulated though, that they felt there was more than one way to behave and different types of 'girl'. The two categories of 'girl' that received the most attention were the oppositional constructs of 'tomboy' and 'girlie girl'. Karla understood a 'girlie girl' as a female who "loves shopping and clothes and make up and always has to have their hair right and couldn't get dirty and always has to have clothes that are the latest fashion". This was the common definition amongst them. It relates closely to cultural stereotypes of femininity and how a girl should be. In contrast the 'tomboy' girl was not concerned with what she looked like "what they wear or how their hair is" (Katherine). Their definitions for tomboys were much closer to masculine stereotypes. The girls see a tomboy as unfeminine. For them, tomboys are associated with male characteristics such as being rough, aggressive and brave.

I explored these definitions in greater depth with the girls using images from magazines. I asked them to comment on pictures they liked and disliked. Generally they preferred pictures that fit with stereotypically feminine images. They concentrated on signifiers of female beauty when discussing why they liked them.

Ella: "I think these two are pretty. They just look pretty. I don't know
            what makes them pretty. Their faces and things, their hair is nice
            and they are thin and their eyes are quite green."

Femininity and a positive body image were associated with perceived physical beauty. Ella struggled to articulate what she finds pretty. Beauty discourses have been so internalised she cannot verbalise them. She just 'knows' what they are when she sees them. The pictures that were criticised generally depicted images that did not fit into the established discourses.

Anna: "I don't like that because she is acting too punky and not being a proper girl."

Ruth: "Really why not?"

Anna: "She is trying to be like a boy, her clothes and her hair and everything. I am not saying that is wrong but I just don't like it."

The girls discussed body shape as being a further essential component of feminine identity. At first they argued that boys and girls should not have a particular size or shape dictated to them: it should be down to individual choice. Using pictures again of different shaped women, it became apparent that in practice the girls had a very narrow framework for what they viewed as tolerable. Body shape needed to fit in with their culturally influenced boundaries. The perfect body was slim. Their definitions of fat were well below what would clinically be described as overweight. Muscular women were also difficult to accept. I asked them to look at a number of pictures of female athletes including a female bodybuilder. None of these were considered suitable body shapes for a woman. The picture of the female bodybuilder produced reactions of disgust and horror. These were justified using 'natural woman' discourses.

Sarah: "Urghh I don't like this one, she is too bodybuilt."

Sian: "I don't like that it is sick."

Susie: "Urgh that is horrid."

Helen: "She is just stupid."

Ruth: "Why?"

Helen: "I don't like that because it looks a lot like a man especially her arms. Her arms just aren't right. It is not natural for a woman to have that strength."

Sian demonstrated the limitations to the girls' liberal attitudes to disregarding feminine stereotypes. "I think women have the right to play games that men do but not have the bodies that men do". In other words, women and girls may take part in activities that defy expected stereotypes, but they cannot move to extremes of feminine body images without it being viewed unappealing. Many of the girls' opinions were attributed to personal choice rather than the effect of cultural expectations. They were horrified that a woman should want to look so muscular and the only way they could explain why she had chosen to look this way was that she must be a man dressed up as a woman. It was impossible for them to believe that women should want to defy femininity so openly and create such a contradictory body image.

The girls highlighted the importance of visual appearance during the story session in which they were asked to write an ending to a story about a girl footballer. Anna felt Rebecca, the central character in the story, could continue playing football, but only if she reinforced her femininity in other aspects of her life. This again was unquestioningly seen as acceptable. It was the only way the girls perceived Rebecca could balance out any challenges to the gender order.

Anna: "Boys want their girlfriends to be girlie girls."

Karla: "They don't want them to be better than them at things that men should do."

Anna: "Yes she has to dress up to show him that she can be a girlie girl so he won't mind so much when he finds out about playing football."

The girls view this as being a priority above football. It is of greater importance because it affects their future lives and may alienate them from leading a 'normal' adult life. They do not want to risk not being 'valid' because they do not have a boyfriend or children. They were worried that not complying with an appropriate girlie appearance and body image would have upsetting future consequences.

Katherine: "If she doesn't do that then she could end up being sad and lonely with no boyfriend at all because they all think she is too boyish and that wouldn't be very nice."

The girls discussed the importance of women ensuring their behaviour fitted gender stereotypes. Not doing this was considered more unpleasant than the sacrifices and changes they would have to make as women to ensure they stayed within the acceptable boundaries of being feminine.

The initial discussions illustrated how girls internalise aspects of restrictive gender stereotypes. They firmly believe stereotypes need to be adhered to, particularly in their future lives. It demonstrates how these beliefs can influence girls' views on body image, appearance and behaviour with the first two being of particular importance to maintain. The girls, when questioned directly, would argue with this. They suggest it is possible and acceptable for girls and women to behave in any way they chose. Once we began exploring the different images, it became clear that this is restricted to a boundary of respectability and what their everyday discourses define is acceptable.

Girls and football

The girls had many ingrained beliefs regarding football and how their definition of femininity fit with the sport. Again their reflections on football reflect the dominant assumption that is unrelated to feminine behaviour. They were also very aware of male attempts to retain exclusivity of the sport.

Ruth: "Why would boys not pass to girls?"
Helen: "Because they think it is their game: It is not a girl's game."
Sonia: "But they think they are better."
Helen: "Yes because they never show them (women's football) on the TV."
Ruth: "Why is that?"
Helen: "It is the pigs at the BBC because they are mostly men."
Ruth: "Do you think that they see women's football as not as good?"
Helen: "I think that yes… I don't think they feel there is a need to show women's football even if it is really, really good."

The girls recognise men have the power within football. This keeps women outside it and prevents them from receiving any recognition. The discourses of football can therefore stay firmly embedded in masculine culture. The girls discussed how playing football was 'cool' for the boys and an essential part of their masculine identity. Equally they recognised that playing football was not necessary 'to be' female and that participating at times could be actively discouraged. They were able to understand and express this eloquently demonstrating that even at a relatively young age they have a firm understanding of the influence of gender discourses.

Ruth: "Why is it not important for girls to play football?"
Anna: "Because it is not in their social stereotypes, their feminine list they should be doing in modern contemporary culture (giggle)."
Ruth: "You are saying about stereotypes, what do you mean by that?"
Anna: "They should be girlie girls, they should stay in the house and cook in the kitchen and paint their nails."

Although the girls may not necessarily see this as correct it was perceived as being 'reality' and as such, should be accepted. Girls were not expected to play football. They did, however, recognise that girls and women who do play present a challenge to masculinity and that is what encourages men to retain such strong hold on it.

Katherine: "They don't like girls being able to do it because they might be better than them and they need football because it helps their masculinity."

Karla: "Yeah the boys just don't like girls playing they don't think they should so they get mean to the girls who do play."

The girls were very accepting of this. They articulated they felt it was unfair but did not believe it could be changed and so it was better to accept it and work with the dominant discourses. They thought that girls should be able to play football if they wanted to and play with boys if they chose. They recognised how discourses of both football and femininity influence society to believe it is inappropriate for them to do so. Interestingly, one girl was aware that this was not a 'natural' occurrence but a result of cultural 'teaching'.

Ella: "Yes they think girls are really weak and stuff and they like skirts and stuff."

Lisa: "We have learnt so much that it is more boys that do this sort of thing."

Working with dominant discourses entailed accessing football through girl-only sessions. They understood how feminine stereotypes could restrict them but they still believed girls should be able to play. They realise however, that females do not often get the space to participate. This is due to football being so successfully defended by males. Disappointingly they believe this will probably continue.

Jo: "Football for girls is growing so I think it will be men's and women's football."

Susie: "More girls are joining in."

Jo: "I don't think women's football will take over men's but I do think it will increase to make it more equal in terms of popularity."

Although they could see more women and girls participating when the opportunities are made available they do not see women being able to gain power in this environment.

The first two sections have examined how the girls understand two key discourses, femininity and football. Using these interpretations I asked the girls to discuss how these discourses influenced their own lives. The following sections document how they construct their own identity around these definitions of femininity and how they fit football in with this identity and the many contradictions that occur in this process.

Constructing a feminine identity?

The girls discussed their own gender identity construction along three themes: body shape, body image and behaviour. They previously defined gender identity as being two extremes: girlie girl that covered all the elements of traditional femininity, and tomboy that was seen as a female who shuns all elements of femininity in favour of a masculine identity. In discussions about their own gender identity it was revealed they devised complicated and multiple personas which are constantly changing and adapting. They cannot place themselves along oppositional definitions. Reflecting the theorising on multiple femininities, the girls cannot provide a singular definition. They do not use one 'femininity' that solely constructs their identity. Instead they draw on many discourses available to them. Even the girls who align themselves more closely to one end of the two opposites admitted they drew on elements of the other identity at times.

Sian felt she enjoyed boys' activities but did not view herself as a tomboy. She did not perceive herself as the latter because she did not want to be a boy. Instead it was being a girl and doing these activities that gave her the most enjoyment rather than adopting boy's behaviour. Anna positions herself very closely to the 'girlie girl' identity. She enjoyed dressing up and putting make up on. She also liked playing sports and doing well at school which "girlie girls shouldn't do". Karla agreed with Anna saying she draws on different gender discourses at different times.

Karla: "And me, when I want to be girly and wear a skirt I am, but I also like playing football as well and doing boyish things sometimes, it just depends on how I feel and what I want to be."

Only Becky positioned herself as a full tomboy and actively wanted to be a boy. Her appearance did not reflect this. Even though she wanted to be a boy, to be accepted within her immediate social sphere of school, friends and family, she had to retain some element of 'being a girl' such as having long hair and wearing appropriate clothes. The girls recognised there was a great deal of pressure to conform to the 'girlie girl' identity, particularly from male expectation.

Heidi: "Boys expect from the girls that they should be into make up, high heels and pop music."

The girls negotiated this by devising a workable gender identity that they could manage in different situations rather than outwardly attempting to defy and challenge all feminine stereotypes. This compromise was problematic for Becky and Helen, who did not enjoy having to adopt feminine personas. The rest of the girls found shifting between identities a pleasurable experience and a way to ensure maximum enjoyment out of every way of 'being'. They liked adopting a 'masculine' persona on occasions and felt doing this gave them a great deal of freedom to try activities such as football which they would not normally participate in. However, being part of the feminine culture of dressing up, looking after their appearance and being part of a group of girls also contained much enjoyment for them and they did not want to lose this element of their lives. Challenging stereotypical identities is not a straightforward process because there were many aspects of this identity that the girls did not want to challenge. They liked and enjoyed the behaviour associated with them.

Heidi: "I like being a girlie girl sometimes but I like doing rough boy things too."
Ella: "I like to be a girlie girl sometimes. I like to do the things that boys do because last night there were four boys and me and we had a B-B gun fight and it was great."

Discussing with the girls their own gender identities helped illustrate that they are not necessarily 'victims' of restrictive gender beliefs. Instead they take advantage of a number of femininities available to them and enjoy the benefits of being able to draw on masculine and feminine discourses and adopt the behaviour available in each. There was, however, a limit on how long they felt they would be able to continue shifting through these multiple identities without causing conflict between the masculine behaviour they adopted and the feminine ideals of getting married and having children. They discussed possible ways to work around this, such as being very feminine around boyfriends but ultimately believed this would be too difficult.

Anna: "I would give up things that my boyfriend didn't like because, well, I don't know if he was that special and he might be a soul mate and I wouldn't want to lose out on that because of football."

Currently they felt able to combine these different identities effectively, apart from Becky, who already saw her lack of interest in feminine pursuit as causing problems. Generally though, identity for them was a process of negotiation and enjoying all the different behaviours available to them in certain situations. This process was built very strongly on ensuring that certain aspects of femininity were maintained and developed and most of the girls chose to achieve this through image and body shape.

Most of the girls wanted to create and develop a body image that reflected the dominant discourses they had discussed. This seemed to be a particularly influential discourse because all the girls expressed a desire to sit within the most accepted version. They varied in how much they worried about being fat relating it to their current body size. This was a concern for all them. Ella, quite a stocky girl but not overweight, was very upset about being fat and felt her body was very unpleasant and unappealing. The boys at school constantly reinforced this to her. The girls saw their desire to be slender as their own choice, stating there was nothing wrong with fat people. Their choice was not to be 'fat'. It was clear in further discussions that being fat was tied in with very negative connotations that they wanted to avoid at all costs.

Ruth: "Would you mind if you were fat then Karla?"
Karla: "Probably. That is just me though."
Ruth: "So you don't mind if other people are but you wouldn't want to be fat yourself?"
Karla: "Yeah."
Ruth: "Why not?"
Karla: "Because I wouldn't feel very nice. You would just feel like you were being stared at sort of thing."

There were certain aspects of their body that the girls felt should reflect the feminine ideals they discussed. As well as being thin they did not want to develop the muscles they had felt were so undesirable when discussing femininity more generally.

Helen: "I don't want to be really big and like butch I don't want
to be like that gross picture we saw. I want to be strong but I don't
want to be horribly muscley."

Whilst Helen did not want to be seen as weak and completely 'feminine'
any strength she attains must be kept hidden otherwise it would not be
accepted. She equated being strong to being butch or not female and this
correlation was important to avoid.

As well as body shape the girls were also conscious of changing other
aspects that may lead to their femininity being questioned. Their hair in
particular, was very important to the girls. When Rebecca, the character in
the story cut her hair they felt she had made a mistake. They did not want
to have their hair short because they perceived it as being unflattering and
associated with maleness. Even the girls who saw themselves as being 'not
girlie' felt it was essential to keep their hair long to retain important visual
elements of femininity within their identity. Long hair was immediately
associated with femaleness and they were anxious that without it they would
be perceived as male.

Helen: "I would never cut my hair all off."
Ruth: "You know the girls in there that are boyish and have short hair
            and stuff, would you want to look like them?"
Helen: "Um not really. I would cut it shorter if someone said I needed
            to like a coach but only a little bit though."
Ruth: "How about the rest of you, would you want short hair?"
Anna: "No definitely not."
Katherine: "No."
Karla: "No."
Ruth: "Why not?"
Anna: "I just don't think it is very nice, I don't think it is very girlie
            and I just wouldn't want to be like that. It is okay to be like that
            if you want to be but I wouldn't and I wouldn't try to be."
Katherine: "Yeah I wouldn't cut my hair really short it just doesn't look
            right on a girl."

The girls do not want to appear critical of different appearances but are swift
to illustrate how they would not like to adopt these themselves. They struggle
to articulate why, other than to say it doesn't 'look right'. It appears a choice
to them but this choice could be seen as fitting with dominant gendered
beauty discourses rather than reflecting preference.

The discussions with the girls illustrate how they draw on different gender discourses at different times. In terms of behaviour the girls moved between and across the girlie girl and tomboy identities depending on the activity they were engaging in. They felt relatively free to take advantage of the different masculine and feminine identities available to them. Appearance though was much more restricted to feminine appropriate ideals both currently and in the future. The final section illustrates how football fits into this identity and how they work around beliefs that it is solely a masculine sport.

Girls, football and identity

The process of negotiating football into a feminine identity was relatively straightforward. The girls, who identified as 'girlie girls', felt that football did not conflict with this identification in any way. They were 'girlie girls' who also participated in football. The sport was very much another activity for them and was placed alongside music and dance as extra curricular activities they enjoyed. They did not view it as presenting a massive contradiction to the gender identity they preferred to adopt.

Ruth: "Of the different football girls in the story which one do you relate to most closely?"

Anna: "The girlie girls who liked to play football but like getting dressed up as well, definitely. Because I really enjoy playing football but I love getting all dressed up and putting make up on."

Karla: "Yes me too I think."

Jo: "I like wearing mini skirts but I still play football."

Susie: "I have got a girlie side and a boy side and football comes into my boy side."

Jo: "I like girlie things but I still like playing football."

Football sits easily alongside more traditional and appropriate behaviour. Some of the girls even find it a way of expressing a different type of femininity, their 'boy side'. They actively enjoy being able to access this without having to lose or challenge their more 'normal' feminine side. For the more 'girlie girls' this is what they see as making it acceptable for them to play. Even though they are participating in this masculine sport they are still retaining the elements of femininity cultural pressures demand. For some of the girls, football was appealing precisely because it gave them the space, for a short time, to forget these ideals without being judged or considered 'not normal'. They could return to their feminine identities, which most of them enjoyed, after they finished playing.

Ruth: "Why do you like football Jo?"
Jo: "Well quite a lot of people consider it is a boy thing, but I think it is a girl thing too. That is why I want to play just to prove that anyone can do it."
Heidi: "You expect from girls that they should be into make up, high heels, pop music not football or anything that the boys like because they find it weird. That is why I like doing it to show them I am not weird."
Mary: "Football is a good sport I think because everyone thinks it is a sport not for girls and they say oh no girls are rubbish at football but I like showing them it is not."

Participating in a sport they are 'not supposed' to be able to play and contradicting these beliefs gave the girls a lot of satisfaction. However, the changes in gender identity apparent as a result of playing did not translate into other areas of their lives.

For the girls who viewed themselves as closer to the 'tomboy identity', football complemented the identity they wanted to construct.

Ruth: "But with football, was that something you thought maybe you shouldn't be doing?"
Sarah: "A few years ago I wouldn't dream of playing football."
Sonia: "I would. I have always thought it is okay for me to play any sport. It doesn't matter if it is a boy's sport."
Lisa: "Yes me too. I've always been not very girlie so I have always played all games. In games we don't get a chance to play so it is good this is available."
Helen: "I am less girlie and like getting dirty so football really suits me. That is why I like it. I don't have to be girlie."

Football, for the girls, provided a chance to construct their preferred identity and reinforce it without the risk of being alienated for doing so. It was a safe space for all the girls involved to adopt and adapt gendered discourses and know that it will have fewer cultural consequences for them. The 'tomboy' girls did construct some elements of stereotypical femininity within their identity. As discussed, this was often achieved using their appearance. However, they did this much less than the other girls and found it more of a necessity to be 'girlie' rather than an enjoyment. Football fitted more fluidly for them into their gender identity. It was not, as it was for the other girls, a break from constructing and enacting the constant demands of stereotypical femininity.

Investigating how much playing football challenges stereotypical gendered identities for the girls is a complex process. Playing alone is defying expected feminine behaviour but the girls have illustrated this often does not last outside of football unless they construct the majority of their identity at a distance from feminine ideals. These girls openly defied stereotypes before becoming involved in football and the sport offered a further opportunity to achieve this. It is inappropriate to state that football helps the girls actively ignore feminine expectations. The process is not as simple as this and it does not have this influence for all the girls involved. Instead gender construction and football have a fluid relationship where girls move in between different feminine identities. Football is sometimes used to construct an alternative identity that allows them some freedom or 'time off' as Anna suggests from being a 'girl'. Although the construction of their own gender identities is heavily influenced by feminine stereotypes and cultural pressures, the girls adopt these to different degrees and not entirely unconditionally. They do feel they can contradict stereotypes at times and football can be the sole or one of many ways to achieve this. The girls illustrate as well that conforming to feminine ideals is not always a negative and restrictive process, but actually gives them a lot of enjoyment and pleasure. In effect they seem to be drawing on what they perceive as the best facets of many identities.

The defiance of femininity is evident at times but is not a complete transgression. However, this is not necessarily negative. The girls are limited by cultural stereotypes but not to the point where they completely dominate their behaviour. Because of this challenge they also suggest football and the perceptions around football may change in the future and it will become more of an accepted sport for females to play. They do not however, see the concept of the 'girlie girl' disappearing completely so all girls would be able to enact the identity they chose. They saw 'girlie girl' as continuing to be the most desirable and easiest gender identity to pursue.

Helen: "Loads of girls are still going to be girlie even if lots of us are playing football. I think that most girls will still be girlie girls in the future because they think they have to be."

Anna: "Yes but I think football will be more like hockey where it is okay
          for girls and girlie girls to play."

Rather worryingly though, the girls did not always feel they could continue
these shifts between contrasting gender identities once they moved into
adulthood. They felt feminine ideals would be too powerful and too risky
to ignore.

Heidi: "I will try to carry on but not for a club, just messing about but
          when girls get older they start getting more umm grown up and
          start going out and I wouldn't want to miss out because of
          football."
Becky: "You don't want to be too much of a boy when you are older."
Ruth: "Why?"
Becky: "I want to get married and have children."

As encouraging as it is to see the flexibility with which they negotiate gender
discourses, it appears that this may not continue into womanhood. Once
moving into this life phase the girls anticipate less opportunity to challenge
and contest or work within a range of feminine identities. Instead they believe
they will have to adhere to the more rigid and restrictive stereotypical
feminine ways of behaving and appearing. They understand gender as no
longer open for negotiation.

Conclusions

The research has illustrated how the girls see masculinity and femininity
as opposites, but they also recognise there is more than one type of femininity
that females can access. They primarily discuss two extremes of possible
feminine identities: the tomboy and the girlie girl. As Davies and Banks (1992)
suggest "humanist discourse constrains each person to constitute themselves
as unitary and non contradictory. These constraints were evident in the
children's talk about themselves and their gender" (p. 5). Reflecting the views
of children in Davies' (2003) research the girls believed they should be able
to do what they want independent of gendered categories (p. 117). The use
of images illustrated that in practice this did not occur and there were
perceived right and wrong ways to behave. The girls' definitions of the images
were similar to the views of children in Davies (2003) and Francis' (1998)

research, with a strong link between appearance and femininity. Visual signs such as appearance and clothes played a crucial part in children's and the girls' understanding of feminine behaviour.

The girls were very aware of the inter relationship between masculinity and football. They understood and articulated the power men hold within the game and the way males of all ages use this power to restrict female access to the sport. These views reflect the majority of literature available on girls' attitudes towards football. As Harris (2002) suggests "the particular place of football in regard to this male/female dichotomy serves as a major signifier of maleness even to children of primary school age" (p. 165). Similarly Skelton (2000) found football reinforced masculine ideals and kept girls excluded. Prior to the sessions the girls saw themselves as completely excluded from football discourses and still felt unable to access the male dominated football sessions available in the school. The girls recognised that playing football could be interpreted as unacceptable behaviour for girls and attributed this to strong links with masculinity.

Constructing a gender identity was not as straightforward as the girls implied in their initial conversations regarding different gender 'types'. They struggled at times to articulate where their identity sat within the extremes they defined, concluding that they were a mixture of both. Davies (2003) suggests children often take steps towards transgressing gender identities but they rarely have the words to legitimate what they were doing (p.148). Davies and Banks (1992) suggest that there is "undoubtedly much more variety, discontinuity and fragmentation in their lived experiences than comes over in their telling of that experience" (p. 22). This appears to have happened with the girls, possibly assisted by the multi method approach which has enabled multi layered discussion, and the relatively long duration of contact with them. Similar to Davies' interpretation, the girls in the group who did position themselves closer to the tomboy identity did not want to be like a boy. They wanted, as all the girls in the research did, to be able to position themselves in a range of ways that includes what we currently understand as masculine and feminine without being deemed inappropriate. There were some differences with previous research. Davies discusses how the girls in her research did not see femininity as being something they could shift in and out of, contradicting the way the girls have been shown to flow between identities during this research. Instead, for Davies' group, femininity had to be embodied not just in dress but in a way of being as well. Most of the football girls saw femininity as being achievable often through appearance only and contradictory behaviour was acceptable so long as traditional appearances were maintained. Similar conclusions could be drawn illustrating that as children learn how to think and act in terms of gender they encounter and can adopt a multitude of contradictory possibilities.

Football and its impact on female gender identity has received little previous attention. Women players provide the majority of available information by reflecting back on their childhood. These women are still playing football and as such have defied the future expectations of gendered discourse discussed by so many of the girls. They have constructed their gender identities differently to the girls involved in this study, who actively have suggested they probably will not continue with football much in adult life. Caudwell's (1999) research with players recognises that playing football, as an activity constructed as male, affects female gender identity. The girls illustrated they were not negatively affected by this but used football to access discourses and ways of behaving that were previously unavailable. The 'tomboy' girls, who had already been accessing similar discourses, used football as a site to continue to develop and enjoy this area of their identity. The results reflect to some extent Harris's (2002) observations that even during the primary years there is the first sign of conflict between football participation and femininity. But whilst the girls anticipate possible future conflict they currently are able to integrate football into their adoption of different types of femininity. Doing this causes them little concern. Renold (1997) suggests football is responsible for reinforcing the constraints on boys and girls experimenting with other ways of being male and female. My research would suggest the opposite has occurred. Football has been the avenue through which the girls have accessed some male ways of behaving and alternative feminine ways of acting they previously may not have been aware of. As Cox and Thompson (1999) reflect in their study of women footballers, the women players have multiple bodies and in the girls case, multiple identities. We can see how they both challenge and dismiss restrictive discourses of traditional femininity, and how they are aware of the tension of doing this. The women footballers in Cox and Thompsons' research and the girls in this research have demonstrated how they manage these tensions. They usually construct themselves appropriately according to the different contexts.

This paper has illustrated how girls' construction of gender identities is a complicated and changing process. The girls illustrate that negotiating different gender expectations is just as complicated as adult gender identification. Gender construction is also not as simple as following the dominant discourse or straying away from it. The girls move between many identities and football has been shown to offer a site to assist them with this. Stereotypical femininity is the foundation though which the girls build their gender identity upon. As a result, the girls cannot achieve a complete challenge or transgression away from these restrictions. The impression given is that they do not want to disrupt the gender order to this extent. They enjoy adopting 'feminine' behaviour and the penalties of not conforming are too intense. Even so whilst previous research demonstrates girls often have a negative experience when involved with football, this paper has shown the freedom and enjoyment girls have attained from engaging in this very masculine of pursuits.

References

Caudwell, J. (1999) 'Women's football in the United Kingdom: Theorising gender and unpacking the butch lesbian image', *Journal of Sport and Social Issues* Vol. 23, No. 4: pp. 390–402.

Cox, B. and Thompson, S. (2000) 'Multiple bodies: Sportswomen, soccer and sexuality', *International Review for the Sociology of Sport* Vol. 35, No. 1: pp. 5–20.

Davies, B. (2003) *Frogs and Snails and Feminist Tales: Preschool children and Gender.* (Revised Edition). Cresskill, New Jersey: Hampton Press Inc.

Davies, B. (2003) *Shards of glass: Children reading and writing beyond gendered identities.* (Revised Edition). Cresskill, New Jersey: Hampton Press Inc.

Davies, B. and Banks, C. (1992) 'The gender trap: A feminist poststructuralist analysis of primary school children's talk about gender', *Journal of Curriculum Studies* Vol. 24, No. 1: pp. 1–25.

Derrida, J. (1982) *Positions.* London: Athlone Press

Fine, G. A. and Sandstrom, K. L. (1988) *Knowing children: Participant observation with minors.* Newbury Park, Beverley Hills, London, New Delhi: Sage.

Francis, B. (1998) *Power Plays: Primary School Children's constructions of gender, power and adult work.* Trentham Books.

Foucault, M. (1979) *The history of sexuality: Vol. I. An introduction.* London: Allen Lane.

Harris, J. (2002) 'No you can't play you're a girl': Some primary school recollections of female football players', *The Bulletin of Physical Education* Vol. 38, No. 3: pp. 161–178.

Mean, L. (2001) 'Identity and discursive practice: Doing gender on the football pitch', *Discourse and society* Vol. 12, No. 6: pp. 789–815.

Renold, E. (1997) '"All they've got on their brains is football". Sport, masculinity and the gendered practice of playground relations', *Sport, Education and Society* Vol. 2, No. 1 pp: 5–23.

Skelton, C. (2000) '"A passion for football": Dominant masculinities and primary schooling', *Sport, Education and Society* Vol. 5, No.1 pp: 5–18.

Swain, J. (2000) '"The money's good, the fame's good, the girls are good": The role of playground football in the construction of masculinities', *British Journal of Sociology of Education* Vol. 21, No. 1: pp. 95–109.

Thomas, N. and Kane, C. O. (2000) 'Discovering what children think: Connections between research and practice', *British Journal of Social Work* Vol. 30: pp 819–835.

'URBAN SURFERS': REPRESENTATIONS OF THE SKATEBOARDING BODY IN YOUTH LEISURE

Ian Macdonald

Canterbury City Council and Bromley College

Introduction

The culture of skateboarding has traditionally been referred to as part of "off beat" (Crosset & Beal, 1997), "alternative", or "extreme" sporting culture (OSM, April 2003), which also includes snowboarding, surfing, motocross, BASE jumping, Ultimate Frisbee, free running — the list goes on –, but more recently as part of a "wheeled" culture which incorporates rollerblading and BMX. Additionally, the links between the development of skateboarding and the development of surfing and snowboarding have been previously documented (Humphreys, 1997), and the crossover potential between these sports remains high today with surfers using skateboards as a training tool when a surfing environment is not available. Therefore skateboarding occupies a variety of spaces within modern sport, but is yet to receive a sustained volume of analysis. It is worth noting that I am using the term 'sport' in its broadest sense here, as the traditional view of skateboarding as "an ideologically 'pure' physical activity, far removed from that tainted institution — sport" (Humphreys, 1997: p. 150), is still prevalent.

The traditional gaze cast over skateboarding has been one based on a body in need of discipline and surveillance. The result of this is often a view of skating culture as deviant and unruly. Such a view is also partly due to the discourses created in wider culture around the skating body, and the lack of a national organising body. Examples of this gaze can be seen through representations of Bart Simpson, and the symbolic, stereotypical representation of the young troublemaker in need of discipline is intensified by frequent representations of him on a skateboard. The disciplined skating body is also seen through recent films such as *xXx* ["Triple X"] and *Kids*, where the *young* skating body is part of a culture of underage sex, drinking and violence. Furthermore, the use by skaters of architecture and public spaces to express themselves serves to disrupt deep-rooted notions of the ways public buildings and spaces should be used (Borden, 2001). The construction and consumption of the skating body in this way serves to cast a disciplinary gaze over the body. The power of wider cultural processes, such as film, to produce not only a gaze, but also a powered gaze, has been previously identified:

> The cinematic apparatus operated as a technology of gender (and race) which reproduced the structure of patriarchy (and racism) by implementing a concept of looking and spectatorship which often made women (and non-whites) the object of the male (white) gaze. (Denzin, 1995: pp. 14–15)

Butler develops this point further, where the camera "trades on the masculine privilege of the disembodied gaze that has the power to produce bodies, but which is itself no body" (1993: p. 136). Indeed, the nature of this gaze is exemplified within cinema through films such as *Rear Window* — an Alfred Hitchcock thriller in which a bed-ridden photographer casts a spying gaze over his New York neighbours through his back window. The film provides an example of the production of the masculine gaze in the development of cinema (Denzin, 1995). It demonstrates the influence of visual culture on wider social spaces in helping to maintain masculine domination. Therefore the representation of the skating body in visual cultures — such as film, television and computer games — can have the effect of producing a gaze, in this case disciplinary, which is cast over it not only in a sporting context, but other social spaces.

The process of classifying the skating body as deviant and disorderly can be understood through an engagement with Foucault's 'Technologies of the Self'. The production of the skating body is achieved as a result of the ways in which such bodies are 'classified, managed, disciplined and regulated by others and also by ourselves' (Pini, 2004: p. 160). The Foucauldian notion that the body is inherently meaningless and that it is the power/knowledge processes of coding elements that give meaning to our bodies, can easily be transferred to the skating body:

> However, when we speak of our bodies in this context, we are not speaking of things which are separate from 'mind' or from 'selves'. On the contrary, selves are always embodied. Different messages are inscribed on different bodies according to society's wider system of classification, and hence different styles are produced. (Pini, 2004: p. 161)

The subsequent coding of skaters' bodies is closely linked to the counter-cultural values highlighted earlier, and their traditional position as cultural anomalies. These values set the skating body apart and, as such, its codes become regulated by the fact that it appears 'out of the ordinary'. The baggy clothes, the unkempt hair style, the body piercings, the second-hand clothing — these common signifiers are subsequently coded and inscribed with deviancy and masculinity. Furthermore, the body becomes inscribed with codes relating to the social spaces in which these bodies operate. Indeed, these acts of power on the body are closely linked to the sense of 'style', which skaters adopt and adhere to and their perceived existence in a 'subculture'.

Previous analyses of skating culture have adopted a combination of subcultural theory and a degree of Marxist theory in order to understand the dynamics of skating's resistance to dominant sporting bureaucracies (Beal, 1995; Humphreys, 1997). This has also included the appropriation of Bourdieu's concept of cultural capital (1984) in explaining the heterogeneity of styles prevalent in skating culture (Beal, 1995; Thornton, 1995). Indeed, the subcultural capital of skaters has been analysed not only through its embodiment in the bodily hexis, but also through wider cultural tastes including music, cinema and poetry. Furthermore, the logic of this cultural capital is revealed through skaters' individual dislikes, and by what the culture of skating does not represent (Thornton, 1995). This is indicative of the modes of resistance espoused by skating culture; it is not competitive, it is not professionalized, it is not organised, it does not have a governing body. Therefore, previous research has suggested the logic of skating culture is revealed in its position as an antithesis to modern sporting forms. In contrast, it is my contention that a lack of theorising on the body within skating culture has negated an important axis of analysis. While the application of Bourdieuian concepts has proved successful, this has been in the context of structural resistance and not to gender. It is through the application of theories of the body and gender performance, including those of Bourdieu (1984, 2001) and Judith Butler (1993, 1997), that I hope to reveal a more recent shift in the dynamics and 'tastes' of skating culture. Indeed, the compatibility of these two theories has been previously identified (Butler, 1997) and is evidenced in the further adaptation of the gendered habitus in sporting contexts (Bourdieu, 2001; Laberge, 1995).

Research methods

Data for analysis was gathered primarily through ethnographic observations of young skaters in practice, through a mobile skate park, and popular skating locations in London and Kent. Where possible, skaters were also engaged in casual conversation about their previous experiences. This was augmented by unstructured interviews with the project managers of organisations that provide skating facilities to public and private customers, and also arrange skating events up and down the country. A similar method of enquiry has been utilised previously and proven successful (Beal, 1995). To enhance the pool of data, an analysis of skating magazines was undertaken, incorporating issues of *Sidewalk* and *Skateboarder*; coupled with wider representations of the skating body outside the sporting context through analyses of the *NME*. The lack of female representations necessitated the use of on-line fanzines and web groups in order to access representations of the female body in its sporting context, including the popular 'www.girlsskateout.co.uk'. This gave an adequate level of data on representations of the skating body to which theories of the body were applied, primarily synthesising the works of Pierre Bourdieu (2001; Jenkins, 2002), Judith Butler (1993; 1997) and Michel Foucault (Dreyfus, 1992). Previous literature on skating culture (Beal, 1995; Borden, 2001) was also analysed in order to contextualise this current research. The issues under scrutiny here relate principally to the shifting gaze cast over the skating body, the process of its 'normalisation', and its subsequent gendered representations.

The normalisation of the 'alternative' body

Despite the traditional disciplinary gaze cast over the skateboarding body, there are indications that cultural shifts are occurring which are transforming this gaze into one of desire. This process can be viewed as a consequence of the 'normalising' of the skateboarding body due to increasing capitalist appropriation of it. The application of 'normalisation' is referred to here in the Foucauldian sense. Dreyfus (1992) summarises this process thus:

> Foucault sees that modern norms supposedly grounded in science
> likewise produce anomalies and then take every anomaly, every
> attempt to evade them, as occasions for further intervention to bring
> the anomalies under the scientific norms. This is normalisation.
> (Dreyfus, 1992: p. 90)

This follows on from Thomas Kuhn's theory of scientific change through
the process of paradigmatic shifts. Under Kuhn's model of scientific
development, the progression of 'normal' science is characterised by the
existence of anomalies outside of the dominant scientific paradigm. These
anomalies are then 'mopped up' and incorporated into normal science, unless
the anomalies are too strong to be incorporated and therefore constitute
revolutionary properties (Smith, 2000). While this view relates more
specifically to the natural sciences, it does fit in with the development of
social science, as it allows for a number of competing paradigms, or theories,
to be in operation at any one moment. This is in essence what Dreyfus is
referring to when discussing Foucault's notion of normalisation. It is at this
juncture where Foucault's ideas can be applied to the shift in the
representation of the skating body. Indeed, this could also be applied to a
wider 'alternative' body including Ultimate, free running and 'freestyle'
football and basketball. All bodies which exist and interact outside of
mainstream sporting representations.

    If we accept that skating culture exists outside mainstream culture, then
it can be considered as a 'cultural anomaly'. This is furthered when the traits
of skateboarding, discussed earlier, are taken into account. At the risk of
introducing binaries to this discussion, the culture of skateboarding has many
traits in direct opposition to modern, consumerist sporting practices.
Examples are its traditional resistance to competition; resistance to
bureaucratic organisation; resistance to professionalism; and resistance to
corporate sponsorship. There is no middle ground here; any skater accused
of not staying true to the principles of skating is vilified (Beal, 1995).
Subsequently, skateboarding exists not only on the margins of mainstream
culture due to its ongoing subjection to a disciplinary gaze, but also due to
its resistance to contemporary sporting politics and economies. It is therefore
justified to talk of this culture as being a 'cultural anomaly'. This location
has more recently seen a process of cultural appropriation by capitalist forces,
which have re-presented the skating body as 'normal' culture, supposedly
free from the disorderly stigmas. As such, the skating body is moving away

from its previous subjection to discipline and surveillance, and more towards a gaze of desire, both sexually and culturally.

The extent of capitalist appropriation of the skateboarding body can be seen through a brief analysis of skateboarding magazines as much as a brief walk down the local high street. Despite the high prevalence of anti-sponsorship and anti-professional values in skateboarding culture (Beal, 1995) there is a surprisingly large volume of product advertisement in skateboarding magazines. Issue 77 of the UK's *Sidewalk* magazine devotes 52% of its 160 pages to advertising. This incorporates products from shoes to t-shirts, and from wheels to grip tape. Perhaps more surprising, in light of previous research into skateboarding culture, was the number of professional skaters used in such advertising strategies (Borden, 2001). Furthermore, the age ranges targeted by the advertisements seem to encompass pre-teens to late twenties, with a number of older skaters being used to advertise products. This represents a highly commodified body, and is testament to the increasing capitalist appropriation of the skating body. The availability of consumer friendly clothing and equipment means it becomes easier for this body, as an object of desire, to be attained, along with the perceived cultural capital attached to it. The occurrence of commodified bodies in print media suggest a *recent* move in the appropriation of the sporting body since resistance to the commodification of skating culture has been documented as recently as the late 1990s (Beal, 1995; Humphreys, 1997). The use of skating bodies as cultural products subject to, and also the subject of, capitalist practices such as sponsorship, competitions and codification exemplify this commodification. Furthermore, this increase in appropriating the body is not just restricted to the print media. More consumer friendly images have been created through the use of skaters in recent BBC programme introductions, and perhaps most significantly, through the entrance of Nike into the skate clothing industry.

Skaters have previously been defined by their resistance to bureaucratic and commercial codes, and as such have traditionally steered away from the logos and insignias of commercial clothing companies. However, as the normalisation of skating bodies becomes more profound, so does the reality of the changing skating culture:

"Well, people say about townies having corporate logos and icons, but so do we." (*Sidewalk* message board, April 2004)

"I have noticed recently the tension between rude-boys and skaters … The superficial label and clothing styles they brand themselves with and live by are being threatened by a similar group of people, skaters. Proudly displaying their own bold logos and brand names in a similar sad way, the skaters are stepping on their toes." (*Sidewalk* message board, April 2004)

"I blame Jackass!" (Skate project co-ordinator, March 2004)

The reference to 'rude-boys' indicates the clash of youth cultures prevalent in youth leisure today. The rude-boy is a label attached to young people who have more recently entered the dictionary as 'chavs', and are identified, among other signs, by the wearing of white trainers and Burberry caps. The skater wearing his or her own example of branded clothing mirrors this 'chav' style. The main justification of 'buying into' the branding of skate clothing centres around the *brand* itself. Skaters justify this through the creation of a separate economy of capital, where 'true' skaters will only purchase clothing from companies set up by skaters, for skaters (Borden, 2001):

"Just as a 'goth' needs Dr. Martens, a skater needs Vans." (Skate project co-ordinator, March 2004)

Therefore, skaters feel they can sleep well at night knowing the money they have paid for their Vans and DC branded clothing will be re-invested in the skating industry. However, the success of larger companies in the normal-isation of the skating body means that these lines are being blurred. Perhaps more importantly, these successes pose a substantial threat to the maintenance of sub-cultural identities within the skating fraternity.

I ague that this shift in the values associated with skateboarding is a consequence of this shift in gaze, characterised by changing representations of this sporting body in wider cultural practice. This is not to deny, however, the existence of traditional values in contemporary skating culture. This shift in gaze will be analysed here in relation to representations of the skating body through popular music and computer games, and the consequences of these representations.

The emergence of the "Sk8er Boi"

The influence of musical cultures on wider cultural trends has been previously identified (Borden, 2000; Rowe, 1995; Frith, 1997; Thornton, 1997). Becky Beal's article (1995) identifies specific influences of musical taste on skating 'style', with some professional skaters partaking in their own bands and musical ventures (*Sidewalk* 77, March 2003). The co-existence between sport and music is evident here in spite of previous suggestions that these cultural spheres are distinctive from each other (Chung, 2003). Indeed, it is not just bands, but also independent record labels and shops that display a cultural crossover. One of the most prominent independent skating shops in London, Slam City Skates, has a close affinity with one of the most famous independent record label/shops, Rough Trade (associated in the past to The Smiths and more recently to The Strokes). The Covent Garden Slam City store houses one of Rough Trade's stores in its basement. Both stores use the same carrier bags, with Slam City advertised on one side, and Rough Trade on the other, pronouncing the affinity between skating and music. In order to reach the music environment, one must first enter the skating environment, linking the experience of purchasing music as a cultural product to skating.

Modern musical influences on skating bodies have been characterised by punk, grunge, metal, and 'stoner' music. Observations of skaters reveal a wide range of musical tastes, including metal bands such as Hell Is For Heroes and Slipknot, and more popular bands (in the context of sales as opposed to musical style) such as Linkin Park, Lost Prophets and The White Stripes. This is unsurprising as the relative marginality of these bands, and the perceived cultural capital imbued in them and their cultural position, reflects the same values traditionally prevalent in skateboarding culture. These bands present themselves as anti-establishment (despite some being signed to major record labels), socially aware, and free from corporate control, thus displaying the same logic of cultural capital as skaters (Thornton, 1997), as well as some contradictions (Chung, 2003). Indeed, the appropriation of skating bodies is somewhat mirrored by the appropriation of former 'independent' music acts and labels by the larger corporations. Furthermore, the shift towards a gaze of desire on the skating body has witnessed a shift in the appropriation of the skating body by the 'major' record companies. The skating body is now prevalent in popular music, as shown in acts from Avril Lavigne to Busted. This represents the eroticised, desirable sporting body. These acts are characterised by their clean-cut images and consumer friendly lyrics and melodies, free from the undesirable and unsociable stigmas attached to the disciplined skating body. A consequence of the production of a desirable skating body is the suggestion of an increased number of subject positions from whence it is possible to consume and enter the skating culture. This suggests entrance no longer has to be through participation in the sport itself, but also through compliance to musical tastes, and the attainment of a skating body via the increase in commercial clothing companies. It is worth noting that these representations embody elements of masculine performance.

Butler argues that the performance of gender cannot be bound in a singular act or occasion, rather, it is a ritualized production "reiterated under and through constraint, under and through the force of prohibition and taboo, with the threat of ostracism and even death controlling and compelling the shape of production" (1993: p. 95). This follows on from Derrida (cited in Butler, 1997), who argues that a performative, in order to become conventional, must be repeated in order to work. This repetition presupposes that this process works in successive contexts, which therefore means that repeat performances are subject to further 'infinite revisions' in subsequent contextualisations. In relation to gender performance, then, the performance of one's gender is not something which can be captured in a single sound bite, or a singular representation of identity. It is, as Bulter argues, a ritualized production. This is complicated further through the countless contexts in which the ritual of gender production takes place. As such, gender and its meanings and values are constantly in flux. This is what Butler refers to when she argues that identifying with a gender involves identifying with an unstable, and ultimately unrealizable, set of norms (Butler, 1993).

While the changing media re-presentations of the skateboarding body have been indicative of the shifting gaze, a further consequence has been the re-presentation of the skateboarding body as a predominantly masculine construction. In skateboarding, repetitive performances aimed at resisting codes of legitimacy and authority, are themselves subject to different contextualisations, or interpretations, with each repetition. The relatively marginalised position of skating culture, in the sense that it has traditionally been impervious to external influences (e.g. capitalism), means that the variety of contexts in which it operates are limited. Its contexts are interiorized, and characterised by its use of internalised 'infrapolitics' (see Beal, 1995). This state of affairs subsequently increases the power of this repetitive performance as it becomes concentrated and reflected back into the same social spaces. However, the important point to make is that while this repetition may resist dominant capitalist and bureaucratic codes, as has been the subject of previous studies (Beal, 1995; Humphreys, 1997), the inherently masculine nature of the performance in skating results in the reinforcing of dominant masculine, patriarchal codes. The performances of masculinity become a ritualized production in skating culture, and as Butler (1993) highlights such conditions allow performative success. It is in this masculine mode of production that skateboarding finds itself, with limited positions of entry for anyone wishing to join the culture.

Observations of skaters in practice revealed a vast over-representation of male participants. This exhibits a correlation with previous research, which has highlighted the sexist behaviour of skaters and resulting in "the transformative benefits of resistance (being) limited primarily to males" (Beal, 1995: p. 265). Conversations with the project manager of a regional based mobile skate park have revealed that out of an estimated 14,000 skaters who passed through their projects in the past year, approximately 98% were male. A further observation was of the present influence of computer games based around the 'extreme' or 'alternative' sporting culture.

Observations were carried out of young people in a community youth project playing on games consoles. The overwhelming popularity of skating, surfing and motocross games suggests the need to further investigate cultural influences. An important point to note is that around half of those observed claimed to take up skating after being introduced to games such as the Tony Hawk (a famous and highly successful skateboarder) series. This increases the probability of these games directly influencing the style of skating adopted by young skaters. The level of competition which is central to these games is therefore likely to impinge on the wider skating culture and may explain the level of competition between the skaters observed, despite previous studies to the contrary (Beal, 1995; Borden, 2001). Games such as Tony Hawk, also display, through a number of ways, the dominant masculine traits of skating. The process of asserting masculinity by subjecting the body to "pain and penetration" (Cook, 2000: p. 182) is reinforced in these games, whereby the skater on screen, under the control of the user, will fall off the board if a trick is performed incorrectly on the keypad. The result is splatterings of blood across the animated pavement, re-enacting real life crashes, and therefore reinforcing masculine traits of bodily "toughness and resilience" (Cook, 2000: 182). Borden (2001: p. 149) makes the link between pain and gender performance — "a form of adolescent male ritual, waging muscular body against muscular body to create pain and so define the skater's own masculinity". The homoerotic nature of this male-on-male ritual should also not go unnoticed, and is worthy of further investigation.

This "pain and penetration" principle was observed in skaters in practice. Out of the 14,000 skaters who passed through the project mentioned earlier, there were only 25 occurrences where first aid was given, and only six of these required hospital treatment. At first glance these figures suggest that the skaters did not express masculinity through "pain and penetration". However, after observing skaters in practice, and reading images and comments of skaters in other texts, it is clear that this masculinity becomes bound in the reaction to pain and penetration. What the figures do not show, and what is prevalent in practice, is the ability for skaters to suppress the affect, and play with pain (Young, White & McTeer, 1994). Indeed, the occurrence of injury was often a source of enjoyment for the group and individual, representing a relief that the stricken skater had proven his masculinity. It is therefore the presence of blood dripping off an elbow, or a scarred knee from a previous injury, that signifies the dominant ritual of masculinity within skating culture:

> All that gravity sucks you down to the cement and makes you fuckin'
> slam, it brings your aggression out. You just go 'Fuck!' ... Blood.
> Getting hurt. Guys need to do that. It's a way of getting together
> to get aggro with your friends. (quoted in Borden, 2001: p. 149)

This is further reinforced when skaters come into contact with members of other youth cultures:

> I saw some kid getting jacked by about 8 rude boys on bikes in the
> tunnel beneath Waterloo. The fucked up thing is skaters never move.
> It's all 'I'm gonna truck him!' Blah blah blah ... If you did you might
> kill him, then what? (*Sidewalk* message board, April 2004)

"Trucking" refers to the axle of a skateboard, called a truck. Trucking therefore normally relates to a process of striking the floor with the underside of a skateboard — a distinctively aggressive, masculine act. The above case however, shows how this aggression is also directed towards other young people, particularly those identifying with other youth subcultures. Bourdieu sums up processes of masculine activity as:

> The primordial investment in the social games which makes a man
> a real man — the sense of honour, virility, 'manliness' ... — is the
> undisputed principle of all the duties towards oneself, the motor or
> motive of all that a man 'owes to himself', in other words what he
> must do in order to live up, in his own eyes, to a certain idea of
> manhood. (2001: p. 48)

This also suggests a process of self-discipline in the construction of the masculine self, while supporting Cook's comment on reinforcing masculinity through inflicting pain on the body.

Avril Lavigne and the "Skate Betty"

A prime example of the 'new' skating body, as constructed by and through the shifting gaze on the skating body, is the Canadian pop star Avril Lavigne. A brief analysis of the skating body represented by Lavigne is offered in order to translate the theoretical concepts of masculine performance and capitalist appropriation into practice. Lavigne evidences the shift in gaze over the body from discipline to desire. The acceptance of Lavigne as the new desirable skating body, however, is beset with a number of complications. Firstly, the existence of a high profile female skating body suggests a point of increased entry for the female body into a previously masculine dominated culture. However, the same processes of masculine domination bind representations of Lavigne. She embodies identifiable traits of a masculine habitus, as displayed in recent publicity shots. General examples show her female skating body presented as 'open', with hands on hips, viewed from below, and have been coupled with an aggressive attitude by way of 'giving the finger' to the photographer and consequently to the reader of the image. This represents the masculine habitus (Bourdieu, 2001; Jenkins, 2002), and reinforces the deviant codes inscribed on the skating body. Furthermore, recent publicity surrounding her single 'Sk8er Boi' — itself an intense example of normalisation through language — involved Lavigne being surrounding by male, masculine skating bodies, further ritualising the practice of masculinity in skating culture. However, it is worth stopping here to note that an analysis of the female skating body through such traditional sexual regimes has been warned against (Butler, 1993), a point to which I will return.

Secondly, representations of Lavigne and colleagues demonstrate a sporting body removed from its sporting context, through the absence of the 'tool of the trade' — the skateboard itself. Iain Borden (2001) has shown how the skateboard can have symbolic properties through his analysis of skateboard advertising, and its use to symbolise offensive weapons in gang culture. Indeed this symbolism has been transferred to reality through the descriptions of 'trucking' referred to earlier. In relation to gender performance, I suggest the skateboard can also have properties of phallic symbolism, which could help to explain, to an extent, the lack of female subject positions in skating culture. Following Butler's theory of phallic identification, the female body in possession of the skateboard would represent the "having of the phallus" (Butler, 1993: p. 103). Therefore the existence of the female body within skating culture serves to destabilise gender construction in this context and represents the threat of castration (Butler, 1993) and, an ascent into the realm of the monstrous feminine (Butler, 1993; Creed, 1990). The normalising of the body, through processes of corporate appropriation, has only been able to re-present the skating body as 'normal' culture because of a removal of the skateboard from the body. This represents a removal not only of the antisocial and undesirable aspects of the disciplined skating body, but also a removal of phallic identification. Therefore, Avril Lavigne, as a female skating body, is subject to cultural acceptance, as her skating body is no longer seen as a threat to the stability of current gender norms and the maintenance of a dominant "exclusive masculinity" (Wellard, 2002). However, the embodiment of masculine traits in Lavigne still causes problems for the entrance of females into skating culture.

Beal (1995) has referred to the role of females in skating culture as the passive "Skate Betty", inhabiting a space of spectator or girlfriend to the active male participants. Observations substantiate this, with few females inhabiting the social space of skaters and fewer taking part. Further research is required in order to uncover the reasons for female non participation, for the time being, a distanced, objectified analysis is offered here. While many of the female bodies occupying skating 'space' exhibited a number of the elements of the masculine skating body such as those exemplified through Avril Lavigne, once more the removal of the phallic symbolism of the skateboard maintains the gendered boundaries of participation. The signifiers of skating culture are inculcated onto their bodies — through musical taste and baggy clothing — yet the threat of castration posed by their presence was not realised. Therefore, the position of the Skate Betty is reinforced. Despite this, a large number of examples can be found of females actively taking part in skating activity.

For Pierre Bourdieu, the construction and maintenance of gender division is rooted in the exertion of 'symbolic violence' or 'symbolic power', which refers to the pervasive force that is exercised often through the unconscious consent of the dominant group (Bourdieu, 2001). As a consequence, "we have embodied the historical structures of the masculine order in the form of unconscious schemes of perception and appreciation" (Bourdieu, 2001: p. 5). Any attempt to analyse this state of affairs is therefore bound by our own thoughts and readings, which are the very products of this form of domination. A similar argument is raised by Judith Butler — "gender performativity cannot be theorized apart from the forcible and reiterative practice of regulatory sexual regimes" (1993: p. 15). Butler suggests there is a need to detach ourselves from these constructions when theorising around gender performance and gender differences. This might be a useful starting place for the next step in analysing the female body in skating culture. Examples can be seen in female only competitions, which exemplify representations of the female skating body in practice, outside of the Skate Betty subject position. Difficulties analysing the female skating body might arise given the phallic identification of the skateboard as part of the body, and representation of the body in terms of clothing and posture. The baggy clothes worn by skaters are discursively constructed as masculine. This might suggest female skaters are to some extent performing masculinity when skating. However, the choice of such clothing should be viewed outside of these "regulatory sexual regimes", and in more practical terms, as the clothing allows more freedom of the body to perform tricks (Borden, 2001). A further point to highlight is that this clothing style masks the specific shape of the female body, therefore disrupting the construction of gender binaries, and representing a threat of castration to male skaters (Butler, 1993). These female identities could also be viewed as a disruption of the functional architecture of the body in the same way as skating a handrail disrupts society's one dimensional view of urban architecture.

Conclusions

While previous research on skateboarding culture has focused on its qualities of resistance, this analysis into the construction of gender identity has shown that the skating body has undergone a process of cultural normalisation and has, to an extent, been removed from its marginal position and been repackaged as part of 'normal' culture. This move has been accompanied by a shift in the gaze cast over the body from one of discipline to one of desire, as exemplified by the increasing commodification of the skating body, and the success of cultural figures such as Avril Lavigne. The shifts might suggest increased points of entry for female skaters. However, the discussions highlight that in practice a dominant, hegemonic masculinity, as documented by Beal (1995), is being maintained. It is the reproduction of masculine traits in the habitus of female skaters that can go some way to explaining this paradox. Furthermore, the removal of phallic symbolism — the skateboard — from the female body has aided this process further by maintaining current gender norms. Subsequently, there is a lack of active female points of entry into skating culture as a *sporting* space that do not contribute to the maintenance of masculine hegemony.

The increase in the popularity of skateboarding has led to an upsurge in local authority provision of skateparks. While the capitalist appropriation of skating bodies may have initiated a change in skating philosophies, the skating industry itself is in a strange situation. The purists will relent against the creation of the skating body as a culturally desirable product, yet find it difficult not to endorse the increasing levels of skate provision being introduced by local authorities:

> 2004 is a damn good time to be a skateboarder in Britain. As we speak there are more skater-friendly construction projects underway than at any time since the first wave of the 70s ... So in the spirit of positive thinking, I want to invite you all to stop whinging, whining and criticising and instead to concentrate on the road ahead. The future's bright, go whistle a happy tune…. (*Sidewalk*, April 2004: p. 12)

It might be undeniable that it is "a damn good time to be a skateboarder in Britain", however the constructions of new social spaces for skating bodies to operate requires further analysis. The increasing use of participation projects in providing the stimuli for skate park constructions would, it seem, give added credibility to this new wave of provision, both for skaters and local authorities alike. Despite this, it could be argued that this new wave of provision is also rooted in the perceptions of the skating body as a deviant body. As such, the good intentions of providing meaningful provision for young skaters can, conversely, signal a return to the disciplined body. The construction of these parks is therefore seen as a control measure for these deviant bodies, no longer in public view. The skating body is in effect being moved from the freedom of the street and Safeway's car parks, and into the controlled space of the skate park. Furthermore, it is also the expectation that the presence of skate provision will lead to a reduction in street skating in urban areas.

Finally, there is a need for future analysis that attempts to remove oneself from dominant, regulatory sexual discourses in order to appreciate the role of young females who do enter into the sporting practice of skating. More specifically, how do these women disrupt normative structures of gender? Further research should also concentrate on the homophobic tendencies prevalent in skating culture (Borden, 2001), and the overwhelming lack of black skaters.

References

Beal, B. (1995) 'Disqualifying the official: An exploration of social resistance through the subculture of skateboarding', *Sociology of Sport Journal* 12: pp. 252–267.

Borden, I. (2001) *Skateboarding, space and the city: Architecture and the body.* Oxford: Berg.

Bourdieu, P. (1984) *Distinction: A social critique of the judgement of taste.* London: Routledge.

Bourdieu, P. (2001) *Masculine domination.* Cambridge: Polity.

Butler, J. (1993) *Bodies that matter: On the discursive limits of "sex".* London: Routledge.

Butler, J. (1997) *Excitable speech: A politics of the performative.* London: Routledge.

Chung, H. (2003) 'Sport star vs. rock star in globalizing popular culture', *International Review for the Sociology of Sport* 38: pp. 99–108.

Cook, J. (2000) 'Men's magazines at the millennium: New spaces, new shelves', *Continuum: Journal of Media & Cultural Studies* 14: pp. 171–186.

Creed, B. (1990) '*Alien* and the monstrous-feminine', in Kuhn, A., ed. *Alien zone: Cultural theory and contemporary science fiction cinema.* London: Verso,pp. 128–141.

Crosset, T. and B. Beal (1997) 'The use of "subculture" and "subworld" in ethnographic works on sport: A discussion of definitional distinctions', *Sociology of Sport Journal* 14: pp. 73–85.

Denzin, N. K. (1995) *The cinematic society: The voyeur's gaze.* London: Sage.

Dreyfus, H. L. (1992) 'On the ordering of things: Being and power in Heidegger and Foucault', in Armstrong, T. J. (ed) *Michel Foucault Philosopher.* London: Harvester Wheatsheaf, pp. 80–94.

Frith, S. (1997) 'Formalism, realism and leisure: The case of punk', in Gelder, K. and S. Thornton, eds. *The subcultures reader.* London: Routledge, pp. 163–174.

Humphreys, D. (1997) 'Shredheads go mainstream? Snowboarding and alternative youth', *International Review for the Sociology of Sport* 32: pp. 147–160.

Jenkins, R. (2002) *Pierre Bourdieu.* London: Routledge.

Laberge, S. (1995) 'Toward an integration of gender into bourdieu's concept of cultural capital', *Sociology of Sport Journal* 12: pp. 132–146.

New Musical Express, 29 March 2003.

New Musical Express, 5 April 2003.

Observer Sport Monthly, No. 38, April 2003.

Rowe, D. (1995) *Popular cultures: Rock music, sport and the politics of pleasure.* London: Sage.

Shots, Internet WWW page at URL: www.girlsskateout.co.uk (accessed April 5, 2003).

Sidewalk, No. 78, March 2003.

Sidewalk, No. 80, May 2003.

Skateboarder, 12, No. 8, April 2003.

Smith, P. K. (2000) 'Philosophy of science and its relevance for the social sciences', in Burton, D. (ed) *Research training for social scientists*. London: Sage, pp. 4–20.

Thornton, S. (1997) 'The social logic of subcultural capital', in Gelder, K. and S. Thornton (eds) *The subcultures reader*. London: Routledge, pp. 200–209.

Wellard, I. (2002) 'Men, sport, body performance and the maintenance of "exclusive masculinity"', *Leisure Studies* Vol. 21, No. 3/4: pp. 235–248.

Young, K., P. White and W. McTeer (1994) 'Body talk: Male athletes reflect on sport, injury and pain', *Sociology of Sport Journal*, 11: pp. 175–194.

ACTIVE BODIES FOR 'REAL' MEN: REFLECTING UPON THE SOCIAL CONSTRUCTIONS OF ACTIVITY AND PASSIVITY FOR GENDERED AND SEXUALLY IDENTIFIED BODIES

Ian Wellard

**Centre for Physical Education Research,
Canterbury Christ Church University College**

Introduction

> From the time I was young, I loved physical activity, especially
> swimming and bicycling. I was not competitive and never raced. I
> just loved moving. There was an intensity in it that was very
> important for me. But the insight that I took in that way of life
> gradually eroded as I approached adolescence and started to realize
> that in my culture physical activity for boys is primarily about sport
> and competition, about building masculinity, about learning to take
> up space in aggressive and domineering ways. That did not appeal
> to me. (Pronger, 2002: p. xi)

Like Pronger, I too have always enjoyed physical activity. My parents were
both enthusiastic sports players and sporting activity was a big part of my
family life. Looking back now, I can see that my abilities in some sports
enabled me to negotiate, relatively successfully, my childhood and especially
my schooldays in ways that others were unable to. Sexuality was not an issue
for me at that time, but rather the performances of what were considered
appropriate masculinity. The sports field was a prime site for such displays
and I was able to navigate this path without the difficulties experienced by
many other men and women, both gay and straight. Individual experiences
of sport, therefore, provide a useful background against which to raise

questions about the body and masculinities and, most importantly, explore the ways in which the social informs the individual experience of physical pleasure and often limits the potential, or 'puissance' as described by Pronger (2002: p. 66).

There remain many taken for granted assumptions within sports about who is able to participate most effectively. The unequal position of girls and women within this equation has been rightly challenged by feminist sports sociologists (Scraton, 1992; Birrell & Cole, 1994; Bedward & Williams, 2000), but an unwanted outcome has been the reiteration of gender binaries which distinguish between boys and girls. Consequently, many investigations into gender and sport have, ultimately, positioned all boys as benefiting from sport and all girls as exclude, which is obviously not the case (Bailey, Wellard & Dismore, 2004).

Post- structuralist accounts have highlighted the extent to which the body has been regulated and disciplined (Foucault, 1984, 1986), and it is through these descriptions that we can explore in more detail the ways in which the gendered and sexualised body is limited in its quest for bodily pleasure by the restraints of heteronormative assumptions (Butler, 1993). This is clearly the case within the arena of sport, where bodily pleasure achieved through physical activity is still regulated by social constructions of the appropriateness of particular bodies and bodily performances considered necessary to participate. Thus, the pleasure or 'jouissance' (Barthes, 1977) or the thrill of physical play (Huizinga, 1970) to be found in sport is often not an option for the majority of gay men, as well as heterosexual men who are unable to present 'exclusive masculinity'.

The main argument presented in this paper is that hegemonic masculinity is maintained through certain bodily practices. As a result, any potential for individuals to experience the body (through physical activity) as pleasurable is often restricted by social constructions of gender performance. This is particularly evident in the field of sport which has established a position within contemporary social discourse as an arena almost exclusively occupied and enjoyed by heterosexual men. Whilst it is apparent that different masculinities are constructed in a range of social spaces, I suggest that the bodily practices formulated in sport reinforce hegemonic masculinity at the expense of other expressions of gender and consequently contribute to gender and bodily based discriminatory practices. Therefore, it is argued that any worthwhile investigation of gender and participation in sports needs to take into consideration the significance of the body and the social performances deemed necessary for participation. Recognising gender and sexuality as constituents in the social construction of bodily performances highlights how exclusive practices are reinforced in sport, whilst at the same time provides the opportunity to challenge these and develop more inclusive strategies.

Methods

Aspects of my own identity such as gender, sexuality and bodily performances not only influence my personal life history, but also the whole research process. Recognising the reflexive processes at play means that I can locate the research within social, historical and political processes and, at the same time, take into account the effect that these have on the research procedure. It is also important to recognise how theory is bound up with the methods of selecting and collecting data, analysing it and writing it up (Bourdieu, 1992).

A commitment on behalf of the researcher to reflexive approaches, now common in qualitative research, owes a huge debt to feminist studies. Feminist methodologies have been significant in their recognition of the social processes at play which have ultimately shaped the way in which all lives are experienced. The focus of much of feminist research has been the specific social and ideological locations which women have historically occupied (for example, areas such as the home (Oakley, 1974) motherhood, (Woodward, 1997) and sexuality (Petchesky, 1986). Much of this research has incorporated a qualitative reflexive approach to fieldwork so that accounts of women's lives can be evaluated in terms of broader social processes which have more often than not determined their subordinate position in comparison to men. I have attempted to incorporate similar methodological approaches in my research by recognising the social spaces which have been significant in my life and which at the same time can be seen to occupy a broader social space for men. Consequently, I consider that active sport participation is an integral aspect in the construction of male identity and is worthy of investigation.

The ability to participate 'inside' the research site is a major strength of observational ethnography. More recently there have been many studies which address masculinity and the body and incorporate participant observation (for example: Aycock, 1992; Fussell, 1992; Klein, 1993; De Garis, 2000). I adopted similar approaches for my research and included interviews, in the form of sporting 'life histories'[1], with a range of men who participated in a mainstream tennis club and a gay tennis club. Consequently, I was able to gain an insight into the relevance of gender and sexuality in relation to the men's everyday practices and bodily performances. I was also able to assess the significance placed on various issues relating to the men's experiences of their bodies, for example, whether the gay men articulated their own sexuality as being a significant factor in their ability to participate in sport in comparison to heterosexual men.

In all, I spent over three years taking part in the sports clubs[2]. During the period between 2000 and 2002, I took an active part in all aspects of the club's activities and maintained a research diary, as well as conducting the interviews. These were tape-recorded, transcribed and analysed.

Exclusive masculinity

In the social arena of sport it is clear that the body plays a central role in determining who the appropriate participants should be. This is not solely based upon the actual physical ability to perform movements related to the specific sporting event. Bodily performance provides a means of demonstrating other normative social requirements which relate to the prevalent codes of gender and sexual identity. Although I am focusing upon examples taken within a sporting context, it is clear that the men I observed and interviewed also performed gender and sexuality outside the sporting arena. However, by focusing upon the centrality of the body in sporting social practices, I have been able to observe a form of what I have termed 'exclusive masculinity' which is expressed through bodily displays, or performances. These bodily displays signal to the opponent or spectator a particular version of masculinity based upon aggressiveness, competitiveness, power and assertiveness. Body practices also present maleness as a performance which is understood in terms of being diametrically opposite to femininity. These constructed understandings of gender appear even more significant when taking into account the value placed upon bodily presentation on the sports field where social activity is established upon principles such as competition, winning and overcoming opponents. The formulation of normative masculinity as superior to femininity and the practice of sport as a male social space create the (false) need for more obvious outward performances by those who wish to participate. This is particularly evident in the displays of the body which act as a central means through which exclusive masculine identity can be established and maintained.

However, it is important to make it clear that this form of masculinity, located as it is in body practices, is not based solely upon physical build or biological sex. Exclusive masculinity can be understood as a version of hegemonic masculinity in that it involves the subordination of competing forms of masculinity as well as femininities. However, what distinguishes it from versions of masculinity in other constructs, for example the patriarch or the corporate leader, is the strong emphasis placed on bodily performance. Exclusive masculinity is expressed through particular types of bodily performance which derive from traditional forms of hegemonic heterosexual masculinity, especially where investment in the male physical body has been valued. This is particularly evident in sport, where the body becomes even more significant and specific displays are considered important. Greater value is placed upon displays of strength, skill and (often) aggression. In consequence, bodily performances which equate with weakness or inability are considered inferior. However, it is the performance of the body which is exclusive, not necessarily the social category such as gender or age. Although these play a role, it is the bodily performance which provides the central focus. For example, in an elite sport such as professional tennis, two current highly ranked players in the men's and women's events, (Lleyton Hewitt and Serena Williams) although being physically small (Hewitt) and female (Williams), both display exaggerated versions of aggressive masculinity through their on court manner. They strut about the court, pump their clenched fists and act aggressively towards their opponents. In the same way, a wheelchair user, although disadvantaged in comparison to an able bodied athlete, can still perform exclusive masculinity in the same manner and, consequently, reinforce the discriminatory practices found in organised sport, in particular those which constantly position hegemonic male bodily performances as exemplary. However, at the same time, evidence which supports the presence of exclusive masculinity raises interesting questions about the extent to which masculinity is threatened or subverted when it is performed by women, gay men, lesbians or the disabled.

With this in mind, I have provided some examples from the research in order to explore exclusive masculinity as well as assess the relationship of the body to performances of masculinity and the extent to which these shape initial entry into active sport. Importantly, the research highlights the social expectations for particular forms of bodily performance which are required in order to participate. This, in turn, often determines the extent to which the individual is able to be 'active'.

Active and passive bodies

Connell's (1995) concept of a 'circuit of body reflexive practices' allows us to understand how new constructions of self identity are formed through bodily experiences. For instance, all the men that I talked to, during the research, expressed their enjoyment of taking part in physical activity, although within the context of sports there were contrasting levels of pleasure. This is an important point and highlights that the individual experience of bodily pleasure during physical activity needs to take into account both biological and social factors. Consequently, specific socially prescribed performances dictated the nature of subsequent participation and contributed to the men's construction of sporting identities in terms of their own understanding of whether they 'fitted in' or not. In this particular case, the 'body-reflexive practice of sport' (Connell, 1995: p. 63) created an understanding of normative identity for some men, whereas for others, it established an identity based upon difference.

I use the examples, taken from the research, of four men (Simon, Gary, Paul and Peter), to provide evidence of the way in which early experiences of sport contribute to the formation of individual sporting identities and, consequently, shape future levels of participation.

Simon (38) and Gary (39) were members of the mainstream tennis club. Simon had been involved with the whole club (football and tennis) throughout his life, whereas Gary had only recently joined the tennis section and, subsequently, left during the course of the research. Although having similar social backgrounds, both men had contrasting experiences of sport.

Gary described how he was aware at an early age of his physical presence by drawing upon comparisons of his own bodily presentation with the other children:

> "I was probably a little bit camp when I was at school. Cos I wasn't aggressive and stuff like that and I was in the lower tier at school, so I was in the 'B' stream and it was more of an aggressive culture and kids didn't wanna learn and so it was very difficult ... . Sport was pretty atrocious ... because it was all cricket, which I loathed, football which I was useless at and hockey which I was crap at."

Gary's use of the term 'camp' suggests that his recollections are shaped by an adult reading of his childhood experiences even if camp was not a concept he would have used at the time. However, we can assume that Gary is describing a sense of being different from other boys that he did have at the time. But what is important is that this sense of difference appears to have derived, to a significant degree, from his experience of his body. Through the physical experience of his body he developed an understanding of it as being weak or inadequate, especially in comparison to other boys when having to take part in organised sport. His awareness of himself as 'camp', or different in terms of the other boy's bodily presentations, also demonstrates that he had developed an understanding of appropriate masculine performance which, in turn, did not relate sufficiently to the experience of his own body. This is similar to Connell's (1995) example of Adam Singer, who was criticised by his father because of his apparent lack of skill at sports. Connell argues that Singer developed an understanding of his body as different from normative masculinity through his inability to throw a ball like a real man:

> The public gender meanings are instantaneously infused with the bodily activity and the emotions of the relationship. Even so, there is a split perception. Adam has learned how to be both in his body (throwing) and outside his body watching its gendered performance. (Connell, 1995: p. 62)

Gary's understanding of his body as weak had been developed through a similar relationship with his own body and its gendered performance. He was aware that he did not present the expected version of masculinity. In the early years of school he was made aware of his difference, specifically through his physical bodily presentation, rather than as a result of any awareness of his sexuality. Indeed, it is difficult to make claims that children are fully aware of their sexuality at an early age or understand the social implications attached to it. For Gary, however, it seems possible that the realisation of his difficulty presenting orthodox masculinity in comparison to the other boys was further accentuated by his placement in the lower stream in the secondary school where the emphasis, within the pupils' culture, was on the presentation of aggressive, physical masculinity rather than the academic. This, again, is similar to Connell's description of Adam Singer, where the attitudes expressed by his father, like the other boys at Gary's school, were located in hegemonic masculinity. In this environment the performance of bodily strength attracted the most cultural capital and in the school curriculum sport was considered a prime area to encourage the boys to let off steam. For Gary, though, his body was a major source of humiliation as he felt he was unable to compete physically with the other (in his words) 'thugs'. Consequently, his experiences of sport as a child were negative:

> I just hated it all. I wasn't very good and so I hated it all … I don't know I just always feel conscious when there's a massive group of people in sport. I feel kind of conscious about my ability.

Gary 'wasn't very good' at sport, but more tellingly the consequence of this was that he could not perform hegemonic masculinity. His loathing of organised sport continued throughout school and during the latter years of secondary school, when he became increasingly aware of his (homo)sexuality, he came to regard sport as something that 'heterosexual' men do. The physical experience of sport created a social understanding of how he should present his body within this context to others and, combined with his interpretation of homosexuality, formed a circuit of bodily reflexive practices which ultimately shaped his ability to interact with the other boys. Because of his feeling that he was unable to 'pass' successfully within this environment, he continued to avoid it:

> "I mean I didn't have any problems coming to terms with my sexuality. But saying that, I thought being gay I wasn't particularly good at sport so I thought well that's part of it."

Gary's account reveals the way that appropriate bodily performance is part of acquiring successful masculine status. Failure in this area signals failure as a 'real' man. For Gary, there was a marked distinction between sport and play. There was pleasure to be gained from his body in terms of physical activity but, for him, sport was associated with negative social expectations and in particular, a pressure to perform hegemonic masculinity. Pleasure through play was found in other areas, particularly in sexual activity which was seen as fun and where the social expectations could be managed. Dunne (1988) describes how young girls are able to take part and enjoy sports as girls, but the onset of puberty creates problems in terms of the social understanding of their bodies, which effectively precludes them from taking part in the same manner. The onset of puberty, if read in terms of bodily practices, directs the individual to experience his or her body in a particular manner. Consequently, many adolescent women begin to understand and experience their bodies as weak in relation to men (Segal, 1993). Gary learnt to experience his body during childhood and adolescence as weak, or feminine. This understanding of masculine identity was also influenced by his perceptions of normative femininity and homosexuality. Gary, therefore, constructed a social identity through an acute awareness of his own body. His bodily performances informed his perception of masculinity in relation to other men and also provide support for the claim that the body is central in the presentation of gendered identity to others. Thus, for Gary, social situations which held the possibility of presenting an inappropriate identity were avoided.

Simon, in contrast to Gary, experienced his body and his abilities in sport as natural. Physical sensations and pleasurable experiences gained from physical activity were seen as positive and normal. Simon's experience of his body enabled him to construct an identity based upon normative masculinity. For example, when he was at primary school, his recollections demonstrate that he was already aware of the performances required. Being active was considered an essential part of his world and was often hampered at school

(S)   "It was mostly games, I mean they did sort of the human movement studies ... A lot of music in the playground, pretending to be a statue."

(I)   "How did you find that?"

(S)   "Well for someone who used to like running around in the countryside I suppose it was a little bit pedestrian ... erm, I played for the school football team."

Football was a space where he could be active and this figured heavily in his childhood memories. For Simon, playing football was considered a natural activity for boys to take part in and he never had any reason to find participation problematic in the way that Gary did. Simon was able to earn respect from other boys and teachers because of his sporting ability. This enabled him to develop an understanding of sport as a male preserve where certain qualities were required. His accounts of his experiences as a young man entering into the world of adult male sport almost suggest a 'rite of passage' to hegemonic masculinity.

(S)   "You sort of see everything there is to see about football. The good side and the bad side. It was er men against boys and er you know they're licensed to do whatever they want to, but you know it sort of conditioned you to er either fall at the wayside or battle through it."

(I)   "Is that good or bad?"

(S)   "Depends what character you are erm .. it did affect a couple of
        friends of mine .. but they did see some very nasty injuries .. erm
        it was particularly scary on a few occasions .. when you've got
        the other team and the supporters you know sort of baying for
        blood, sort of thing. But all in all it was erm it was just good for
        me, I just erm … if I got fouled or whatever, I just got up and
        got on with it and erm and that seemed to wind the opposition
        up even more and it actually helped us get the result we wanted
        … because they totally lost it … from that point if view it set the
        team up for later on in life. And we had a lot of success later on.
        That was quite good grounding from that point of view."

Simon was able to make the transition to adult sport successfully and because
of this was able to justify the process. Those who 'fell by the wayside' were,
for Simon, considered unsuitable for participation and the selection process
merely sorted them out. Simon learnt that successful participation in adult
sport required a performance of exclusive masculinity as a means of
demonstrating to others his ability to take part.

What emerges from the accounts of Gary and Simon is the way that
exclusive masculinity is significant throughout the life course. The emphasis
upon the body as a means of presenting 'natural' or 'unnatural' masculinity
reinforces the hierarchical structure of gender relations and simultaneously
contributes to the dominance of a hegemonic masculinity. At the same time
it is also important to acknowledge the way in which both men experienced
their bodies and the way this played an integral part in the construction of
their own masculine identities as well as wider social understandings of other
men and women. Gary's attempts to conform to hegemonic masculinity
through his efforts to avoid problematic social situations, such as sport, and
in adult life his dislike of 'camp' acting men and reluctance to join a gay
tennis club, reveals the complex nature of those who are both disadvantaged
by hegemonic masculinity but are also inextricably bound to it.

It could be claimed that sexuality was a main factor in the experiences
of sport for Gary and this is in contrast to Simon. However, I suggest that
Gary's bodily awareness and inability to perform 'real' masculinity were
more significant. If it was the case that sexuality was the main factor in
determining entry into sports participation, then it could be assumed that
all the gay men in the sample would have had similar experiences to Gary.
However, a contrasting range of experiences were recounted by the men who

participated in the gay tennis club. The significant factor in terms of 'successful' sports participation was the ability to perform hegemonic masculinity. I use the examples of Paul (34) and Peter (33) to provide support for this claim.

Paul shared similar experiences to those of Gary and was one of several men in the gay tennis club who had experienced taunts during his schooldays and, occasionally, hostility because of his inability to present a particular version of masculinity based upon the body.

> "I remember the first, when I joined junior school and er they wanted me to play football. I cried and cried and cried and tried to get my mother to write me a letter so I didn't have to play … Erm, cos I knew I was going to get picked on. It was going to put me in the spotlight, I couldn't kick a ball, therefore I was going to be called a poof and, you know, I'd get all the aggression from the other boys … I kind of … I suppose was fed up with it … fed up with all the bullshit you get from the sports teachers, you know they were quite bolshy and they gave boys nicknames, er and you just wanted to get away from characters like that, you know, they, a friend of mine, they called 'Doris', one kid they called 'stickweed'. It was kind of like subtle, or just humiliating the kids… ."

Purposeful participation in school sports was inextricably related to the shared understandings of the abilities considered appropriate to it. These were based upon constructions of traditional, hegemonic masculinity, which dictated that successful practices included knowledge and skill in specific sports (often presented in an expectation to be able to perform basic movements, such as kicking a ball) and the ability to 'act' in particular ways, notably through being aggressive or competitive. Consequently, for Paul, school sports were unpleasant as he was both unwilling and unable to conform to the expected practices. Significantly, it was not only the other boys who contributed to the reproduction of exclusive masculinity but the Physical Education teachers. This was reported by many other men in the sample, both gay and straight.

Peter, however, in contrast to Paul, experienced sport as both enjoyable and successful. The main concern for Peter was being able to present a normative version of masculinity. The fear he held was based on being seen by others as presenting 'gay' rather than the broader understanding of his sexuality. Probyn (2000) talks of the importance of 'shame' in constructing self identity, particularly in sport. It is based on an understanding of the body as incompetent, which for many needs to be concealed at all times. The sense of shame in relation to bodily performance was a central theme among all the respondents. Shame related to the presentation of 'unmanly' behaviour and a subsequent threat of ridicule. The notion that Peter needed to avoid being caught suggests that 'gayness' presents itself in some physical form which is manifested through the social presentation of the masculine body. For Peter, this meant learning about ways to present his body in a 'non-gay' manner and become more aware of what being a 'normal' young male involved. Peter was able to adopt strategies for this:

> "Well you just don't look (at other men) longer than you should look … I didn't actually physically do anything … quite secretive … and because I was quite sporty anyway and quite good academically, I wasn't gonna get picked on. I'm a fairly big … you know I was OK.. I was quite keen to fit in."

Learning how to act within an environment heavily laden with conventions of hegemonic masculinity was important. Peter's accounts of how he maintained a furtive approach to containing his sexuality corresponds with additional observations I made at a health club where rules of masculine bodily conduct are constructed without reference to explicit texts. They are learnt within the context of a 'natural men's world'. In this case Bourdieu's (1990) concept of the taken for granted social world (doxa) maybe more relevant than hegemony, within the context of the boy's lives. The concept of hegemony implies an awareness of alternatives, but these are overlooked because of continued acceptance of dominant prevailing social practices. From all the men's accounts, it would appear that awareness of alternative sexuality was limited in comparison to the awareness of a need to demonstrate appropriate masculine bodily performances. Peter's physical presentation was, therefore, a primary means through which he could maintain an outward appearance of normative masculinity. He was physically strong and 'sporty' so his outward physical performance did not conform to stereotypes of the feminised gay body. This is not to say that the problems Peter had to negotiate in order to keep his sexuality hidden are confined only to gay men. Homophobia is often used to police a range of subordinated masculinities (Redman, 1996). Boys learn from an early age how to present their bodies to others, particularly in more intimate settings which arise in sport. Peter's example highlights the way forms of masculinity are learnt and then acted upon. In Peter's case his physicality and ability in sport enabled him to 'pass' as a 'normal' young male without conflict. Probyn (2000) uses the example of the Australian rugby player, Ian Roberts, who came out in public as gay and notes how his body 'functioned as a 'beard' for his gayness, and for a while it was used to hide the possible shame of being gay' (Probyn, 2000: p. 17)

Peter was able to use sport and his body as a similar 'beard' to mask his gayness. At the same time, Peter also recognised the cultural capital to be achieved from his bodily displays. Even within the context of an interview with another gay man, where sexuality was not problematic in the way that it may be within a heterosexual sporting environment, Peter was still keen to demonstrate to me how sport had been a large part of his life and importantly that he had been good at the ones he took part in. Sport was not just fun and games, but was an activity to be taken seriously.

> "I also used to do swim training. So, er, that was like twice a week, serious stuff till I just grew sick of it in the end."

Consequently, in the context of the interview, Peter was concerned with presenting himself as a 'legitimate' gay male, but much of this entailed identifying with heterosexual masculinity and presenting himself as 'manly' in an orthodox fashion. There were numerous ways in which he was able to do this, but his body and sporting deeds provided the main sources. At the same time, it appeared that Peter recognised the significance of sporting capital and was keen to provide evidence of this in his conversations with me. Thus, the reference to swimming training and the serious nature of the participation was included more as an indication of Peter's legitimate place within sport and, to an extent, his ability to be a 'real man'. Peter's general confidence in his own body, his ability to participate in mainstream sport and his enjoyable experiences of school read more like those of Simon, described above.

Conclusions

Listening to adult sporting recollections is revealing in that it draws our attention to the contrasting range of experiences faced by young people. Claims that all children benefit through sport fail to recognise the differing experiences faced by boys and girls, particularly in organized sports and school physical education.

Sport was significant in the lives of all the men in the research, even though some had not taken part in sport at school or as children, but had expressed a sense of enjoyment in physical activity. The research supports arguments which suggest that young people develop an early understanding of their own bodies and how bodily performances often determine the extent to which they are able to actively participate in sports.

Ability to successfully take part in physical activities is determined by many factors. Most notable are performances of gender, where traditional, hegemonic masculinity is favoured, and specific skills based performances are required. Often, within Physical Education, sporting ability is positioned as a form of intelligence. As Evans points out:

> Thinking of this kind now runs through a multiple of grouping and tracking practices that separate the 'able' and the 'less able' within schools, providing the opportunity for teachers and senior managers to identify the winners and losers at the earliest possible stages. (Evans, 2004: p. 99)

Consequently, the negative effects of competition are still overlooked. Competitive sport places direct emphasis upon winning, with the result that taking part can produce a fear of losing and shame about one's performance (Probyn, 2000). Taking into account that young people are generally entering sport as novices and the majority of adults participate in sport at an amateur level, the context of participation in a sporting activity is distorted and the emphasis upon enjoyment is often neglected. Although these sentiments are supported by liberal approaches to sport, the notion of competition is still considered as an aspect of society that is essentially positive. Consequently, competition in sport continues to reflect broader values which are believed to be 'character' building. If this is the case, then little has really changed from the early Victorian sporting practices in the nineteenth century.

Failure to recognise the gendered practices within traditional sports ultimately favours those who are able to perform 'exclusive masculinity'. Consequently, there continues to be a large section of young people (boys and girls) who are excluded because of their inability to 'perform' in the expected manner.

Gorely, Holroyd and Kirk (2003) propose that a step forward would be to apply a 'gender relevant physical education' (p. 443) where the common goal could be to educate both boys and girls to utilise their full bodily capacities. However, the focus upon gender is problematic in that it continues to surreptitiously consolidate existing gender binaries. As such, I believe that a further step forward is needed where 'body relevant' physical education is incorporated. Gorely et al, appear to be moving in this direction when they suggest that the key features of gender relevant physical education should be a 'common goal of physical empowerment while recognising that the realization of this goal will require different kinds of programmes relevant to the groups of young people in specific locales' (Gorely *et al.*, 2004: p. 445). However, it may be worthwhile to adopt 'body relevant' forms of physical education which would place more emphasis upon the central issue, the individual body, whilst at the same time continuing to take into account the influence of other social factors such as gender, race, age and class, upon the body.

In a recent report to the World Health Organization (Bailey, Wellard & Dismore, 2004) on girls' participation in sports and physical activities, attention was drawn to the fact that evidence suggested girls *do* enjoy taking part in physical activities, but more often than not it is the sporting practices which ultimately deter or exclude participation. The continued emphasis upon who is 'able' or not to take part within current sports affects a disproportionate number of young people, who in different circumstances may relish the opportunity to engage in physical activities. A number of recommendations were made in this report which applies to young people in general and it may be appropriate to conclude with the following:

- Practices should be established which recognise the importance of fun, health and social interaction in sports participation.
- Any strategies concerned with raising participation among young people need to remember that neither girls nor boys are 'the problem'; rather, the difficulty lies with the ways in which physical activities are constructed and presented;
- It is important to examine and highlight the practices inherent within sports which might deter children from participating. Sports provision may need to be adapted to encourage and accommodate all young people. (Bailey, Wellard & Dismore, 2004: p. 9)

Notes

1 I adopted a form of sporting 'life histories' in a similar manner to the life history approach adopted by Connell (1995).

2 The research was conducted as part of a PhD investigation into masculinities, the body and sport. The research was funded by the Pavis Centre at the Open University 1999–2003 (see Wellard, 2003).

References

Aycock, A. (1992) 'The confession of the flesh: Disciplinary gaze in casual bodybuilding', *Play and Culture* No. 5: pp. 338–357.

Bailey, R. Wellard, I. & Dismore, H. (2004) 'Girls' participation in physical activities and sports: Benefits, patterns, influences and ways forward', Technical paper for the World Health Organisation.

Barthes, R. (1977) *Image Music Text.* London: Fontana.

Bedward, J. & Williams, A. (2000) 'Girls' experience of physical education', in A.Williams (ed) *Primary school physical education.* New York: Routledge/Falmer Press.

Birrell, S. & Cole, C. (1994) *Women, sport and culture.* Champaign: Human Kinetics.

Bourdieu, P. (1990) *The logic of practice.* Cambridge: Polity.

Bourdieu, P. and Wacquant, L.J.D. (1992) *An invitation to reflexive sociology.* Cambridge: Polity Press.

Butler, J. (1993) *Bodies that matter.* New York: Routledge.

Connell, R.W. (1995) *Masculinities.* Cambridge: Polity.

Connell, R.W. (2000) *The men and the boys.* Cambridge: Polity.

De Garis, L. (2000) 'Be a buddy to your buddy: Male identity, aggression and intimacy in a boxing gym', in McKay, Messner and Sabo *Masculinities, Gender Relations and Sport* London; Sage.

Dunne, M. (1988) *An introduction to some of the images of sport in girls' comics and magazines.* Centre for Contemporary Cultural Studies papers: University of Birmingham.

Evans, J. (2004) 'Making a difference? Education and "ability" in physical education', *European Physical Review* Vol. 10, No. 1: pp. 95–108.

Frosh, S., Phoenix, A. & Pattman, R. (2002) *Young masculinities.* Hampshire: Palgrave.

Fussell, S. (1992) *Muscle.* London: Abacus.

Gorely, T. Holroyd, R. & Kirk, D. (2003) 'Muscularity, the habitus and the social construction of gender: Towards a gender-relevant physical education', *British Journal of Sociology of Education,* Vol. 24, No. 4: pp. 429–448.

Hammersley, M. & Atkinson, P. (1995) *Ethnography, principles in practice.* London: Tavistock.

Huizinga, J. (1970) *Homo ludens* London: Paladin.

Klein, A. (1993) *Little big men: Bodybuilding subculture and gender construction.* Albany: State University of New York Press.

Oakley, A. (1974) *The Sociology of Housework,* Oxford: Martin Robertson.

Petchesky, R. (1986) *Abortion and woman's choice: The state, sexuality, and reproductive freedom.* London: Verso.

Probyn, E. (2000) 'Sporting bodies: Dynamics of shame and pride', *Body and Society,* Vol. 6, No. 1: pp. 13–28.

Pronger, B. (2002) *Body fascism: Salvation in the technology of physical fitness.* Toronto: University of Toronto Press.

Redman, P. (1996) 'Empowering men to disempower themselves: Heterosexual masculinities, HIV and the contradictions of anti-oppressive education', in Mac an Ghaill, M. (ed) *Understanding masculinities.* Buckingham: Open University Press.

Scraton, S. (1992) *Shaping up to womanhood: Gender and girls' physical education* Buckingham: Open University Press.

Segal, L. (1997) *Slow motion: Changing masculinities, changing men.* London: Virago.

Wellard, I. (2002) 'Men, sport, body performance and the maintenance of exclusive masculinity', *Leisure Studies Journal* Vol. 21 Jul/Oct pp. 235–247.

Wellard, I. (2003) *Game, set and match to exclusive masculinity: Men, body practices, sport and the making and remaking of hegemonic masculinity.* PhD thesis, Open University, September 2003.

Woodward, K. (1997) 'Motherhood myths and meanings', in Woodward, K. (ed) *Identity and difference.* London, Sage.

MAKING SENSE OF *'NUTS'* AND *'ZOO'*: THE CONSTRUCTION AND PROJECTION OF HOMOGENISED MASCULINITY[1]

Fiona Jordan and Scott Fleming
University of Gloucestershire, UK

Introduction

In January 2004 two new weekly publications were launched. Targeted at men, and young men in particular, *Nuts* and *Zoo*, were (and continue to be) 'tabloid-esque' weekly magazines. In essence, as Robinson (2004: p. 7) puts it, they are dominated by: "girls and, er, bawdy humour […] Plus football … ". Each had the explicit intention of capturing a niche market and from the outset they were in competition with each other. *Nuts* was the first to get under way (by a week[2]) and its publicity material promised that it would be "the world's first general interest weekly magazine for men", and that "Every Thursday for the price of a half-pint of beer, you can get your hands on a unique mix of sexy women, gritty real-life stories, sport, news and complete TV listings for men" (www.ipc.co.uk — 21st May 2004). *Zoo* followed suit. It was represented as "a general interest weekly aimed at men" and pledged to provide its readers with "100 pages of girls, football and funny stuff" (www.emap.com — 21st May 2004). Although there were some differences in the description of the content, the two magazines were essentially very similar in tone, presentation, subject matter and sales figures — it was reported by the publishers that the first issues sold around 150,000 copies each (*Marketing Magazine*, 11th February 2004).

About three months after the launch it was estimated that circulation figures had stabilised at around 260,000 copies per week for *Nuts*, and 160,000 for *Zoo* (*Marketing Magazine*, 5th May 2004). For the latter, this success was

133

not achieved without risk. *Zoo* originally sold on Wednesdays but in March changed to Tuesdays, and there were concerns amongst media agencies that this would reduce the capacity for the inclusion of weekend football stories and features. This was significant because football had been identified as a key selling point for its target market[3].

As commercial ventures, both *Nuts* and *Zoo* achieved unprecedented initial success. At the time of writing [September 2004], it is too soon to comment unequivocally about the extent to which that has been sustained, and is sustainable into the future. More important than the profit-making effectiveness of the magazines, however, is the wider set of socio-cultural values, norms and expectations that they embody and celebrate, and the effects on the construction of identities[4]. It is clear, for example, that it is often in leisure where young people 'find themselves' (Hendry *et al.*, 1993). That is to say, it is in leisure where many young people are able to establish and confirm their own individual identities. It is also clear, of course, that not all young people are able to exercise real choice over their leisure; as Miles *et al.* (1998: p. 83) observe, "the freedom enjoyed by young people is overstated, thereby reproducing the myth of individual choice".

Writing about football fanzines specifically, Haynes (1993) noted the major role that magazines play in the development of masculinities. The same may be argued for *Zoo* and *Nuts*, especially as the former (and by implication the latter) is aimed at the 16–30 year old male consumer (Robinson, 2004), a time of life when adult roles are being explored and consolidated. Moreover, the linkages between forms of popular culture, like magazines, and the wider societal context in which they are situated are not new. Almost fifty years ago Hoggart (1966 [1957]) observed the inter-connectedness of various forms of public culture and the structure of an individual's private everyday life, gender relations, community and so on. Miles *et al.* (1998) have also argued that consumption of everyday experiences allows young people to feel as though they 'fit in' whilst simultaneously giving them some semblance of individuality. They contextualise these observations by noting the interrelated structural changes on a societal level that have affected young people very directly: youth unemployment; reconstituted families; participation in Higher Education; and changing school-to-work transitions.

In this paper we explore some of the relational themes and issues concerned with the construction and projection of gender identities — or, more accurately, a particular masculinity. We do this by undertaking a preliminary analysis of the overt messages that are contained within one comparable section of *Nuts* and *Zoo*: the television reviews. Described as

'Unmissable TV' (in *Zoo*) and 'Must See TV' (in *Nuts*), content analysis of the television programmes that are recommended (indeed even exalted) followed by some preliminary discourse analysis of the key themes sheds light on the cultural production and reproduction of contemporary youthful masculinity. We begin, however, with an overview of the men's magazine market since the 1980s and a theoretical contextualisation informed especially by Benwell (2003) and, to a lesser extent, by Stevenson *et al.* (2000).

Men's magazines: (selective) history and UK market

A Mintel (2002) report on *Men's Lifestyle Magazines — UK* identified 23 titles prior to the launch of *Nuts* and *Zoo*. These magazines reflect a genre that found expression during the mid-to-late 1980s and early 1990s, and were starkly different from magazines for men[5] that preceded them. Typically, the latter dealt with commodities thought to be of interest to (some) men: cars, fishing and Do-it-Yourself. Though, as Stevenson *et al.* (2000) note, there were also 'style' magazines such as *I-D* and *The Face*, as well as music bulletins such as *New Musical Express* [*NME*]. It is reasonable to conclude, then, that the men's lifestyle magazine sector is relatively new and dates back only to 1986 and the launch of *Arena*. However, two magazines were to change the cultural landscape dramatically: *For Him Magazine* launched in 1988, and *Loaded* in 1994.

Re-branded as *FHM*, the first of these was estimated to sell 3 million copies a month worldwide in 2004. Its audience in the UK alone exceeded 600,000 (greater than its three closest competitors combined). More than *FHM*, however, it was the launch of *Loaded* that is widely accepted to have changed the face of men's lifestyle media. The intention was to appeal to young men whose interests were football, cars, drinking, music and lusting after women, and the magazine deliberately promoted excessive behaviour. Robb (1999: p. 41) explains:

> *Loaded* editor James Brown's Britain was a country of football, pubs, all-night parties, cheeky quips, crap sitcoms, great pop, Carry Ons, and endless in jokes — in other words it was the real Britain.

As if to ape the editorial style of *Loaded* itself, Robb (*op. cit.*) explains further that "*Loaded* was the men's mag that walked it like it talked it. It spoke in the language of the bars and clubs of the UK" (p. 45). Its long-term impact has been substantial as many (if not all) men's magazines since have borrowed from its presentational style, irreverence and editorial stance. It moved away from the focus on fashion and grooming that characterised some of the earlier magazines[6]; and though it is over-stating the case to conclude that the cutting edge of men's culture is sold through men's magazines (as Robb does), the *Loaded* effect has nonetheless been profound and far-reaching.

More specifically, this new breed of magazine was aimed directly and overtly at a heterosexual male readership, using white hegemonic masculinity as a marketing tool (cf. Nayak 1999). Seen by some to be a negative force through their objectification and sexualisation of women, they were (and continue to be) openly sexist. They represent the 'new lad' at least partly as a backlash against the portrayal of 'new man' in the previous, more fashion-conscious magazines such as *GQ* and *Esquire* (Stevenson *et al.*, 2000)

The Mintel (2002) report listed five underlying positive factors that have stimulated the development of men's lifestyle magazines: changing attitudes amongst men; advertising revenue; personal disposable income and economic trends, population trends, socio-economic trends. In terms of male attitudes, the key driver was found to be an interest in style and grooming articulated by over 50% of the men surveyed, chiefly in the younger age group. This also resonates with the corresponding trend towards advertising male style, fashion and grooming products in the magazines. Importantly too, according to this research, men are much more likely than women to be impressed by an attractive and informative front cover (see also Stevenson *et al.*, 2000).

Between 1997 and 2001 the total market for men's magazines grew by 14% in volume to 26.67 million, though between 1998 and 2000 there was a fall of around 8% (attributable, at least in part, to the plethora of undifferentiated products). Within this market segment around 67% of the sales were generated from the 'younger general' market, the most prolific purchasers of men's magazines. This may be evidence in support of the assertion from Mintel that there is a social trend towards men adopting younger, often single lifestyles for longer and therefore remaining consumers of these magazines for longer. Most men's magazines are bought by A, B and C1 men, but it is probable that an increasing proportion of the market is being bought by C1, C2 and D men. Inevitably (given the similarity in presentational style and content), tabloid newspaper readers are more likely to purchase men's magazines than broadsheet readers. In terms of the sensitivity to the market, prior to the launch of *Nuts* and *Zoo*, sports coverage was limited. Yet this was the most popular single interest item amongst 15–24 year old men, ahead of 'female celebrities', 'motoring' and 'health and fitness' (Mintel, 2002).

Nuts and *Zoo* were launched as 'new and innovative' products at a time when the men's lifestyle magazine sector appeared to be suffering from declining sales. The intention was that there would be complementarity between *Zoo* and its stable-mate in the Emap house, *FHM* (Robinson 2004), in much the same way that IPC's *Nuts* was launched not to compete with *Loaded* [7]. There is already evidence, however, that the success of the relatively new weekly men's magazines has hit comparable monthly publications quite hard.

Brief theoretical comments

> In its 1990 heyday, *FHM* was more than a magazine, it was a cultural event, helping to shape the *zeitgeist* ... the journal of choice for young men who thought *Men Behaving Badly*[8] was a documentary. (Robinson 2004: p. 7)

Leaving aside the hyperbole of Robinson's analysis, the sentiment of the remark is significant. In a social climate that saw the affirmation and reassertion of traditional masculine styles linked to Thatcherism and individualism (Haynes, 1993), there was a reaction to growing disaffection with 'new man' and the associated rhetoric (Robb 1999), and a celebration of the 'new lad'. As Carrington (1998: p. 120) puts it:

> 'New Lads' were supposed to be a reaction against the 1980s creation of the caring, sharing and socially reformed man — the so-called 'New Man' who fully respected the rights of women to be his equal, and even superior, and did not mind adopting previously considered 'feminine' roles such as child-rearing and house-keeping.

He continues to explain that one of the features of 'new laddism' meant that it was then possible to continue to be sexist and misogynist and to argue that this was not to be interpreted at 'face value':

> The 'new lad' then was a partial reversion back to the traditional 'laddish' masculinity of old, although the 'new lad' was now supposed to have accepted the basic claims of feminism and so any behaviour, gestures or actions that appeared to be sexist were now deliberately ironic and not to be taken literally. (*ibid.*)

As McRobbie (1999) has explained, the use of irony in men's magazines is the primary narrative tone and editorial style. It allows the reader superficially to engage with topics of importance, and by reducing the seriousness of the discourses, enables levity to characterise consideration of substantive issues[9]. Moreover, failure of the reader to appreciate irony can then be interpreted as humourlessness — what Stevenson *et al.* (2000: p. 381) have described as "an ideological defence against external attack" as well as an "internal defence" against uncertainty about constructions of masculinity.

The portrayal of masculinity in relation to the 'new lad' was characterised by a fierce protection of his independence (eschewing commitment), excessive drinking, interest in sports and a predatory pursuit of heterosexual conquests. This 'new lad' had a dry ironic sense of humour and was not afraid to laugh at 'stuff' that had hitherto been designated as out of bounds for 'new man' with his politically correct (often deemed by 'new lad' to be correspondingly effeminate) agenda. As Stevenson et al (2000: p. 377) state: "Whereas the 'new man' welded together narcissism and nurturance, the 'new lad' offers a rather different cocktail of staunch independence, masculine nostalgia and ... misogyny".

Yet the temptation to characterise 'new lad' as the antidote to 'new man' did not mean that they were necessarily, or even logically antithetical. The danger was that false dichotomies ensued. The editor of *Loaded* was quick to rebut them:

> We like football, but that doesn't mean we're hooligans. We like drinking, but it doesn't mean that as soon as the pub shuts we turn into wife-beating misogynists. We like looking at pictures of fancy ladies sometimes, but that doesn't mean we want to rape them. (cited in Creeber, 2002: p. 182)

The theoretical terrain has been mapped out by Benwell (2003). She argues that men's lifestyle magazines are more than carriers of cultural shifts in masculinities, they are actually in the vanguard of them. Furthermore, she argues that popular culture, in all "its instantiations, plays a key role in the constitution of modern identities" (p. 7) — including youthful masculinity and gender politics. That is to say, men's magazines are both a site of (re)presentation of masculinities and also play a significant part in (re)creating those masculine identities. As such, men's magazines, and for our purposes *Nuts* and *Zoo*, can provide cultural spaces and/or artefacts in which various articulations of masculinity are asserted.

To elaborate on the substantive position, Benwell (*op. cit.*) argues that there are five competing explanations to account for the cultural significance of lads' magazines.

a) Crisis accounts

The 'crisis' thesis of changing masculinity focuses on the reconstruction of 'new man' into 'new lad' as a reaction to the gains made by second wave feminism in relation to reclamation of societal power by women and a corresponding confusion amongst men about their new position in society. Nixon (1996) and Rutherford (1997), amongst others, have posited that this explains the regressive adolescent tendencies of men's magazines. However, the crisis theory is rejected by some (for instance Kimmel, 1987) as being too simplistic in that 'crises' in masculinity could be argued to have occurred throughout time in response to a variety of social changes — not least those identified above.

b) Backlash to feminism

The semi-pornographic and overtly misogynistic tone of many of the images in 'new lad' magazines has resulted in them being viewed as potentially the product of a backlash to feminism — an attempt by men to move away from what was widely regarded as the politically correct posturing of new man. This, though, is acknowledged to be an incomplete account (see also Jackson *et al.*, 2001) because the 'lads mags' are rejecting 'new man' rather than feminism per se, and that some of the discourses of feminism are actually evident in the magazines[10].

c) Risk society individuation relationship conflict and constructed certitude

Beck's (1992) work on the rise of global risk and fear in today's society and a consequent self-surveillance of the prevention of risk and harm to the individual may assist in explaining changing masculinities as evidenced in the men's magazines (Benwell, 2003). The concept of 'constructed certitude' here relates to the (re)creation and (re)invention of individual identities as a means of providing a fixed point in an otherwise uncertain social landscape. In the case of men's magazines this relates to a return to simplified biological determinism whereby male and female roles are clearly defined in sexual terms in order to reinforce notions of heterosexual masculinity as the norm. Benwell (*op. cit.*) suggests that this may at least in part explain the discourses around homophobia and the near-invisibility of 'race' and ethnicity.

d) Consumer imperative

The consumer imperative thesis is predicated on the notion that men's magazines are not the product of sexual revolution or reactive sexual politics but were simply created in response to a gap in the market. This argument must, of course, be context sensitive. Many advertisements in men's magazines are for grooming and styling products reflecting an interest in the presentation of the self, though not overtly endorsed in masculinity discourses prior to the creation of 'new man'. It is, however, difficult to say which came first, an increased interest in male physicality by men themselves or the validation of masculinities where men were encouraged to take more care of their appearance and physical well-being.

e) Haphazard / unreflexive account

The haphazard / unreflexive account of the development of men's magazines suggests that they reflect not one revolution in lifestyle publishing but that they emerged in a fragmented way and responded to many different economic and societal factors rather than being a reaction to, or consequence of, just one.

Notes on method

The interrelationships between leisure, sport and the media have been explored in work examining the formation of identities and representations of gender (see for example Maguire, 1999; Rowe, 1995; 1999; Whannel, 1992). Some empirical studies have focused specifically on magazines and/or comics and have dealt with themes as diverse as nudity (Eck, 2003), surfing subcultures (Henderson, 2001), class relations and cooking (Hollows, 2002), health (Bonner & McKay, 2000) depictions of athletes (Buysse & Embser-Herbert, 2004), advertising (Bolla, 1990), diseased bodies (Cook, 2000) and gendered occupations (Massoni, 2004).

One study in particular, by Stevenson *et al.* (2000), addressed the genre of men's lifestyle magazines in the UK. The purpose of this ESRC-funded project was to "analyse the mags *stylistically* (in terms of the development of a certain 'look') and *narratively* (how the mags use story-telling as a device to discuss the negotiation of sexuality)..." (p. 367). It is from this study that the on-going investigation of *Nuts* and *Zoo* draws its epistemological point of departure, as well as some methods of enquiry.

All of the studies listed above illustrate (to a lesser or greater extent) the power of cultural forms in shaping the nature of leisure consumption. In the present study we provide a systematic quantitative account of one aspect of the magazines' content (the television reviews), and offer some observations about the discourses contained therein. That is to say, our multi-method approach is based on (a) content analysis, and (b) discourse analysis. The purpose of the former was to chart the main thematic content that was endorsed by the magazines as central (even essential) to the television viewing of their readership. The purpose of the latter was to interrogate, in a more nuanced and sophisticated manner, the implicit and explicit messages about the construction of the masculinity embedded within these editorial recommendations.

Both *Nuts* and *Zoo* have dedicated sections in which the forthcoming week's television is previewed. Subtitled variously 'A man's guide to the best on the box', 'Only TV worth watching!' and 'Previews of TV you have to see' (in *Nuts* [11]) and 'Full 7-day listings PLUS the best on the box for blokes' (in *Zoo*), these sections typically feature three or four specific programmes from terrestrial or satellite / cable television networks. Each programme identified in this way had some sort of associated visual image (e.g., a 'still' from the broadcast, a photograph of one of the stars), a short caption (often incorporating some of the 'funny stuff' to which reference has been made above), and an indication of the kind of programme (e.g., war, crime, sport). Data were gathered from both magazines between the time of their launches until mid-July 2004. This sample yielded 15 editions of *Nuts* and 17 of *Zoo* — and included 830 and 795 television items respectively.

At the risk of over-simplification, this approach to content analysis seemed a relatively uncomplicated method/technique that required data items to be interpreted and tallied. The magazines' own classifications were used in the first instance to categorise the data types, but it soon became clear that this was problematic in at least two ways: first, the categorisation presented in the magazines was too blunt an instrument with which to differentiate amongst the data; and second, it was possible to classify the same programme within different categories. For instance, 'No Angels' might have been categorised as drama (as *Zoo* did), but the description of it might lead to a different listing — sex:

> We're getting close to the final episode of the adventures of slapper nurses so it time to 'fess up and admit you're only watching this seemingly girl-type-drama because you fancy one of them. Our money's on the nice blonde — who tonight reveals her breasts. (*Zoo* 16th April: p. 77)

Our interpretations of the data set were informed by our subjectivities (see Parry 1986) as white researchers older than the intended target age for the magazines — a feminist woman and an anti-sexist man. It was anticipated that the discourse analysis might have proved to be the more challenging interpretivist endeavour (cf. Macdonald, 2003; Rosselson, 2000), but it was actually the more straightforward.

As a biographical aside, we both found ourselves experiencing a mixed set of emotions in the process of collecting the artefacts from which the data were gathered. The purchase of the magazines was a site of some internal conflict as (independently) we wrestled with feelings of disgrace and embarrassment associated with buying the weekly edition and, what might be worse, the feelings associated with being seen to be buying it. We each adopted strategies to conceal our activity: buying other magazines or news-papers at the same time; hiding the 'offending' item amidst other shopping until reaching the check-out; buying the magazine from a retail outlet in which we were neither known nor likely to be recognised. All of this may seem rather bizarre, and even indulgent, but there are, of course, some important gender dynamics in the transaction that are relevant to our task. Quite apart from the impact of the content of *Nuts* and *Zoo* on the intended consumers, there is an important set of expectations about the purchasers evident from the behaviour of different vendors and other purchasers. All of these were compounded by the feelings of shame described above, but include Monty Python 'knowing smiles / winks' from a young man (to SF), discernible discomfort and surprise from a different young man (to FJ), comedic 'double-take' from a female supermarket check-out operator (to FJ), and thinly disguised disapproval from a matronly middle-aged woman who looked as though she was sucking a piece of fresh lemon (to SF).

The findings: (a) content

Broadly, the television viewing recommended in *Nuts* and *Zoo* can be organised around the key themes identified in Figure 1.

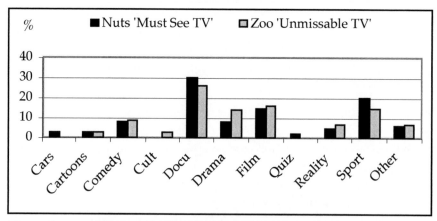

Figure 1:   'Must see' / 'Unmissable' TV in Nuts and Zoo
                 (January to July 2004)

Some of them require further elaboration and illustration. There were striking, if predictable, patterns:

- Sport featured prominently — this is unsurprising given that there was a perception that other men's lifestyle magazines did not cater satisfactorily for sports coverage. In reality, however, sport was limited to magazine coverage and occasional documentaries (e.g., *England's Dream Team, Football Diaries, Ultimate Warriors*), and live action from football (overwhelmingly), and occasionally to boxing, cricket, motor sport, rugby league, rugby union, and tennis; all featured the expression of physical masculinity.
- Comedy programmes were cited frequently (e.g., *Bo' Selecta, Da Best of Ali G, Little Britain*) and were characterised by masculine irreverence. These resonated with another popular genre, cartoons (e.g., *The Simpsons, South Park, King of the Hill*).
- Films were also recommended — but these were also of specific kinds, and were characterised by violent action (e.g., *Bully, Bloodsport, The Way of the Gun*), war (e.g., *Platoon, The Thin Red Line, To End All Wars*), science fiction (e.g., *Planet of the Apes, The Matrix Reloaded, Alien*), sex (e.g., *Sex Files — Pleasure World, The People vs Larry Flint, Crash*), crime (e.g., *Goodfellas, Hannibal, The Corruptor*) and horror (e.g., *The Omen, Dawn of the Dead, Frailty*).
- Drama productions also shared these themes (e.g., *Sex, Footballers and Videotapes, Crime Scene Investigation, Bad Girls*).

Other patterns were less predictable, but consolidated the preoccupation with some of the themes already listed:

- Documentaries — and their emphases on celebrities (e.g., *It's Good to be Pamela Anderson, The Truth about George Best, Punk'd*), crime (e.g., *Underworld Rich List, World's Most Daring Robberies, The Notorious Kray Twins*), natural world (*Anatomy of a Snake Bite, Massive Nature, Webs and Fangs / Stings and Claws*), sex (e.g., *Sex with Strangers, Back in the Saddle, Porn: a Family Business*), violence (e.g. *Mind, Body and Kick Ass Moves, Snipers, Aggro*), extremes of physical suffering (e.g., *101 Things Removed from the Human Body, High Adventure, Fear Factor*), survival (e.g., *Ray Mears' Extreme Survival, Superhuman, World of Pain 2*) and war (e.g., *Greatest SAS Missions, Monte Cassino: the Soldiers' Story, Secret History — Britain's Boy Soldiers*).
- Reality television (e.g., *Big Brother, Bad Lads' Army, Britain's Toughest Family*) and chat/talk shows (e.g., *Friday Night with Jonathan Ross, The Keith Barret Show, Fantasy Football*).

- Cars (e.g., *Top Gear, Motor Mag's International Classic Car Show, Monster Garage*) and gadgetry (e.g., *The Gadget Show, Playboyz, Fifth Gear*)

There were also some interesting, if also predictable, intersections of these characteristics: sport and violence (e.g., *Sports Disasters*), violence and nationalism (e.g., *Weapons that Made Britain*), celebrities and physical challenge (e.g., *Celebrity Fear Factor*), celebrities and sex (e.g., *The Celebrity Penthouse*), sex and science fiction (e.g., *Sex Files — Pleasure World*), sex and cars (e.g., *Street Fury*) and crime and cars (e.g., *Getaway Drivers*).

The findings: (b) discourses

There is widespread acknowledgement that there is no one single 'masculinity', but rather there are multiple masculinities (e.g., Berg & Longhurst, 2003). Yet the construction and projection of gender identities in *Nuts* and *Zoo* is characterised by a homogeneous, youthful, hegemonic, predominantly white, heterosexual masculinity with some key thematic emphases (identified above). These are depicted diagrammatically in a tentative preliminary model showing some of the relational linkages where the thickness of the lines is indicative of the strength of the relation (see figure 2). Additionally, there are three key prevailing mediating influences through which the reader is required to engage with the material.

First, there is a recurrent approach in *Nuts* and *Zoo* to the way that women are presented and discussed. More specifically, there are programmes being recommended that are concerned explicitly with the voyeuristic sexualisation and objectification of women. The visual images have many of the recognisable features of 'subordinated' women adopting ultra-feminine postures and gestures as well as the sensuous symbolism to which Hargreaves (1993) has referred in the sporting domain. When combined with the written text that accompanies them the sexualising effect is even more significant. For instance:

[Under the heading 'Bums'] *Kylie Night* — We love Kylie. Tonight's two docs look at the ever-evolving pert little lovely, beginning with her *Neighbours* mechanic (mechanics have never looked like Kylie), through to Waterman's pop tart, misguided indie chick and US-conquering, unrivalled queen of rump. (*Zoo* 4th June: p. 81)

Footballers' Wives — Well whaddya know, the artist formerly known as Jordan appears once again, joining the outrageously dressed footie crew as a guest at Shannon and Harley's wedding. Remember to switch over to the show on the left [*Tabloid Tales*] to see the jungle goddess in her more natural environment. (*Nuts* 27th February: p. 67.)

Moreover, even when programmes appear to have a different thematic emphasis, there is a preoccupation in the description with sexualising women who star in the shows:

Hell's Kitchen — ... But we do get to vote them off the show, one at a time, and that means you need to get dialling in an effort to keep such beautifully garnished dishes as Abi Titmuss, Jennifer Ellison and '80s icon Belinda Carlisle on the menu. (*Nuts* 28th May: p. 69)

Fifth Gear — Can you believe people get paid to do this? Tiff Needell and chums not only get to drool over Vicki Butler-Henderson, but also test sports cars in exotic locations. (*Nuts* 9th April: p. 67)

The Gadget Show — Whoever persuaded Suzi Perry to get tarted up in a sexy leather catsuit while stroking even sexier gadgets deserves some kind of masturbatory medal. In this new series, the Kylie of petrol-heads leads a team of eager gizmo geeks itching to try out anything and everything from the latest plasma TV to pen-sized surveillance cameras. (*Zoo* 4th June: p. 73)

This objectification of women is both 'absolute' and 'comparative'. For there is even a directly offensive reference to a female tennis star whose physical appearance is asserted in the description to be less desirable than that of some of her fellow competitors at the Wimbledon tournament:

Wimbledon Semi-Finals — It's semi time, when the hallowed SW19 turf starts to look ropey and, traditionally, so does Tim Henman. The ladies kick things off and even ZOO crystal ball can't predict who you'll see. But on a purely aesthetic basis, let's hope it's not Lindsay Davenport. (*Zoo* 25th June: p. 83)

In contrast to other men's magazines (e.g., *Loaded*) where sexual liberation from the structures of relationships is celebrated, in *Nuts* and *Zoo* women are presented primarily for the sexualised gaze and the discussion is taken no further. The heterosexual masculinity in these magazines is represented not so much as being in a heterosexual relationship but by enjoying consumption of those cultural forms and activities proscribed by the magazines as macho or manly. Second, there is a specific lens through which all of the subject matter is projected. Reference has already been made to the use of irony as narrative tone and editorial style for men's magazines, and in *Nuts* and *Zoo* this presentational technique is especially evident. Often, in all but the most distasteful images, text captions allow (even encourage) the reader to resist the weightiness of the particular story being depicted. For instance:

[Against a backdrop of a panoramic view Vinson Massif (the biggest mountain in Antarctica), four scientists are walking across a barren snow-scene] "I don't care what you say, I think the off-licence was the other way." (*Nuts* 11th June 2004: p. 65)

[Two large family cars involved in a high-speed head-on crash]."Magnetic cars: rubbish." (*Zoo* 26th March 2004: p. 71)

[Deep-sea diver searching amongst artefacts at the 'sunken city of Atlantis'] "OK, (blubalub) who left the bath running?" (*Zoo* 19th March 2004: p. 79)

In this way the use of irony constitutes a contradictory discourse whereby potentially serious stories on say, heroism, survival or exploration, are rendered less challenging (cognitively and emotionally). An alternative to the spirit of so-called 'harmless fun' that the use of irony is intended to propagate however, is the much more problematic discourse reinforcing, for example, homophobia and xenophobia[12]:

[Two soldiers in desert combat gear sitting holding sub-machine guns looking into the distance] "I can't go fighting till I've had my nails done!" (Nuts 27th February 2004: p. 61)

[Re-enactment of the D-Day landings with British soldiers wading through the sea] "Those Jerries wouldn't get anywhere near the sun beds this time." (*Zoo* 4th June 2004: p. 69)

The third mediating influence that characterises *Nuts* and *Zoo* is the use of voyeurism and a carnivalesque engagement with 'freak-shows'. In this way, as Benwell (2003) has argued of other men's magazines, the voyeuristic visual consumption of, for instance, gory injuries and physical deformities relates to the 'Othering' of those not conforming to the rigid norms of physical able-bodied masculinity. This tendency also illustrates a "ritualistic rejection of fragile embodiment" (Benwell, 2003: p. 15) as it can be the subject of the gaze in a way that does not actually threaten the reader. It therefore contributes to the discourses of man as macho enough to withstand pain and injuries. There are, of course, ethical concerns that can (indeed should) be raised by this characteristic of *Nuts* and *Zoo*. These relate to the changing nature of social acceptability *vis-à-vis* voyeurism and sexism in men's 'lifestyle' magazines, and especially those that are not 'X' rated.

Concluding comments

Through these magazines young men are exposed to powerful socialising influences linked to images of what 'homogenised masculinity' actually is. Consumption of sport features prominently (albeit delimited, in the main, to football), but the most ubiquitous characteristic is the sexualisation and objectification of women. Acts of physicality, courage and heroism are valorised and validated — for instance, withstanding pain, overcoming extreme circumstances (life-threatening accidents, being lost in the Arctic, and so on) and bravery, often expressed through militarism and nationalism. Anti-heroism is also celebrated, even venerated, through the apparent fascination with violent criminality.

Gender identities are not fixed; they are both context-sensitive and historically situated. Yet as Benwell (2003) concluded in her analysis of 'new lad', *Nuts* and *Zoo* confirm the return to traditional masculine values of sexism, the distinctiveness of the language of 'new laddism' with its roots in ironic cynicism, a focus on working class values and culture and a tendency towards excessive hedonism. There is an additional, potentially political and overtly cultural agenda within these new magazines. They make a greater claim to 'expert' status through their critical reviews of television and seek to set a cultural agenda through their proscription of what constitutes appropriate viewing. There is a more explicit attempt to articulate and define the boundaries of 21st century youthful heterosexual masculinity here. In common with the 'new lads' of the late 20th century, however, this cultural agenda also regards women purely as sexual objects, makes no reference to relationships, is ethnically white and is determinedly able-bodied.

Notes

[1] We wish to acknowledge our gratitude to Ben Carrington, Jayne Caudwell, Gill Lines, Geoff Nichols, Helen Pussard and Doug Sandle for their valuable contributions to the discussion at the LSA 2004 Conference at Leeds Metropolitan University that followed our presentation of an earlier version of this work, and to Malcolm MacLean for some helpful suggestions.

[2] After the publishers Emap had announced their intention to launch *Zoo* at the end of January, IPC beat them to it by launching *Nuts* a week before on 22nd January.

[3] It would be misleading to suggest that *Nuts* did not cover football related items. The point, though, is the amount of the coverage in *Zoo* — which

was extensive. Current sports stories (rather than features about sports stars) were characteristic of both *Nuts* and *Zoo* that set them apart from the other monthly men's magazines.

4   As early as 2nd April 2004 the fortnightly satirical magazine *Private Eye* described the success of *Nuts* and *Zoo* in its 'Hackwatch' section: "...already the two mags between them are selling around 1.6 million copies a month, or 400,000 a week. It may make grim reading for adults, but tits, ass and the occasional rectal prolapse really are what little boys want" (p. 5).

5   We want to make a distinction here between those magazines that were principally pornographic in nature and those that were concerned with men's lifestyles more generally. We therefore exclude from this discussion magazines such as *Playboy* and *Penthouse* as well as their more explicit cousins such as *Knave* and *Black Label* and those that market their 'hardcore' contents such as *Wild Cherries* and *Girly Girls*.

6   Indeed the editor, James Brown, remarked dismissively that 'grooming is for horses' (cited in Stevenson *et al.*, 2000).

7   *Nuts* is published by IPC as part of their Ignite! brand, which also encompasses *Loaded*, *Loaded Fashion*, *NME*, and *Uncut*. With their Ignite! publications, IPC claim to have 'practically invented the Men's Lifestyle sector' with the launch of *Loaded* and their aim is to be "the leading media player in the key men's sectors of Lifestyle and Entertainment". Their motto is that "love 'em or loathe 'em you can't ignore the *Loaded* generation" (*www.ipc.co.uk* — 21st May 2004).

8   Thought by many to be one of the most successful UK situation comedies of the 1990s, *Men Behaving Badly* was first broadcast by BBC TV in 1992. A thumbnail sketch of the from the 'beebfun' website sheds some light:

> Tony and Gary are a couple of likely lads who definitely do not fall into the category of 90s modern man! ... The main theme running throughout this sitcom is the interaction between two young men and two young women and err, well male hormones and beer!! To say that Gary and Tony lack some of the finesse necessary to win the hearts and minds of the Totty upstairs would be putting it mildly. Their flat is usually a tip and their manners gross to say the least. But love wins through in the end and the girls get their men. (http://www.beebfun.com/mbb.htm — 8th September 2004)

9   The sociology of humour was a neglected avenue of academic enquiry (Fox, 1990), and there is always the possibility that a preoccupation with an analysis of humour will take the 'fun' out of it (Mulkay, 1988).

10 As an aside, this is not the case with *Nuts* and *Zoo*, indeed the high profile television advertising campaign used to launch *Nuts* had the imperative strap-line "women, don't expect help on a Thursday" [because *Nuts* is published on that day]. The imagery in this advertising showed women as unable to complete basic household tasks such as drilling a hole in a wall or making a cup of tea for their (male) partner without the help of their man.

11 Indeed *Nuts* goes further and makes reference not only to those pro-grammes that are 'Must see TV', but also to those that should be actively avoided 'Time to ditch the duff telly' and 'Avoid the girly show crap'.

12 Here, of course, we will be accused of 'not getting it' — that is, failing to understand the nature of the humour. Indeed, it has become fashionable in some quarters to ridicule 'right-on' politically correct, do-gooders. The double-bind here is that those who would level such a criticism are themselves guilty of 'not getting it', in this case the objection, either. Or if they do get it, they disregard it.

References

Beck, U. (1992) *Risk society: Towards a new modernity*. London: Sage.

Benwell, B. (ed) (2003) *Masculinity and men's lifestyle magazines*. Oxford: Blackwell Publishing.

Berg, L. D. and Longhurst, R. (2003) 'Placing masculinities and geography', *Gender, Place and Culture* Vol. 10, No. 4: pp. 351–360.

Bolla, P. A. (1990) 'Media images of women and leisure: an analysis of magazine advertisements 1964–87', *Leisure Studies* Vol. 9, pp. 241–252.

Bonner, F & McKay, S. (2000) 'Challenges, determination and triumphs: inspirational discourse in women's magazine health stories', *Continuum: Journal of Media and Cultural Studies* Vol. 14, pp. 133–144.

Buysse, J. A. M. & Embser-Herbert, M. S. (2004) 'Constructions of gender in sport: an analysis of intercollegiate media guide cover photographs', *Gender & Society* Vol. 18, pp. 66–81.

Carrington, B. (1998) 'Football's coming home' But whose home? And do we want it? Nation, football and the politics of exclusion', in A. Brown (ed) *Fanatics — power, identity and fandom in football*. London: Routledge, pp. 101–123.

Cook, J. (2000) 'Men's magazines at the millennium: New spaces, new selves', *Continuum: Journal of Media and Cultural Studies* Vol. 14, pp. 172–186.

Creeber, G. (2002) 'Old sleuth or new man? Investigations into rape, murder and masculinity in *Cracker* (1993–1996)', *Continuum: Journal of Media and Cultural Studies* Vol. 16, pp. 169–183.

Eck, B. (2003) 'Men are much harder: Gendered viewing of nude images', *Gender and Society* Vol. 17, pp. 691–710.

Fox, S. (1990) 'The ethnography of humour and the problem of social reality', *Sociology* Vol. 24, pp. 431–446.

Hargreaves, J. (1993) 'Bodies matter! Images of sport and female sexualisation', in C. Brackenridge (ed) *Body Matters: Leisure Images and Lifestyles* (LSA Publication No. 47). Eastbourne: Leisure Studies Association, pp. 60–66.

Haynes, R. (1993) 'Every man (?) a football artist: football writing and masculinity', in S. Redhead (ed) *The passion and the fashion — football fandom in the new Europe*. Aldershot: Avebury, pp. 55–76.

Henderson, M. (2001) 'A shifting line up: Men, women and Tracks surfing magazine', *Continuum: Journal of Media and Cultural Studies* Vol. 15, pp. 319–332.

Hendry, L., Shucksmith, I., Love, J.G. & Glendenning, A. (1993) *Young people's leisure and lifestyles*. London: Routledge.

Hoggart, R. (1966 [1957]) *The uses of literacy : aspects of working-class life with special reference to publications and entertainments*. Harmondswoth: Pelican

Hollows, J. (2002) 'The bachelor dinner: masculinity, class and cooking in *Playboy*, 1953–1961', *Continuum: Journal of Media and Cultural Studies* Vol. 16, pp. 143–155.

Jackson, P., Stevenson, N. and Brooks, K. (2001) *Making sense of men's lifestyle magazines*. Cambridge: Polity Press.

Kimmel, M (1987) 'The contemporary "crisis" of masculinity in historical perspective', in H. Brod (ed) *The making of masculinities: The new men's studies*. London: Allen and Unwin,, pp. 121–153.

Macdonald, M. (2003) *Exploring Media Discourse*. Abingdon: Arnold.

Maguire, J. (1999) *Global sport: Identities, societies, civilizations*. Cambridge: Polity Press.

Massoni, K. (2004) 'Modelling work: occupational messages in *Seventeen* magazine', *Gender & Society* Vol. 18, pp. 47–65.

McRobbie, A. (1999) *In the culture society*. London: Routledge.

Miles, S., Dallas, C. & Burr, V. (1998) "Fitting in and sticking out': Consumption, consumer meanings and the construction of young people's identities', *Journal of Youth Studies* Vol. 1, pp. 81–96.

Mintel (2002) *Men's magazines — UK*. London: Mintel.

Mulkay, M. (1988) *On humour: Its nature and its place in modern society*. Cambridge: Polity Press.

Nayak, A. (1999) "Pale warriors': skinhead culture and the embodiment of white masculinities' in A. Brah, M.J. Hickman & M. Mac an Ghaill (eds) *Thinking identities — ethnicity, racism and culture*. Basingstoke: Macmillan, pp. 71–99.

Nixon, S. (1996) *Hard looks: Masculinity's, spectatorship and contemporary consumption*. London: St. Martin's Press.

Parry, J. (1986) 'Philosophy and sport science'. *Annali* Vol. V, pp203–220.

Robb, J. (1999) *The nineties — what the f**k was that about?* London: Ebury Press.

Robinson, J. (2004) 'Power to the Lads', *The Observer* 4th July, p. 7.

Rosselson, R. (2000) *Discussions Arising from a Discourse Analysis of my Diary from Nepal: or What I Did on my Holidays by Ruth R. aged 29 1/2*. Unpublished dissertation, MA in Women's Studies, Manchester Metropolitan University.

Rowe, D. (1995) *Popular cultures: Rock music, sport and the politics of pleasure*. London: Sage.

Rowe, D. (1999) *Sport, culture and the media: The unruly trinity*. Buckingham: Open University Press.

Rutherford, J. (1997) 'Introduction: avoiding the bends', in R. Chapman & J. Rutherford (eds) *Male order: unwrapping masculinity* (2nd ed.). London: Lawrence & Wishart.

Stevenson. N., Jackson, P. and Brooks, K. (2000) 'The politics of 'new' men's lifestyle magazines', *European Journal of Cultural Studies* Vol. 3, pp. 366–385.

Whannel, G. (1992) *Fields in vision: Television sport and cultural transformation*. London, Routledge.

III

YOUTH AND
SOCIAL CHANGE

RE-INVENTING 'THE GAME': RUGBY LEAGUE, 'RACE', GENDER AND THE GROWTH OF ACTIVE SPORTS FOR YOUNG PEOPLE IN ENGLAND

Karl Spracklen
Leeds Metropolitan University

Introduction

In historiographical terms, rugby league in England is rich in invented traditions, both in the game and in its origins in the coal smoke of the late nineteenth century (Delaney, 1993), and for the game's detractors, who dismiss it as merely a professional adjunct of 'proper' rugby: rugby union. Supporters of rugby league, and those who write about it, are clear that rugby league is an expression of working-class defiance, of northern working-class culture and celebration of working-class masculinity (e.g. Bamford, 2002; Hinchliffe, 2000; Kelner, 1996). Equation of 'the game' with northernness and northern identity, however, does not stop people within the community of rugby league from also adopting the language of equality and diversity and boasting of the historical and current involvement of black people. In a publication to celebrate and recognise black players in rugby league, it is stated that:

> ... then [in the past when the Northern Union split from the Rugby Football Union in 1895], as today, many people in rugby league shared Huck's defiance [Huckleberry Finn, from the anti-slavery book written by Mark Twain in 1885] towards authority and his belief in doing the right thing ... And this is one of the reasons why rugby league [has] ... a proud record of black players, captains and coaches for the best part of a century. (Melling and Collins, 2004: p. 10)

Following Hobsbawm and Ranger (1983), it can be seen that this is an invented tradition that conflates rugby league's origins in the north of England in the nineteenth century with a mythical 'northernness' founded on resistance. This invented tradition has become normalised: rugby league is seen by Melling and Collins as a model of inclusivity, despite continued references to belonging that associate the game's imaginary community with northern, working-class masculinities (Spracklen, 1996; 2001); and despite the 'small but significant' problem with racism and stereotyping and lack of minority ethnic supporters and officials, identified in research by Leeds Metropolitan University (Long *et al.*, 1995).

That this 'northernness' is also in essence a culture and community of whiteness has been observed and discussed elsewhere (Spracklen, 2001). Rugby league in its traditional English heartlands remains a predominantly white game. But just because rugby league is based on symbolic boundaries (Cohen, 1985) and invented traditions that are embedded in normalised whiteness (cf. Long and Hylton, 2002), it is not necessarily a sport exclusively for white, northern working-class men. Any imaginary community based on a sport is inevitably susceptible to change, and symbolic boundaries will always be sites of contestation over meaning and interpretation, between insiders and outsiders.

This paper examines rugby league development activity aimed at young people via the medium of Active Sports, and highlights key issues of participation and exclusion at the interface between policy, sports equity, belonging and exclusion. Drawing on previous research by Spracklen (1996) on construction of social identity in rugby league through creation of an imaginary community (cf. Anderson (1983) on use of myth in imagining community and Cohen (1985) on use of symbols in constructing community), this paper shows that rugby league, traditionally viewed as a northern, white, working class male game (Spracklen, 1995; 2001), has had to re-imagine its symbolic boundaries to accommodate young people from non-traditional rugby league areas. The paper uses rugby league development activity through Active Sports as a site for exploring tensions around top-down policy commitment to equity and targets to increase participation in the sport (Hylton and Totten, 2001; Spracklen, 2003), and racism and sexism normalised by symbolic boundaries and myths of belonging to the imaginary community. 'Race', gender and class are used throughout in a critical sense, as constructs used in definition of belonging and exclusion (cf. McDonald and Carrington, 2001), both within the imaginary community and in wider networks of power in society (e.g., gender order, cf. Connell, 1987).

The structure of argument in this paper, in spite of attempts by qualitative researchers to introduce innovation into epistemological practice (cf. Fuller, 2000; Willis, 2000), retains some conservative and positivistic affectations. After a brief discussion of the policy context, I describe the methods adopted in research. An exposition of statistical data on participation rates follows, and then a qualitative analysis and critical, theoretical discussion using the framework provided by previous writing on this subject.

Policy context

Development of sports policy in the United Kingdom following election of a New Labour Government in 1997 has already been mapped and analysed by sociologists. Hylton *et al.* (2001) identified a shift in emphasis in sports development through a number of hegemonic models of relationships between providers of sport, the purpose of sport and demands of local communities. Houlihan and White (2002) have shown that New Labour's policy towards sport, underpinned by both the 1999 Policy Action Team 10 report and the Department for Culture, Media and Sport's policy statement *A Sporting Future For All*, was underpinned by commitment to social inclusion and belief that sport could "specifically address" those issues (Houlihan and White, 2002: p. 94). This shift from performance to social inclusion was replicated by changes to the way Sport England worked and distributed Lottery and Exchequer funding, and acceptance by the organisation that it needed to widen access to sport and reduce inequalities in sport (Collins and Kay, 2003). Along with attempts to foster equality and diversity through centralising control of equity projects and organisations and development of the Racial Equality Standard (Long *et al.*, 2003; Spracklen, 2003), Sport England attempted to introduce a commitment to equity and equity outcomes as a condition of funding in its new Active framework. This framework attempted to influence sports development across a continuum of participation and performance (Hylton *et al.*, 2001; Houlihan and White, 2002), with Lottery funding to develop community sports projects (Active Communities), pathways to improvement and clubs (Active Sports), and specialist sports colleges and teachers (Active Schools).

However, Active Sports was the only programme that had equity targets specifically written into its funding and evaluation framework. The programme attempted to bridge the gap between the demands of national governing bodies with a focus on excellence and development squads, and the Government's agenda of widening access and using sport as a vehicle for social inclusion. Research commissioned by Sport England identified need for a framework that supported young people who already had some experience of a sport but wished to continue to take part and perform to the best of their ability. Active Sports Partnerships were established across England, often but not necessarily based on geographical counties, that brought together local delivery agents to work together to produce development plans, including a specific action plan for equity, with identified activities and initiatives to meet equity and other targets agreed with Sport England (Houlihan and White, 2002). So from its inception, Active Sports forced local partnerships and delivery agents to consider initiatives that increased participation by young women, young people with disabilities, young people from ethnic minorities, and those from socially disadvantaged areas.

Initially, rugby league was not considered part of Active Sports, but when the final ten sports were announced, rugby league was alongside rugby union and eight others as an Active Sport. Why this decision was made will be discussed later, but it is important to note that since the switch from winter to summer rugby, following development of Super League and involvement of Sky Television, rugby league had started to claim a national supporter base and a national focus. The Rugby Football League (RFL) and the British Amateur Rugby League Association (BARLA) finally reunited, after a period of working together on, amongst other things, racial equality and the Tackle It campaign (Spracklen, 2004). A summer amateur competition, the Summer Conference, was launched in 1998 for teams playing outside the game's traditional areas, and by 2004 this became the Rugby League Conference, with 57 teams, including an elite division consisting of top southern-based clubs alongside a handful of northern-based BARLA clubs playing either exclusively in summer or all-year (National League Three). NL3 was in turn immediately below the semi-professional, traditional RFL club dominated National League Two, as part of a 'pyramid' structure: providing a club pathway that theoretically could see the Bristol Sonics or Cambridge Eagles progress all the way up to Super League. This was not the first rugby league expansion into the south of England — in the 1980s teams had been established as part of a Midlands and South-West Amateur Rugby League Association, and in the 1990s an Eastern Counties League had affiliated to the RFL (Spracklen, 1996) — but these teams either folded through lack of numbers or joined other leagues. So, under the aegis of the Active Sports programme, rugby league soon established a network of professional development officers working in eleven Active Sports Partnerships across the country, including four officers in London and others in 'expansionist' areas of Durham, Tees Valley and Tyne and Wear. It is the work in London, and its relationship to other RFL development work under the Active Communities banner in Slough and voluntary work undertaken by Rugby League Conference clubs in London and the south, that forms the focus of qualitative analysis and critical discussion at the end of this paper.

Methodology

The paper draws on statistics gathered by the London Active Partnership on gender and ethnicity of participants in rugby league activities, and uses other participation information on amateur rugby league in England, collated by interviews, examination of team photographs and attendance at matches. Participation data are analysed and compared to data collected previously by Long *et al*. (1995), as well as other research on 'race' and gender in rugby league (Spracklen, 1995; 2001). The paper also draws on qualitative interviews undertaken with seven key respondents involved in developing Active Sports and rugby league both at Sport England and the Rugby Football League (through the London Active Partnership), and in a voluntary capacity through four southern-based rugby league clubs. An eighth respondent was identified and interviewed for insider knowledge of rugby league in London and the south of England. Respondents were approached through contacts within rugby league and personal knowledge, and through a snowball sampling process (Willis, 2000) and interviewed either through e-mails, phone or face-to-face, depending on availability and ability to provide additional information.

Participation Rates

For this paper, all white ethnicities have been conflated under a single 'fictive' ethnicity: white (Balibar and Wallerstein, 1988; Cohen, 1999). Doing this fails to distinguish the significant level of participation in rugby league by people of Irish descent and people from Australia and New Zealand. The Irish are the biggest minority ethnic group in England (defining ethnic groups according to the 2001 Census), and it may seem perverse for a critical discussion of ethnicity and community to ignore their role in English sport. Indeed, other work has demonstrated that the Irish played a significant role in development of rugby league in both England and Australia (Moorhouse, 1989). However, the focus of this paper is Asian and black involvement in rugby league and the challenge this poses to the existing imaginary community (a community that includes large numbers of Irish working-class in northern towns like Wigan, Dewsbury and Leeds, as evidenced by famous amateur clubs such as Wigan St Patrick's). White Australians and New Zealanders are also part of 'the game' and have been since the first tour of England by New Zealand in 1905. It should also be noted that Other BME participation rates in professional rugby league reflect involvement of Papuan professionals, Australian Aboriginals and New Zealand and South Pacific professionals of Polynesian origin.

Although these participation rates are only partial and more detailed analyses of youth rugby, amateur rugby league and off-field participation are needed, a number of salient points about rugby league's community can be demonstrated by reference to data gathered in this research (see Table 1).*

Firstly, there is continued under-representation of ethnic minorities and in particular British Asians in the game's senior and professional ranks. This, of course, is not just an issue for rugby league. English sport in general fails to attract participants from a wide demographic base (Long *et al.*, 2003); this is partly due to differing experiences of social exclusion between different ethnic groups, but is also a symptom of the imaginary community that 'sport' represents in England, a community based around symbolic boundaries that define middle-class, white masculinities (Spracklen, 2003). Most sports fail to attract and retain British Asian participants (Fleming, 1995). Soccer, like rugby league, has failed to recruit significant numbers of British Asians into its spectator base and professional ranks, though there is evidence that British Asians play football at junior and amateur levels (Johal, 2001). Absence of British Asians from rugby league is even more worrying when the game's traditional heartlands are examined. Although the traditional National League Three profile shows some British Asian involvement, this is due to the work of one development officer for Bradford Council, Ikram Butt, and

---

*   It should also be noted that these figures refer to the men's game only: development of the women's game has not tracked development of the men's game, either in traditional northern heartlands or in new expansion areas mapped out by growth of the Rugby League Conference, Active Sports activity or National League Three. For female participation on the terraces, Long *et al.* (1995) identified 30% as the number of female fans. In this limited survey of the current spectator base, random sampling produced a slightly higher figure of 36% (based on a sample of 200 supporters coming into a ground at a National League 3 match, 18th May 2004).

Table 1   Participation Rates (to one decimal place. Please note that due to rounding the totals may not equal 100%)

Level/ Area of Rugby League	White (including White Other)	Black	Asian	Other BME
London Active Partnership Youth Development [i]	36.0%	64.0% (includes small number of British Indian)	N/A	N/A
RL Conference — London and south clubs sample [ii]	86.8%	13.2%	0.0%	0.0%
National League 3 — Expansion Areas [iii]	79.4%	17.6%	1.5%	1.5%
National League 3 — Traditional Areas [iv]	92.6%	4.4%	2.9%	0.0%
National Conference — northern amateur [v]	97.1%	2.9%	0.0%	0.0%
National League 2 — Northern clubs Semi-Professional [vi]	91.9%	4.4%	0.0%	3.7%
Super League 2004 [vii]	86.8%	4.9%	0.0%	8.3%
Professional RL, 1995 [viii]	83.8%	7.9%	0.4%	7.9%
Spectator Base, 2004 [ix]	>99%	<1%	†	†
Spectator Base, 1995 [x]	>99%	<1%	†	†
National Demographic (2001 Census, Table s104)	91.3%	3.5% (n.b. includes Mixed category)	4.4%	0.9%

[i]   Data provided by London Active Partnership and the Rugby Football League. Information collated from player registration forms for 2003/2004 rugby league development activity.

[ii   Based on a sample of four clubs in the South and East Divisions of the Rugby League Conference. Information gathered through interviews and analysis of club websites.

[iii]   Based on team sheet sampling exercise, 5 June 2004. Information gathered via the League Express (07/06/2004), interviews and analysis of club websites.

[iv]   As above.

[v]   Based on team sheet sampling exercise, 13 March 2004. Information gathered through fieldwork, the League Express (15/03/2004) and analysis of club websites.

[vi]   Based on team sheet sampling exercise of NL2, 19 June 2004, excluding London Skolars and their opponents. Information gathered through reports in the League Express (21 June 2004) and personal knowledge of the game based on doctoral research, lifetime watching the game and eight years involvement as a rugby league journalist/writer.

[vii]   Based on team sheet analysis for Super League matches, 19 June 2004. Information gathered from the League Express (21 June 2004) and through personal knowledge, as above.

[viii] Adapted from Long et al. (1995).

[ix   Based on personal observation at matches and therefore an indicative figure only.

[x]   From Long et al. (1995).

work he has done in Bradford and West Yorkshire with the South Asia Bulls development team — a team that has become an informal support network to identify potential players in the local South Asian community and to encourage those players to remain in the game. Much growth of Britain's Asian and black communities in the last fifty years has been in traditional rugby league towns and cities (Spracklen, 2004): to the west of the Pennines — Salford, Oldham and Rochdale; in Yorkshire — Leeds, Bradford, Keighley, Batley, Dewsbury and Huddersfield. The black community in rugby league towns and cities is quite dispersed except for a few places in bigger cities, but the Asian community, and in particular working-class British Pakistani and Kashmiri communities, is heavily concentrated in urban areas around rugby league grounds and in streets where rugby league clubs once drew fans and players. Figures for the 2001 Census show that British Pakistanis alone make 14.5% of the population of Bradford (including Keighley), 7.7% of the population of Rochdale and 6.8% of the population of Kirklees (Huddersfield, Batley and Dewsbury, concentrated in the latter two) — factor in British Asians from Indian and Bangladeshi communities and it is clear that there are thousands of British children from the Asian community growing up a drop-kick away from rugby league.

The second participation issue is related to the first: representation and involvement of black players in rugby league. Although there is evidence that black players face discrimination, both overt and institutionalised (cf. Long *et al.*, 1995; Spracklen, 2001), that black players are encouraged to play in positions that perpetuate stereotypes about natural attributes of black people (their speed, their physicality — all myths perpetuated in sport, with no scientific basis whatsoever — see Marks, 2003), participation data show that black people are involved in rugby league at some levels and in some roles. For Melling and Collins (2004), this is evidence that rugby league has always been an inclusive game. But, as argued elsewhere (Spracklen, 2001), this participation maps the extent to which black people are allowed to participate in making the game's symbolic boundaries, its myths and invented traditions, and the route through which individual black players become accepted as part of 'the game', by playing the role of the 'northern, working-class man'. Rugby league has always been, and continues to be in many places, a game of close-knit localities. In areas where the black community have settled, new traditions and networks have developed over the past thirty years that allow black people to become involved in rugby league. Black players and supporters have become associated with certain amateur clubs such as Queen's in the Burley district of Leeds, or Huddersfield St. Joseph's and

Moldgreen in Huddersfield, or Queensbury on the edge of Bradford where the Pryce family has become a well-known source of rugby league talent. But this adoption of black players is limited, and outside those networks — in amateur rugby league in the old mining towns, in southern Lancashire and northern Cheshire, in the spectator base and ranks of administrators, and even in the key tactical role of scrum-half (Long and Spracklen, 1996; Spracklen, 2001) — the whiteness of the game is still one of its defining characteristics.

The third and final issue, and the focus of discussion in this paper, is the huge difference between participation rates in traditional, northern areas and those in the development area of London. Work of southern-based clubs and the Rugby Football League and London Active Partnership on the Active Sports programme has resulted in significant change in the game's demographic profile in London and the south of England. How this happened, why this happened and what this may mean for survival of the imaginary community associated with 'the game' — that based around northernness, whiteness and working-class masculinity — is the subject of qualitative analysis and critical discussion in the rest of this paper.

Barriers and stereotypes

Rugby league faces a number of barriers that hinder its development in London and the south of England. For instance, one respondent, a professional sports development officer, suggested that lack of club infrastructure meant that people interested in playing rugby league, or young people attending development activities, often had nowhere to go or nowhere to progress to. Active Sports was seen by this officer as a way of overcoming this barrier, although as another professional officer claimed, it is "still early days yet". Another respondent claimed that rugby league has, ironically, struggled to expand because of the bad image rugby union has in the eyes of many people. This respondent, a volunteer at a Rugby League Conference Club, became interested through watching Super League on television and live in the north, despite his background as a "staunch" unionist. He felt many in the south didn't know the difference between league and union, and so associated any sort of 'rugby' with the "violence and snobbery" they perceived in rugby union. This was supported by another respondent, an activist of the Rugby League Supporters Association based in London, who pointed out that "working-class Londoners dislike union intensely" and believed they could be turned from following soccer to following rugby league. This was one of the reasons respondents believed rugby league was proving attractive to ethnic minorities in London and the south of England: because, as one club volunteer put it, "when they realise league isn't as stuck up as union they know they'll be made to feel welcome, because the black working-class in London are outcasts like notherners". For this respondent, the conditions of social exclusion and discrimination faced by London's many black communities, and the struggle for recognition and social identity (cf. Carrington, 1998), was analogous to the struggle faced by white working-class followers of league in getting their game recognised and respected outside its northern heartland.

However, the biggest barrier, mentioned by all respondents, was the southern perception that rugby league was a minority sport. Most, but not all, respondents associated this with a perception that rugby league was a northern sport, "a northern stereotype," as one respondent said, "like whippets", or to another, it was the shadow of Eddie Waring looming over every conversation. This northern stereotype, however, was not always described as negative: as the activist from the RLSA explained, rugby league, because of its association with northern toughness and honesty, "could play on its solid northern strengths without having to become a pastiche". Another respondent, interestingly, also suggested that the perception could be that rugby league was "Australian", and as obscure and alien to the south of England as Australian Rules football.

Changing traditions

All respondents recognised the success of Active Sports in London — and other initiatives such as the Rugby League Conference and the work of the RFL in Slough's Asian community — in bringing ethnic minority players into rugby league. Most volunteers believed that rugby league was welcoming and inclusive, and referred to historical instances of black involvement. However, one respondent, the fan activist, admitted that it was "easy to point to these successes and say all is well. Yet it isn't. Spectators are predominantly white ... terraces and grounds, like other sports grounds, are generally the preserve of white males and the racist baggage that attaches itself to such gatherings". Another respondent based at a Rugby League Conference club also suggested there were still problems with racism in rugby league in the north. After citing the instance of Batley, surrounded by streets of Asian families but with none on the terraces, and the use of Bernard Manning in previous years by the club as a fundraising highlight, this respondent went on to describe an incident of "ignorant and offensive language on the touchline" he witnessed at a BARLA National Conference match between two top amateur clubs from the game's northern heartlands.

Growth in the number of black players coming into the game in London and the south was welcomed by all respondents. A professional development officer explained that there had been a deliberate attempt to "tap into London's black communities" as it was believed these communities were generally ignored by other sports and were "a goldmine" for rugby league. Another respondent debated that "it may be that coaches are seeing black people as athletic", suggesting that this may be part of the reason why some development decisions have been focussed on London's black communities and not, say, London's Asian community (although the Rugby Football League does have an Active Communities initiative in the south targeted at the Asian community in Slough). Most respondents expressed the view that the proportion of black players coming through Active Sports and London-based Rugby League Conference Clubs was simply a reflection of London's diverse nature. One respondent suggested that in London and the south, rugby league had to "work from scratch to attract any players", so it had to embrace positive community development, compared with league clubs in the north where a steady trickle of new players and supporters came from traditional white working-class communities:

"Up north they don't need to work for players, they'll just turn out."

Lack of Asian players coming into the game — either in the north or south — was something that respondents were less willing to analyse and discuss. "Cultural issues and families" were cited by two respondents as barriers to getting Asians involved in rugby league. Work in Slough was, according to one respondent, "at an early stage". Others provided a counter example and spoke of Ikram Butt and the South Asia Bulls, and the Tackle It campaign in Bradford, but one admitted that "there seems a long way to go before the barriers are broken down" and Asian people start to participate in significant numbers.

Belonging

Not all respondents were northerners in exile in London and the south. However, half of them were, and became involved in rugby league at an early age, taken by their families to local professional rugby league grounds.

The small sample means any conclusion about nostalgia and belonging needs to be written in cautious tones; but it is clear that for those northerners who were engaged in rugby league in the south, this sustained their social identity and position within the imaginary community of 'the game'. But none of the respondents believed that 'the game' was necessarily equated with 'northernness' — not surprisingly, as they were all involved in selling rugby league to the south. All respondents acknowledged that black players coming through into the game were, as one respondent put it, "guardians of the game's identity", even though that identity was potentially changing because of the presence of those players.

How much this trend in London and the south would change rugby league was still, for most respondents, a hypothetical question. Most admitted that change in the local demographic profile of rugby league was not yet a sustainable trend, but as one argued, "these kids will come through and with a bit of luck they'll be running the clubs, then they'll be bringing a whole new set of people into the game". Another suggested that the trend posed "a challenge to all those clubs in the north that have been around for years, and all those people who think rugby league should always be the same, like it always has been". One respondent pointed out that London Skolars had already made an impact by being admitted to National League Two, and this was forcing traditional clubs to "come to terms with the fact that southerners, black and white, can play the game to a professional standard".

What this trend does not change is the game's position as an imaginary community that (re)creates gender order and a narrowly defined, hegemonic masculinity. One respondent spoke at length about the strength and ability of "young black lads, channelling their aggression". Another said that the focus of his club was the men's game because "historically, rugby league has been a man's game, and women don't want to play it, there's just no demand". The fact that the black communities targeted by the Active Sports programme were working-class was a matter of some pride for one professional development officer who believed rugby league was reaching out to its "own kind": working-class men. However, as the ex-unionist respondent argued, "we've developed a men's team because it's easier, but it shouldn't have to be so: there could be a much bigger market for women".

Conclusions

Previous work on rugby league has examined the way in which the sport established a sense of belonging and identity through creation of an imaginary community (Spracklen, 1995; 1996; 2001). This community of belonging is both imagined, in a historical sense (Anderson, 1983) and constructed through the (re)production of symbolic boundaries (Cohen, 1985) that define both belonging and exclusion. Insider texts such as player biographies collated by Mellings and Collins (2004) reinforce invented traditions that define the imagined, but also reproduce the norms and values associated with 'the game', that create the symbolic boundaries. But, of course, Mellings and Collins' account of the heroic working-class nature of rugby league, in constant rebellion against the Establishment, is a contested one. The imaginary community of 'the game' could also be described using more conservative rhetoric, being a community that maintains and perpetuates the existing, hegemonic gender order (Connel, 1987), for instance, or one in which whiteness is normalised and made invisible, as in so many other sports (Long and Hylton, 2002; Spracklen, 2003).

Taking this more critical stance, work being done in London and the south of England can be seen to be challenging the imaginary community of 'the game', but also replicating it. Black players coming into rugby league in London and the south of England do not bring with them invented traditions about 'northernness', northern working-class pride and whiteness. In that sense, involvement of these players could present a challenge to the symbolic boundaries of 'the game', provided those players come through in significant numbers and remain in 'the game' and are not excluded or marginalised (as has happened in other sports such as cricket — see McDonald and Ugra, 1998). However, existing black involvement in rugby league has been limited by narrowly defined symbolic boundaries — that is, black participants playing roles defined by 'northernness'and its white, working-class masculinity — which has excluded British Asians from becoming fully involved (Spracklen, 2001; 2004). It is therefore too early to tell whether the changing demographic profile in London and the south of England will have a lasting impact on 'the game' itself, or whether these players will be absorbed into the existing culture and community of rugby league. This may, in fact, already be the case, given comments made about their working-classness, and their hegemonically correct fit with rugby league's own stereotypes about manliness and masculinity (Spracklen, 1995).

For the Rugby Football League, Active Sports has been a way to fund and ultimately mainstream development work already started, albeit in a patchy and unsustainable way, in London and the south. But by taking Sport England silver, the Rugby Football League has been forced to abide by policy commitments to equity, central to the Active Sports framework. Tension between the ideals of a well-meaning policy and practice of sports development is well-documented (Hylton and Totten, 2001). For rugby league, this tension is as much about meanings and symbols associated with the imaginary community of 'the game' as it is about power, autonomy and control. Ultimately, more research needs to be done — with black players themselves, with British Asians and with others such as white, middle-class southerners, as well as more detailed auditing of development work across the country — to establish whether the Rugby Football League's work is sustainable, and whether it will have any lasting impact on the imaginary community of 'the game', its invented traditions and its symbolic boundaries.

References

Balibar, E. and Wallerstein, E. (1988) *Race, nation, class: Ambiguous identities*. London: Verso.

Bamford, M. (2002) *Bamford: Memoirs of a blood and thunder coach*. Manchester, Parrs Wood Press.

Carrington, B. (1998) 'Sport, masculinity and black cultural resistance', *Journal of Sport and Social Issues* Vol. 22, No. 3: 275–298.

Cohen, A. P. (1985) *The symbolic construction of community*. London: Tavistock.

Cohen, P. (1999) 'Through a glass darkly: Intellectuals on race', in P. Cohen (ed) *New ethnicities, old racisms*. London: Zed Books, pp. 1–17.

Collins, M. and Kay, T. (2003) *Sport and social exclusion*. London: Routledge.

Connell, R. W. (1987) *Gender and power*. Stanford: SUP.

Delaney, T. (1993) *Rugby disunion*, Keighley, self-published.

Fleming, S. (1995) *'Home and away': Sport and South Asian male youth*. Aldershot: Avebury.

Fuller, S. (2000) *The governance of science*. Milton Keynes: Open University Press.

Hinchliffe, D. (2000) *Rugby's class war*. London: LLP.

Hobsbawm, E. and Ranger, T. (eds) (1983) *The invention of tradition*. Cambridge: CUP.

Houlihan, B and White, A. (2002) *The politics of sports development: Development of sport or development through sport?*. London: Routledge.

Hylton, K., Bramham, P., Jackson D. and Nesti, M. (eds) (2001) *Sports development: Policy, process and practice*. London: Routledge.

Hylton, K. and Totten, M. (2001) 'Developing sport for all? Addressing inequality in sport'. In Hylton, K. *et al.* (eds) *Sports development: Policy, process and practice*. London: Routledge, pp. 37–65.

Johal, S. (2001) 'Playing their own game: A South Asian football experience', in I. McDonald and B. Carrington (eds) *'Race', sport and British Society*. London: Routledge, pp. 153–169.

Kelner, S. (1996) *To Jerusalem and back*. Basingstoke, Macmillan.

Long, J. and Hylton, K. (2002) 'Shades of white: An examination of whiteness in sport', *Leisure Studies* Vol. 21, No. 2: pp. 87–103.

Long, J., Robinson, P. and Welch, M. (2003) *Raising the standard*. Leeds: LMU/CRE.

Long, J. and Spracklen, K. (1996) 'Positional play: Racial stereotyping in rugby league', *The Bulletin of Physical Recreation* 32: pp. 18–22.

Long, J., Tongue, N., Spracklen, K. and Carrington, B. (1995) *What's the difference?.* Leeds: LMU/CRE/RFL/LCC.

Marks, J. (2003) *What it means to be 98% chimpanzee: Apes, people and their genes*. London: UCP.

McDonald, I. and Carrington, B. (eds) (2001) *'Race', sport and British Society*. London: Routledge.

McDonald, I. and Ugra, S. (1998) *Anyone for Cricket? Equal opportunities and changing cricket cultures in Essex and East London*. London: UEL Press.

Melling, P. and Collins, T. (eds) (2004) *The glory of their times: Crossing the colour line in rugby league*. Skipton: Vertical.

Moorhouse, G. (1989) *At the George*. Sevenoaks: Hodder and Stoughton.

Roberts, K. (2004) *The leisure industries*. Basingstoke: Palgrave Macmillan.

Spracklen, K. (1995) 'Playing the ball, or the uses of league: Class, masculinity and rugby', in G. Mc Fee, W. Murphy and G. Whannel (eds) *Leisure cultures: Values, genders, lifestyles* (LSA Publications No. 54). Eastbourne: Leisure Studies Association, pp. 105–120.

——— (1996) *Playing the ball: Constructing community and masculine identity in rugby*, unpublished PhD thesis, Leeds Metropolitan University.

——— (2001) 'Black pearls, black diamonds: exploring racial identities in rugby league', in I. McDonald and B. Carrington (eds) *'Race', sport and British Society*. London: Routledge, pp. 70–82.

——— (2003) 'Setting a standard?: Measuring progress in tackling racism and promoting social inclusion in English sport', in A. Ibbetson, B. Watson and M. Ferguson (eds) *Sport, Leisure and Social Inclusion* (LSA Publication No. 82). Eastbourne: Leisure Studies Association, pp. 41–57.

——— (2004) 'Ikram Butt', in P. Mellings and M. Collins (eds) *The glory of their times*. Skipton: Vertical, pp. 164–176.

Willis, P. (2000) *The ethnographic imagination*. Cambridge: Polity.

FOOTBALL FANDOM, WEST HAM UNITED AND THE 'COCKNEY DIASPORA': FROM WORKING-CLASS COMMUNITY TO YOUTH POST-TRIBE?

Jack Fawbert
De Montfort University, Bedford

West Ham United: a metaphor for a traditional working-class community?

Until recently, for the 'parent generation', attachments to and identification with particular football clubs were, by and large, toponymic. Moreover, fan identity was always largely dependent on the topophilic pre-dispositions of supporters in opposition to other places (Armstrong & Giulianotti eds, 2001; Bale, 1991; Bale, 2000; Brick, 2001; Clarke, 1976; Dimeo, 2001; Giulianotti, 1997; Hughson, 1997). In addition, as a consequence of the game's history, it was working-class communities in particular that football clubs traditionally represented. This ontologisation of working-class community was central for many working-class men in communicating a sense of football identity to their male progeny. 'Local pride' and 'family' have always been by far the predominant reasons given by fans in surveys asking why they support particular football clubs (www.le.ac.uk/snccfr/resources/factsheets/fs3.html).

The constituency that West Ham United 'represented' was one such community. It was the East End of London, which for outsiders:

> ...is an amorphous term that has been used by generations of historians, sociologists and welfare workers to describe the vast area that lies east of the Aldgate Pump and stretches out into rural sections of Essex. The area has held a fascination for outsiders, who have used

it as a virtual laboratory for their social theories and research. There
has been a strange combination of revulsion at the poverty and
degradation that was rife in the East End and attraction to the social
structure that allowed people to develop a sense of community and
shared enterprise that is almost unique in London. (Korr, 1986: p. 213)

But it wasn't just the poverty that defined the area. It was the archetypal
working class community (Young & Willmott, 1957; 1960); a heartland of
what Goldthorpe *et al.* (1968) called 'proletarian traditionalism'. It was the
regional specialisation of work and industry, in this case docks and ship repair
yards rooted in the industrial revolution, that formed the basis of the historical
emergence of this type of traditional working-class community. And it was
waves of poor immigrants from all over the globe coming into the biggest
docks complex the world has ever seen that drove out any remaining pockets
of affluent residents, especially in the early 20th century. It subsequently made
London a socially segregated place with, "… the whole of East London
[being]… a vast one-class quarter" (Young & Willmott, 1957). As jobs,
particularly in docks and ship repair yards, were 'passed down' from one
generation to the next, the degree of homogeneity of the area in social class
composition and reproduction was assured.

This encouraged a locale characterised by counter-hegemonic forms of
mechanical solidarity as opposed to more organic kinds of solidarity of social
life in general in modernity. This manifested itself in strong bonds of working
class solidarity and longstanding loyalties to trade unions and the Labour
Party. It was the area from which the last Communist MP, Phil Piratin was
elected. In the 1950s every single constituency in East London returned a
Labour member to Parliament and every Council was controlled by Labour.
It was the scene of many historic labour disputes. From the winning of the
eight hour day by gasworkers, the dockers' 'tanner' strike and the Bryant
and May 'matchgirls strike', all in the 1880s, to the 'battle of Wapping' against
the Murdoch empire in the late 1980s, the East End working class stood firm
in solidarity 'with their own'. Even the shiny new corporate and 'postmodern'
Wetherspoons public house in Barking Road that leads up to West Ham's
ground, where many fans gather before games, has portraits of Labour
pioneers Kier Hardie and Will Thorne hanging from its walls. As O'Neill
says:

If a history of labouring people and their struggle for fair pay and
conditions was being written the East End could provide enough

material for several volumes. In short, it was an area where close bonds were forged between people (O'Neill, 2001).

As a consequence, not only were people in the East End, "… loyal and value comradeship…" (Belton, 1998: p. 11) but also they had a keen sense of 'territoriality' and 'fierce local pride' (Clarke, 1976) rarely seen in middle class culture. The force of these social orientations had always been evident in local support for West Ham United; a support that was passed down from generation to generation. In such a habitus the club had "political overtones" (Korr, 1986: p. 213). It was an integral part of and focus for the emotional loyalty of the whole East End community. Korr goes on to say that West Ham United:

> …has touched the lives of tens of thousands of people in ways that have nothing to do with what happens on the field. The Hammers have been part of something much larger than the club, the League, or even the game of football. (Korr, 1986: p. 207)

If, as is often claimed, the football grounds of England were the Labour Party at prayer, then the Boleyn ground at Upton Park was the High Temple.

The East End was also a community where supportive working class networks and working class commitment to extended family were at their most "ideal typical" (Young & Willmott, 1957: p. 104). Social life was much less privatised; to a great extent, the community shared supervision of children and acts of generosity and a readiness to help others in need were commonplace. For example, it was commonplace for neighbours to 'take in' others who had been evicted (O'Neill, 2001). The football club was a metaphor for this notion of the East End as 'one big family'. Writing in 1981 Trevor Brooking said:

> No club in the Football League has such an affinity with its fans as West Ham. It is truly a family club and the 24,000 fans who regularly attend matches at Upton Park are part of that family. The spirit derives from a variety of factors, from the club's location in the East End of London, from its people and from its history. (Brooking, 1981: p. 48)

The notion of West Ham United as a 'family club' was indeed shaped by this culture of the East End and the club itself consciously and conspicuously tried to foster the loyalties that are involved in working class extended families (Korr, 1986; Lyall, 1989). In her ethnographic study of West Ham supporters Maye Taylor says the fans that she travelled to away fixtures with, "… appeared to be a very large extended family …" that was "… most certainly … contrary to the media portrayal of West Ham supporters…" as new folk devils (Taylor M., 1994: p. 44). The notion prevailed amongst supporters that, like relatives and the East End more generally, "West Ham are *always* [my emphasis] there for you" and if you've got no family "you can *always* [my emphasis] turn to West Ham" (testimony of fans to Williams *et al.*, 1986). As Belton so eloquently puts it:

> Fidelity is sacred in the East End. The Hammers emerged from, and are an extension of, the same… Loyalty is ingrained in the institutions and movements of the working class. Notions of 'family', the network of blood loyalty, the traditional bastion in the face of grinding need, are important around the West Ham heartlands. (Belton, 1998: p. 11)

Furthermore, the East End culture of "associations of a lifetime" where "…fathers still want their sons to carry on the family tradition…" (Young & Willmott, 1957: p. 99) in work was reflected in patterns of support for West Ham United. Former West Ham United manager John Lyall expressed what the club meant to supporters in terms of loyalty and being bound together as a part of their social identity when he said:

> The club is an institution… It gives the local people a sense of identity, and they have responded over the years with their loyalty… I can't think of another club that has established a greater rapport with the local community. (Lyall, 1989: p. 57)

These sentiments were, once again, confirmed by research undertaken by Korr (1986: p. 41) and Trevor Brooking has also expressed similar sentiments when he said:

> I remember growing up in East London and going with my dad and friends to watch my local team — West Ham — play. It was a big part of the world around me… There was a local rapport and understanding. (Brooking, 2000: pp. 24–25)

The club represented a sense of belonging characteristic of working class communities, handed down from generation to generation. West Ham United was always more than just a football club; it was a collection of traditions shared between players, supporters and management rooted in a very specific geographic and cultural setting. It was, "... a manifestation of ... collectiveness and connectiveness that we have come to call 'community'" (Belton, 1998: p. 176). The constituency of West Ham United was thus one of the "... more traditional working class footballing enclaves..." (Williams & Neatrour, 2002a: p. 5).

Farewell to the East End?

Back in the 1930s the London County Council (LCC) promised to demolish the slums of the East End within 10 years (O'Neill, 2001). In the event the Luftwaffe's V1 bombs did much of the job for them; one, symbolically, destroying part of the Boleyn Ground. In the 1950s and 1960s the government embarked on a major programme of slum clearance and resettlement of the East End's population. Very few new homes were actually built in the old East End. It was easier to build on vacant ground, on 'greenfield' sites within the expanded boundaries of the Greater London Council. Consequently, residents were firstly moved to suburbs (ironically West Ham was originally such a suburb where East Enders had moved out to in the latter half of the 19th century) such as South Ockendon and Harold Hill (the latter being the 'Greenleigh' of Young and Willmott's 1960 study). Eventually they were moved even further abroad into 'New Towns' such as Basildon and Harlow in more rural parts of Essex and Hertfordshire.

What became known locally as 'the great exodus' had begun. The old working class did not leave because they disliked the milieu. In their research Young & Willmott found the main attractions or motivations for leaving were practical ones; work, better accommodation with 'all mod cons', gardens, and a better physical environment for their children. When kin came to visit from the East End they were often persuaded to follow the example of these 'pathfinders' (Young & Willmott, 1957: p. 127). Although Young & Willmott's research was undertaken in the 1950s this policy of relocating London's 'overspill' population to suburbs and New Towns was still progressing apace until recession and consequently the anti-welfarism of Thatcherism began to bite in the late 1970s and early 1980s. This spread of the 'East End' was fuelled by policies of many local authorities as well as the London County Council to give preference to those relocating from the East End over the children of residents of the new estates.

Later on in the 1980s, as a consequence of 'privatisation' of housing by the Thatcher government, many residents bought their new Council houses, then later still sold them on and bought houses on private estates, first in places such as Stanford-Le-Hope, Corringham and Braintree and then much further afield. As a consequence of these changes, adopting a 'cockney identity' became less a matter of coming from a bounded territory and more a matter of self-definition as:

> ... nowadays the East End seems to include not only Hackney, Newham, Redbridge, Barking and Dagenham but much of urbanised Essex as well. It once seemed odd to hear broadcasters referring to Romford as East London... But claims to being from the East End now come from people as far apart as those who live in the shadow of the Tower itself and Essex cockneys right out in Southend; the result no doubt of all those families, like my own, that moved out to the new housing estates in the post-war slum clearances. (O'Neill, 2001)

Many, like O'Neill's family, were eventually able to move much further because of upward social mobility occasioned by the Butler Education Act of 1944 that gave working class children the opportunity to receive a grammar school education (Young & Willmott. 1957; O'Neill, 2001). A number of studies have found there is a symbiotic relationship between geographical and social mobility (Young & Willmott, 1957; O'Neill, 2001; Southerton, 2002). With each fuelling the other, consequent 'hyper-mobility' created a *cockney diaspora* spread far and wide across the map of Britain and beyond.

But this was true only for a minority. For many there were 'push' as well as 'pull' factors at work. At the same time as slum clearance and re-location of the East End's population was going on, capitalism was restructuring (Lash & Urry, 1987; Crow & Allan, 1994; Massey, 1994). This led to the destruction of strongly integrated communities of the East End associated with capitalism's more organised, 'Fordist' phase. The gradual 'disorganisation' of capital included the break-up of traditional industries associated with docks, engineering workshops and small craft workshops. Dock work was first moved down river to Tilbury, then 'containerisation' dispersed loading and unloading. At the same time, 'new' container ports such as Felixstowe began to take much traditional trade away from the London Docks.

'De-industrialisation', in particular the 'downsizing' of engineering workshops, was also part of restructuring capitalism that affected the East End more severely than many other areas. Production was relocated to more peripheral areas in Britain, but more especially moved overseas. The giant Ford plant at Dagenham is a good example of this 'post-Fordist' trend. In the early 1960s over 75,000 men and women were employed there (Greenslade, 1976: p. 13). Now, car production has come to an end after three-quarters of a century (*The Dagenham Post,* 16 April 2003). This "...exceptionally rapid de-industrialisation in the late 1970s and early 1980s... created a profound sense of loss..." (Urry, 1990: p. 103).

This is the case for the overwhelming majority for whom the tripartite education system had offered only confirmation of 'failure'. For these East Enders social and geographical mobility were more likely to be achieved via 'proletarian entrepreneurship" (Hobbs, 1988) than the 'credentialed' route of the middle classes. Indeed, in 2001, compared to all other Premiership clubs, West Ham United fans were in the top three in earnings but, with the exception of Ipswich Town supporters (there is no university in Suffolk), they were less likely than fans at any other Premiership club to be university qualified (Williams & Neatrour, 2002a: p. 8; Williams & Neatrour, 2002b: p. 1). As Williams and Neatrour (2002a: p. 8) comment, "at West Ham United and Charlton Athletic, especially, higher earnings for middle-aged men are, in fact, not very strongly tied to a university education...".

As capital was relocating manufacturing operations elsewhere, 'control functions' of companies were increasingly relocated to the South-East and this led to an influx of the professional-managerial class to the area (Savage & Warde, 1993; Deakin & Edwards, 1993). This was partly to do with the East End's proximity to the City. But this 'yuppification' of the area was also cemented by that 'flagship' of 18 years of Conservative 'urban regeneration' policies, the 'Docklands Development' project. The foundations of the London Docklands Scheme were laid in 1988. This development has resulted in significant numbers of new jobs going to middle class 'outsiders' (Deakin & Edwards, 1993) because the jobs required higher qualifications than were held by most people in the area (Coupland, 1992). Docklands has become a prestige location for offices, art galleries, expensive riverside apartments, yachting marinas and the like. Former working class neighbourhoods have been gentrified to become suitable addresses for executive lifestyles of the growing managerial and service class.

Though similar 'sexy', 'brochure led' developments have occurred in many other places such as Liverpool and Cardiff's Tiger Bay area, the East End Docklands scheme remains, "the largest example of this process of gentrification" in the world (Morris & Morton, 1998: p. 65). As older communities have been displaced there has been a consequent fragmentation of social class cohesion. This is reflected in many areas of social life, not least in politics where the Liberal Democrats captured and have subsequently controlled Tower Hamlets Council for the past few years.

Other poorer areas of the East End have been 'colonised' by an influx of several waves of new immigrants over the last 30 years. The more recent have come mostly from the Indian sub-continent. Bengalis have been arriving since the 1970s to be joined in the 1990s and the 2000s by Somalis and refugees from Eastern Europe, the Balkan states and Afghanistan. West Ham United's ground is situated in Newham where 59% of the population is now from minority ethnic groups.

The majority of traditionally white respondents in O'Neill's study felt that the East End was now a place where they no longer belonged (O'Neill, 2001). Antipathy to the newest arrivals has often manifested itself in support for fascist political parties and racist views as well as greater intensity of support for West Ham United. Despite their numerical superiority in the area, less than 1% of fans who attend matches at Upton Park are from minority ethnic groups. Indeed, Lash and Urry have emphasised how 'intense' communities of place can often turn out to consist of no more than a collection of "race-baiting neo-tribes" (Lash & Urry, 1994: pp. 317–8). Indeed, when travelling to away games West Ham fans have recently taken to changing the words to the sexist song "Oh, East London is wonderful…" to "Oh, East London is like Bengal…".

However, one incident recently suggests that it may not be as simple as that. The editor, contributors and readers of the popular West Ham United fanzine, *Over Land and Sea*, reacted angrily to reports of an Asian *OLAS* seller being racially abused outside the ground before a game (*Over Land and Sea*, 10 April 2004; *Over Land and Sea*, 17 April 2004). The point was made by everyone that "he is West Ham" regardless of race, ethnicity, class, sex or where he comes from. This suggests that for the younger generation a 'West Ham United' identity overrides all others and that identities and support based on long-standing familial connections to working-class communities of the East End are declining or have become defunct. It suggests the new fandom for younger supporters may be based on neo-tribal identities of a wholly different kind.

'Nouveau' fans: from working-class community to youth post-tribe?

The neo-tribe, post-tribe, postmodern tribe or pseudo-tribe or tribus, depending on who one reads (Bauman, 1992; Maffesoli, 1996; Hetherington, 1998; Bennett, 1999; Hughson, 2000), is said to have replaced identities based on attachments to long-standing familial connections and working-class communities. Despite the 'disappearance' from the East End of the old, white, working-class communities that supported West Ham United, attendances at Upton Park have increased considerably in recent years. This is despite the fortunes of the club having been more mixed than during the 1960s, 1970s and 1980s, not having won a major trophy for 24 years and currently languishing in Nationwide Division I, having been relegated from the Premier League at the end of the 2002/3 season. Yet, on average, home attendances are higher than ever. Perhaps this increased level of support is because, "... occupational identities with particular places are being displaced" (www.le.ac.uk/snccfr/resources/factsheets/fs3.html) by neo-tribal forms of support by young people not based on fixations with class, locality and long-standing familial connections.

Bauman (1992), Maffesoli (1996) and Bennett (1999) claim that as class identifications have declined, the consequent privatisation of fears amongst the younger population has resulted in a search for new communal shelters. In a more risky and uncertain world it is argued that 'rampant tribalism' has become the new way of embracing contingency; that in the post-modern world sociality is no longer based on class-bound geographical communities with historic familial connections but based on the neo-tribe or tribus (Maffesoli, 1996). For Maffesoli, the tribus is unlike the tribe in the traditional anthropological sense because it is:

> ... without the rigidity of the forms of organization with which we are familiar, it [*tribus*] refers more to a certain ambience, a state of mind, and is preferably to be expressed through lifestyles that favour appearance and form. (Maffesoli, 1996: p. 98)

More specifically, as Hetherington says:

> Michel Mafessoli has [argued]... that the decline of class and class identities has seen its replacement by different types of identifications: neo-tribes based around interests and outlooks not determined by one's class background. (Hetherington, 1998: p.7)

Unlike the gemeinschaft of modern class communities, it is argued that the puissance of the postmodern tribe is 'choice' rather than class, family and territorial ascription; that neo-tribalism is 'intentional' and based on an 'elective sociality'; that identities are 'constructed' rather than 'given'. These postmodern tribes are said to 'pick and choose' and 'mix and match' from the symbolic properties of a multitude of products and lifestyles that are available in the post-Fordist marketplace (Bauman, 1988; Beck, 1992; Giddens,

1991; Hall *et al.*, 1992; Lash & Urry, 1994: p. 316; Shields, 1992; Chaney, 1994; Willis, 1990). The neo-tribe is thus a 'do-it-yourself' culture where support for particular ideas, culture or lifestyle exists because of individual decisions. Therefore, unlike class communities based on locality and family tradition, neo-tribes tend to be more cryptic and ill-defined with membership being more 'fickle' and 'ephemeral'. The existence of a neo-tribe is thus said to be 'fluid' rather than 'fixed'; 'transient' or 'fleeting', arbitrary and unstable and always in flux and prone to dispersal. The *neo-tribe* is also said to be 'occasional' rather than dominating the whole persona of the individual.

It is argued that the nomadic character of the neo-tribe is a consequence of the polydimensionality of the lived experience of the younger generation which encourages 'choice' in contrast to the mono-cultural experiences and composition of older working-class communities. Membership of a neo-tribe is based on the puissance of carnivalesque rather than serving as an expression of working-class culture. Members of neo-tribes are said to base their affiliations on emotion and sentiment rather than rationality and that such aesthetic and expressive forms of collective identity and sociation are thus 'affectual' rather than rational. What Shields (1992) calls a 'postmodern persona' moves between a succession of 'site specific' identifications. These, "multiple identifications form a dramatic personae — a self which can no longer be simplistically theorized as unified" (Shields, 1992: p. 16). The identification is thus just one of a number of foci in which the postmodern subject can experience a selected, temporal identity before moving on to another, just as temporal, role.

A community of 'feeling' divorced from the supposedly now defunct local working-class family and community is thus said to be the new basis of shared experience for the younger generation. Indeed, most youth neo-tribes are actually imagined communities. They are said to be like Bunds or groupings based on communion rather than community. In the words of Maffesoli, they are:

> …a succession of territories in which people in a more or less ephemeral way take root, close ranks, search out shelter and security. In using the term "village", I have made clear that it is only a meta-phor. Indeed, it can of course delineate a concrete space; but this can also be a *cosa mentale*, a symbolic territory… (Maffesoli, 1996: p. 139)

In the Foreword to Maffesoli's seminal work, *The Time of the Tribes*, Shields, refers to "sports clubs", "associations of hobbyists" and "the crowd of fans at a sports match" as examples of neo-tribes (Maffesoli, 1996: p. ix). Hetherington

(1998: p. 57) uses 'sporting allegiances' as an example of 'neo-tribal lifestyles'. More specifically, Hughson (2000) uses the notion of the post-tribe to examine 'expressive fandom' between rival club supporters in Australian soccer's A-League. In such contexts, the "football post-tribe" is said to be dependent on an ongoing attraction of tribal-related activities to the extent that, "... when the attraction wanes..." as it frequently does for young people "... members leave and such tribes can die" (Armstrong, 1998: p. 306).

Commodification, gentrification and the de-localisation of football fandom

As well as what has been happening to old working-class communities, a number of developments in football itself have also undermined traditional culture. Though commercialisation of the game in general has been going on for many years (Taylor I, 1971) it has accelerated in the past decade. Commercialisation and hyper-commodification have transformed football clubs from community organisations with organic relationships with their fans to companies concerned more with balance sheets than communal representation (King, 1998). This has resulted in the establishment of a different kind of relationship with supporters; one more akin to producer-consumer relationships typical of late-capitalist societies.

The fierce opposition in the early 1990s from traditional West Ham United fans to such aspects of commercialisation is well-documented (Campbell & Shields, 1993; Taylor R, 1995). Although this opposition wasn't entirely futile, its impact was limited. One of the consequences of these changes has been that in the last decade or so football in general has been, "... shedding its working class iconography and associations at an unprecedented rate" and appears, "... poised on the brink of a definitive and stable breakthrough into middle-class markets" (Robson, 2000: p. 35). In particular, "... new fans are disproportionately recruited from the ranks of the higher classes, suggesting a gradual gentrification of football in England" (Williams & Neatrour, 2002a: p. 7). Furthermore, only 44% of new fans compared to 70% of long-time fans were born in the locality of clubs they support, suggesting that there is also, "... a gradual longer term shift in the importance of birthplace in connecting football supporters with a club" (Williams & Neatrour, 2002a: p. 9).

With regard to West Ham United, some residual enclaves of the traditional East End remain and it is this that forms much of the Hammers support, but as far back as 1981 Brooking commented that:

West Ham supporters come from all over the South-East of England. Our catchment area extends to Hertfordshire in the north-west and to Southend in the east. (Brooking, 1981: p. 54)

Brooking's anecdote was validated by research undertaken more recently. Commenting on the 1997 National Fan Survey that showed that only 21% of season ticket holders live within five miles of Upton Park (Williams *et al.*, 1997: p. 53) the authors said that:

Generally speaking, London clubs have fewest 'local' fans; as we have seen, many of the families of supporters of the major London clubs have probably long since moved out of the central area itself and now live around the motorway system which feeds the capital. This goes for traditionally "local neighbourhood" clubs such as West Ham United almost as much as it does for other, larger, London clubs. (Williams *et al.*, 1997: p. 52)

Recent evidence, when West Ham were still in the Premier League, showed that only three clubs, Tottenham Hotspur, Manchester United and Chelsea, have a lower percentage of fans who live within 10 miles of their ground and have fewer fans who live within one hour's travelling distance of the ground (Williams & Neatrour, 2002a: pp. 13–14). As the authors said:

West Ham United attracts a much stronger *regional fan core* [my emphasis] than is nationally the case... 45% of West Ham United fans take *less than one hour* [my emphasis] to travel to home matches, rather below the national average. (Williams & Neatrour, 2002b: pp. 1–2).

But as the cockney diaspora has continued to spread, West Ham United supporters locally born now live even further afield. By 1997 36% lived more than 50 miles from Upton Park (Williams *et al.*, 1997: p. 53).

Thus, on the surface at least, fandom is gradually being divorced from its traditions rooted in class affiliation (Malcolm *et al.*, 2000) and locality (Bale, 2000). New types of younger fans may be more likely to 'choose' the club they support on the basis of criteria other than propinquity and family tradition. 'Freed' from normative group attachments inherent in traditional football communities the geographically mobile football fan is increasingly able to construct his or her own identity. In such a 'culture' football can provide a focus for a wider variety of identificatory possibilities that depend on the more fluid habitus and whims more consistent with neo-tribalism.

But it is not just geographical mobility that has stretched the symbolic expression of social relations through football across space. Saturation coverage of football on television, ease of access to football products through the Internet and the arrival of a networked society have all provided a multiplicity of football styles and 'attachments'. Given declining certainties of particularistic forms of identity founded on class, gender, ethnicity and familial based local communities, postmodernists argue that it is no longer the exception but the rule that individuals have "little choice but to choose" their lifestyles and personal identities (Giddens, 1991: p. 80). Such choices result in 'neo-tribal affiliations' (Bauman, 1991) to particular football teams, rather than class, family and geographically based 'attachments'.

Uninhibited by social and geographical categories, the postmodern football fan presumably selects his or her team from a whole menu of possibilities. His or her sense of belonging results from a much more reflexive project of identification with the specific stylistic properties of teams and the puissance of continuing support. This is a supposed culture that has a 'depthless' quality to it. Rather than representing and attempting to reproduce particular class and geographical communities, it is a culture that is concerned with mere surface style and image. It is a culture in which football is 'consumed' not in terms of its use value but in terms of its semiotic capacity to appeal to an audience. Support for a particular football team thus becomes merely a matter of taste.

Supporting West Ham United: an example of a "neo-tribe"?

'Market' and 'brand' leaders such as Manchester United, Liverpool and Arsenal are bound to do well in this marketplace where attachment is based on 'elective association' rather than 'blood tradition'. Conversely, at West Ham United one would have thought that the postmodern fan is likely to be more of a rarity. Indeed, perhaps if the 'postmodern football neo-tribe' exists with regard to clubs like West Ham United it is more likely to be found amongst groups of fans furthest removed from the 'family of origin'. Because "...there is little consensus on what impact geographical mobility has on senses of belonging..." (Southerton, 2002: p. 173) to traditional working class communities, I have used the Northern Hammers group as a case study.

The main problem with the concept of the neo-tribe is that there is a dearth of empirical research to test the theories of various protagonists. The rationale for using Northern Hammers as a case study is not only because they are a mixture of 'fans' and 'supporters' (it is difficult to draw an easy distinction between the two) but they are also, "… a mixture of Londoners who have moved North and born and bred Northerners who like the West Ham *style* [my emphasis] of football" (www.hammernorth.demon.co.uk).

I am not suggesting that Northern Hammers are perfectly representative of either cockney émigrés or those with no connections to the East End working-class. But they are an organised group that get tickets for games collectively, travel to games together, socialise in pubs before games and organise other 'communal' events such as a summer picnic and 'meet the players' evenings. In other words, they have all the outward characteristics of a neo-tribe searching for some sort of 'communion', apart from the fact that they are an organised group that fans become members of.

In addition, members, certainly in a national context, are at greatest remove from the locale of West Ham United or from any central geographical location. Membership stretches from one end of the M62 to the other and from Carlisle in the North to Nottingham in the South. In many ways, by necessity, it is a *cosa mentale*. To some extent the group was used because it was convenient and provided for an easy entrèe because I was already a member. But, the sampling frame was also a convenient size (117 members) that was easily identifiable. This precluded the problem of distinguishing between 'eligibles' and 'ineligibles' — i.e. how many matches a person has to attend before he/she is described as a 'supporter of West Ham United'.

At least two-thirds of members supplied their email addresses for use by other members. With such a dispersed population this enabled contact to be maintained more easily and was a useful tool in trying to ensure a good response rate. The profile of the group was compared with profiles of the club's fans in general as well as Premier League club fans in general produced in national surveys by researchers at the Sir Norman Chester Centre for Football Research. All members of Northern Hammers receive a regular newsletter. Questionnaires were sent out with these.

The results show that support for West Ham United from this group is hardly 'ephemeral'. 85% said they had supported the club for more than 20 years with the majority having first attended a match before the age of 14. Less than 5% described themselves as 'new' or 'returned' fans compared to "around one-quarter" of all Premier League fans (Williams & Neatrour, 2002a: p. 9) and 16% of West Ham United fans in general (Williams & Neatrour, 2002b). Whilst only 34% said that they came from families who supported West Ham and only 32% had fathers who had supported the club, only 27% said that their fathers had supported other clubs. 87% of the group had never supported another club themselves.

In addition, intensity of support seems to belie the notion of 'fickleness'; over 60% said that West Ham United was either "one of the most important things in their lives" or "very important" compared to 52% of West Ham United supporters generally (Williams & Neatrour, 2002a: p. 12). Indeed, whilst their identities seem to be multi-dimensional (localities they live in, the jobs they have etc.) and "occasional", support for West Ham United seems to be the over-riding identity that consumes their lives, with all other identities regarded as secondary.

However, on the surface it appeared the group were not overly 'topo-nymically ascribed'. Only 30% said that they supported West Ham United because they originally came from the East End. Only 32% were actually born in the locality of the club, compared to 67% for all Premier League fans (Williams & Neatrour, 2002a: p. 8) and only 5% of those who had no family connection to the East End had ever lived there. Nearly half said they were attracted to supporting West Ham United because of the style of football played. However, almost half the respondents were born in the 'extended constituency' of the club of the East End, London in general and the South East and Essex. In addition, 60% of respondents had connections to the club through one or more 'traditional' routes: a father who supported West Ham; other family connections; because it was originally their local club; or because they were born or at one time lived in the locality.

It seems the case that class, gender and ethnicity have played a part in the 'identity choices' of Northern Hammers fans. The majority come from manual working-class backgrounds and 73% of them had not been to university; higher than for fans in general of all Premier League clubs (Williams & Neatrour, 2002b). Over 90% are male, a higher percentage than for Premier League fans in general (Williams & Neatrour, 2002a: p. 5) or West Ham United fans in particular (Williams & Neatrour, 2002b).

Only one of the 82 respondents described himself as coming from a minority ethnic background; not dissimilar to the national picture for Premier League football fans (Williams & Neatrour, 2002a: p. 6) and West Ham United fans in particular (Williams & Neatrour, 2002b). The latter, however, in the case of West Ham United fans, could be evidence of a 'race-baiting neo-tribe'. Also, mirroring the national picture (Williams & Neatrour, 2002a: p. 7; Williams & Neatrour, 2002b), the fact that over two-thirds have non-manual occupations suggests some degree of divorce from traditional working-class fandom associated with West Ham United supporters.

Whilst they may not overtly regard support for West Ham United as an expression of their gender, ethnicity or social class background, it is certainly true that such 'traditional' factors have ascribed their identities to a large extent. Hetherington's critique of Maffesoli is particularly apposite with regard to Northern Hammers when he says:

> The main weakness in Maffesoli, however, is that he ignores power relations, constraints and uncertainties placed on identity choices when he indicates that such factors as class, gender and ethnicity are no longer relevant in establishing styles of life… Neither class nor gender determines all that we do in our lives but they still have some hold over us. Their efforts are real enough. Equally, we do not have complete freedom of choice in terms of the tribes we can choose to join, but we do have some choice independent of issues such as class and gender. (Hetherington, 1998: pp. 53–4)

Indeed, there is 'choice' in the sense that not everyone who is white, male, working-class and comes from the East End of London will choose to express their identity through support for West Ham United. Again, as Hetherington says later, in a quote that is totally apposite to Northern Hammers members:

> All the cultural, political and religious enthusiasms that can be associated with neo-tribalism are elective in that individuals make choices as to whether they want to become involved. This does not mean, however, that one's social class, gender, ethnicity or locality are of no significance. While these structural categories do not inevitably lead to neo-tribal involvement, it can be established that involvement in particular neo-tribes is related to such factors. (Hetherington, 1998: p. 57)

One could be critical of these 'findings' as they are based on very small numbers. However, although the sampling frame of 117 was small, the return of 82 questionnaires represented a very high (68%) response rate, giving the data greater validity. But, it could be argued, even if they are representative, maybe they are only representative of a specific group of West Ham United fans who live in the North of England and who belong to an organisation that represents their interests. The essence of neo-tribalism is a 'community of feeling' outside formal groups. Perhaps 'members' of the 'West Ham United neo-tribe' are out there as an amorphous army who 'choose' not to join groups like the Northern Hammers. Nevertheless, one can draw tentative conclusions about this group that could be used as a guide to further research.

'Communion' as a means to a 'magical recovery' and 'magical discovery' of 'community'?

Whilst it is true that group identifications are now more consistent with the notion of communion than with the concrete existence of 'community', it is mistaken to believe that such 'feelings' and 'emotions' are divorced from the past of strong and ascribed attachments to family, class, gender, ethnicity and locality as the concept of the neo-tribe implicitly suggests. In a situation of increasing 'ontological insecurity' working-class youth who have been upwardly and geographically mobile, unlike the traditional middle classes, continue to display a preference for "... continuity, stability, cohesion and relatively bounded identifications" (Robson, 2000: p. 110).

Until the late 1980s sociologists had been inclined to think of 'community' as something that was passé or at least in decline because it was incompatible with increasing social and geographical mobility inherent in late modern societies. Recent studies have suggested that this stance was not just premature but was also misplaced because 'community' is not something that should necessarily be bounded by clearly recognisable geographical limits but should be defined as communion or 'shared meanings' (Cohen, 1985).

Previously, researchers tended to assume that this sense of 'community' was conditional on geographical proximity. But, 'community' can persist as, "... a group in which factors which unite people are stronger and more important than anything which may divide them" (Bauman, 1990: p. 72) even where the first sense of 'community' is absent. The 'quintessential referent of community' is, thus, not necessarily found in terms of 'territoriality' or 'local social systems' (Stacey, 1969) but is to be found in that it:

> ... exists in the minds of its members, and should not be confused with geographic or sociographic assertions of "fact". By extension, the distinctiveness of communities, and, thus, the reality of their boundaries, similarly lies in the mind, in the meanings which people attach to them, not in their structural forms... This reality of community is expressed and embellished symbolically. (Cohen, 1985: p. 98)

This notion of 'community of the mind' or the construction of symbolic rather than 'real' "... boundaries which inhere in the mind" (Cohen, 1985: p. 17) is nothing new. Tonnies (1955) himself distinguished between a *'gemeinschaft of locality'* and a *'gemeinschaft of the mind'*, the existence of the latter being borne out by research undertaken long ago with East End émigrés. When East Enders initially moved out they tried to retain a culture of 'East Endedness' (Young & Willmott, 1960). It was found that, "... in Bethnal Green, the one-time villages which have as elsewhere been physically submerged and their boundaries usually obliterated... live on in people's minds" (Young & Willmott, 1957: p. 111). As each new generation of cockney émigrés has since been dispersed further and further from their communal roots to areas of lower and lower population densities and as intra-generational geographical mobility has become more and more the norm, the yearning for a recreation of such a 'communal sociability' has become an increasingly urgent project. Unable to assert physical boundaries any more, the construction of a 'cockney identity' by use of 'symbolic boundaries' has thus become much more prevalent.

Indeed, it is precisely in contemporary conditions of existential doubt, uncertainty and 'ontological insecurity' that cockney émigrés and their offspring have turned more to the comfort of cognitive constructions of community which may have spatial dimensions but just as importantly involve metaphorical and rhetorical elements. In the contemporary world more and more relationships are held together by the use of such symbols, not necessarily because of a loosening of spatial and class 'affiliations' occasioned by the 'disorganisation' of capitalism, but more often because there is simply no alternative. In particular, the construction of a 'non-geographic' cockney community is not a question of spatial or class indifference but of what is possible and realisable in very practical terms. The wealth of examples provided by Cohen from across the globe suggests that when 'real', objective or structural boundaries of a community become impossible to retrieve people generally act in this way. They become more, not less, assertive in declaring the symbolic dimensions of their community as, "... a resource and a repository of meaning and a reference for their identity" (Cohen, 1985: p. 118).

This longing for at least a symbolic recovery of community out of the contingencies of rapid demographic and social change has long since found its expression by young people in support for football teams (Clarke, 1976; Robins & Cohen, 1978; Day, 1996: pp. 148–9; Giulianotti, 1999: p. 70). It is here that social relations are 'disembedded' from the 'real' community context and 'restructured', not across indefinite spans of space and time that Giddens (1990; 1991) suggests is increasingly the case, but in the much more 'intense', geographically bounded world of the football ground. The football ground has become the 21st century's new 'locality'; a service centre that can perform some of the social and cultural functions of the traditional geographic community for the armies of what Giulianotti (1999: p. 95) calls "rootless football fans". So, Maffesoli is right that neo-tribal affiliations are often cosa mentale. However, in this case, 'community of the mind' is a nostalgic recovery of a very real geographical community that does have a surrogate, 'concrete' (sic) home in the form of the Boleyn Ground at Upton Park in London, E13. To be fair to Maffesoli, he does say that neo-tribes can sometimes represent specific concrete spaces.

However, because in such symbolic constructions the boundaries of 'community' are artificial or imaginary, they are attempts to recreate something that goes far beyond the world of football and football clubs themselves. The breaking of geography and an 'absence' from localities does involve a 'stretching' and 'deepening' of community at one level. In particular, West Ham United is a place where cockney émigrés and their offspring have attempted to re-create social relationships and boundaries between 'us', 'the true inheritors of the East End', and 'them', 'the invaders'. It is here that attempts to strengthen resistance to change and to practically cultivate or structurate a new sense of 'ontological security' to replace that which has been destroyed as a result of post-war 'reconstruction' is at its greatest.

West Ham United has become a surrogate for a lost gemeinschaft; an attempt to transcend the rupture of ontological continuity as well as a scene for creating a heightened form of working-class sociality. It helps keep alive not only very personal senses of history but also recreates the feeling of attachment to a community. This 'recreation' is strikingly poignant for the sons, daughters, grandsons and granddaughters of émigrés who may have merely inherited an oral tradition of the area and its community self image where the East End is still regarded as the "family of origin" (Lyall, 1989: p. 57). 53% of season ticket holders at West Ham come from families with a 'tradition' of supporting the club (Williams *et al.*, 1997: p. 30). For many of these, West Ham United is the focus for this dispersed extended family and the kinship network is expressed through attachment to the club. To a great extent fans of West Ham United are an émigré community that is constantly concerned with the quest for recreating their former 'homeland'.

The fortnightly ritual of flocking to Upton Park as a 'home away from home' is like Muslims going to Mecca; a way of recapturing their lost heritage; 'United' (sic) once more. Though talking about Millwall, for Robson, "such ritual visits to symbolically charged ancestral stamping grounds resonate with the voices and atmosphere of the past" (Robson, 2000: p. 149). A similar phenomenon can be observed at Arsenal, where Hornby says:

...because their occupation... has removed them far away from where they belong or where they have come from... football seems to them a quick and painless way of getting back there. (Hornby, 1992: p. 186)

Indeed, at West Ham United, 72% of season ticket holders said that they were born within 20 miles of Upton Park, the club's ground (Williams *et al.*, 1997: p. 31). So, "the space they share... is [still] a way of magically retrieving the sense of group solidarity and identification that once went along with living in a traditional working class neighbourhood" (Robins & Cohen, 1978: p. 137). Pilgrimages to the Boleyn ground are thus still a, "magical way of expressing collective ownership" through a "magical recovery of community" (Clarke, 1976; Robins & Cohen, 1978). Émigrés are attempting to exhume a community and set of values, beliefs and lifestyle that stand in danger of oblivion. The term 'magical' was originally used ironically because a traditional working class community couldn't be recreated in any 'real' sense. It is 'magical' or, put another way, fanciful, because it is a form of self-delusion; an imagined community (Anderson, 1983: p. 7). West Ham United is an exemplar of Giulianotti's premise that:

... football supporters of the modern age belong to an 'imaginary community' of those that follow the same club. They may never encounter these fellow fans, nor even attend the club's home fixtures, yet the sense of communitarianism continues undiminished. (Giulianotti, 1999: p. 70)

But it is also imagined or fanciful in the sense that processes of interaction and narrative between the club and its supporters promote "shared memories" creating a "collective imaginary" (Bromberger, 1993: p. 118) that identifies the team and the club with an 'ideal', rather than a 'real' image of collective life. Symbolic constructions of identity and community are never exclusively individual but invariably are mechanisms of aggregation. They are always, to some degree, collective and negotiated phenomena. And, like all such collective and negotiated phenomena, imagined communities "...bring with them characteristic amnesias" (Anderson, 1983: p. 204); in this case particularly, amnesias of cultural difference and social conflict occasioned by the long history of autocratic rule at West Ham United (Korr, 1986). In particular, the 'social memory' of 'deep horizontal comradeship' may indeed appear to outsiders to have a 'folkloric' appearance, but it does assume the status of fact used to legitimate the present and provide a map to guide future social practices in the minds of supporters. It is not that such 'social memories' are without substance, but that they are distorted, one-sided accentuations of the past.

It may be that for the other 40% of Northern Hammers who have no family or residential connections to West Ham United, that their affiliation represents a search for a communal shelter in the manner of the neo-tribe. However, their 'choices' are certainly not made in a class, gender or ethnic vacuum either. Neither are such choices 'ephemeral' or 'occasional'. Support for the club and its institutions are deep and seem to dominate many aspects of their social being with a life-long commitment as strong as that of any cockney émigré. For these Hammers supporters it is a 'magical discovery of community' or rather communion that fuels their search for 'authenticity'. As with the Scandinavian Liverpool FC supporters in Nash's study (2000), they are no less contemptuous than cockney émigrés of the fickle, post-modern 'tourist' fan who they regard as 'inauthentic'.

However, it may be premature to suggest that football fan groups like Northern Hammers will never display all the characteristics of the so-called neo-tribe. The overwhelming majority of members are in the 31–50 age range and are therefore likely to be trying to preserve the culture of their youth. The question is, will the next generation of supporters prove to be more like the neo-tribe than the present 'parent' generation? These younger supporters are, in the style of the neo-tribe, probably less likely to belong to organised groups like Northern Hammers. However, the fact that 73% of West Ham United fans usually or sometimes still take their children to games (Williams & Neatrour, 2002b), suggests that the preservation of a 'cockney identity' through support for West Ham United is still important enough to take several generations to peter out, if indeed it peters out at all.

References

Anderson, B. (1983) *Imagined communities.* London: Verso.

Armstrong, G. (1998) *Football hooligans: Knowing the score.* Oxford: Berg.

Bale, J. (1991) 'Playing at home: British football and a sense of place', in J. Williams & S. Wagg (eds) *British football and social change: Getting into Europe* Leicester: Leicester University Press, pp. 130–144.

—— (2000) 'The changing face of football: stadiums and communities', in J. Garland, D. Malcolm & M. Rowe (eds) *The future of football: Challenges for the twenty-first century.* London: Frank Cass, pp. 91–101.

Bauman, Z. (1988) *Freedom.* Milton Keynes: Open University.

Bauman, Z. (1990) *Thinking sociologically.* Oxford: Blackwell.
———— (1991) *Modernity and ambivalence.* Cambridge: Polity Press.
———— (1992) *Intimations of postmodernity.* London: Routledge.
Beck, U. (1992) *Risk society: towards a new modernity.* London: Sage.
Belton, B. (1998) *The first and last Englishmen.* Derby: Breedon Books.
Bennett, A. (1999) 'Subcultures or neo-tribes? Rethinking the relationship between youth, style and musical taste', *Sociology* Vol. 33, No. 3: pp. 599–617.
Brick, C. (2001) 'Can't live with them. Can't live without them: reflections on Manchester United', in G. Armstrong & R. Giulianotti (eds) *Fear and loathing in world football.* Oxford: Berg, pp. 9–21.
Bromberger, C., Hayot A. & Mariottini J. (1993) '"Allez l'O.M., forza Juve": the passion for football in Marseille and Turin', in S. Redhead (ed) *The passion and the fashion: Football fandom in the new Europe.* London: Avebury, pp. 103–151.
Brooking, T. (1981) *Trevor Brooking: An autobiography.* London: Pelham.
———— (2000) 'United for change', *Soccer and society* Vol. 1, No. 3: pp. 24–29.
Campbell, D. & Shields, A. (1993) *Soccer city: The future of football in London.* London: Mandarin.
Chaney, D. (1994) *The cultural turn: Scene setting essays on contemporary cultural history.* London: Routledge.
Clarke, J. (1976) 'The skinheads and the magical recovery of community', in S. Hall & T. Jefferson (eds) *Resistance through rituals: Youth subcultures in post-war Britain* London: Hutchinson.
Cohen, A. (1985) *The symbolic construction of community.* Chichester: Ellis Horwood.
Coupland, A. (1992) 'Docklands: Dream or disaster', in A. Thornby (ed) *The crisis of London.* London: Routledge, pp. 149–162.
Crow, G. & Allan, G. (1994) *Community life: An introduction to local social relations.* Hemel Hempstead: Harvester Wheatsheaf.
Day, G. (1996) 'Community, locality and social identity', in M. Haralambos (ed) *Developments in sociology: An annual review* Vol. 12: pp. 131–154.
Deakin, N. & Edwards, J. (1993) *The enterprise culture and the inner city.* London: Routledge.
Dimeo, P. (2001) 'Team loyalty splits the city into two: football, ethnicity and rivalry in Calcutta', in G. Armstrong & R. Giulianotti (eds) *Fear and loathing in world football.* Oxford: Berg, pp. 105–118.
Giddens, A. (1990) *The consequences of modernity.* Cambridge: Polity Press.

———— (1991) *Modernity and self identity.* Cambridge: Polity Press.

Giulianotti, R. (1997) 'Enlightening the North: Aberdeen fanzines and local football identity', in G. Armstrong & R. Giulianotti (eds) *Entering the field: New perspectives on world football.* Oxford: Berg, pp. 211–237.

———— (1999) *Football: a sociology of the global game.* Cambridge: Polity Press.

Goldthorpe, J., Lockwood D., Bechhofer F. & Platt J. (1968) *The affluent worker.* Cambridge: Cambridge University Press.

Greenslade, R. (1976) *Goodbye to the working class.* London: Marion Boyars.

Hall, S., Held D. & McGrew T. (eds) *Modernity and its futures.* Cambridge: Polity Press.

Hetherington, K. (1998) *Expressions of identity: Space, performance, politics.* London: Sage.

Hobbs, D. (1988) *Doing the business: Entrepreneurship, the working class and detectives in the East End of London.* Oxford: Oxford University Press.

Hornby, N. (1992) *Fever pitch: The best football book ever written.* London: Victor Gollancz.

Hughson, J. (1997) 'The bad blue boys and the "magical recovery" of John Clarke', in G. Armstrong & R. Giulianotti (eds) *Entering the field: New perspectives on world football.* Oxford: Berg, pp. 239–259.

Hughson, J. (2000) 'A tale of two tribes: expressive fandom in Australian soccer's A-League', in G. Finn & R. Giulianotti (eds) *Football culture: Local contests, global visions.* London: Frank Cass, pp. 10–30.

King, A. (1998) *The end of the terraces: The transformation of English football in the 1990s.* London: Leicester University Press.

Korr, C. (1986) *West Ham United: The making of a football club.* London: Duckworth.

Lash, S. & Urry, J. (1987) *The end of organised capitalism.* London: Polity.

———— (1994) *Economies of signs and space.* London: Sage.

Lyall, J. (1989) *Just like my dreams: My life with West Ham.* London: Viking.

Maffesoli, M. (1988a) 'Jeux de masques: postmodern tribalism', *Design Issues* Vol. 4, Nos 1–2: pp. 141–151.

———— (1988b) *Les temps des tribus.* Paris: Meridiens Klincksieck.

———— (1996) *The time of the tribes.* London: Sage.

Malcolm, D., Jones I. & Waddington I. (2000) 'The people's game? Football spectatorship and demographic change', in J. Garland *et al.* (eds) *The future of football: Challenges for the twenty-first century.* London: Frank Cass, pp. 129–141.

Massey, D. (1994) *Space, class and gender.* Cambridge: Polity Press.

Morris, A. & Morton, G. (1998) *Locality, community and nation.* London: Hodder & Stoughton.

Nash, R. (2000) 'Globalised football fandom: Scandinavian Liverpool FC supporters', *Football Studies* Vol. 3, No. 2: pp. 5–23.

O'Neill, G. (2001) *My East End.* London: Penguin [Audio]. Robins, D. & Cohen, P. (1978) *Knuckle sandwich: Growing up in the working class city.* Harmondsworth: Penguin.

Robson, G. (2000) *"No one likes us, we don't care": The myth and reality of Millwall fandom.* Oxford: Berg.

Savage, M. & Warde, A. (1993) *Urban sociology, capitalism and modernity.* Basingstoke: Macmillan.

Shields, R. (ed) (1992) *Lifestyle shopping.* London: Routledge.

Southerton, D. (2002) 'Boundaries of "us" and "them": class, mobility and identification in a new town', *Sociology* Vol. 36, No.1: pp. 171–193.

Stacey, M. (1969) 'The myth of community studies', *British Journal of Sociology* Vol. 20: pp. 134–147.

Taylor, I. (1971) 'Soccer consciousness and soccer hooliganism', in S. Cohen (ed) *Images of deviance.* Harmondsworth: Penguin, pp. 134–164.

Taylor, M. (1994) 'Ethnography', in P. Banister (ed) *Qualitative methods in psychology.* Milton Keynes: Open University Press.

Taylor, R. (1995) *Kicking and screaming: Whose game is it anyway?.* London: BBC2 [VHS video].

Tonnies F. (1955) *Community and association* London: Routledge & Kegan Paul.

Urry, J. (1990) 'Urban sociology', in M. Haralambos (ed) *Developments in Sociology: An Annual Review* Vol. 6: pp. 91–104.

Williams, J., Dunning E. & Murphy P. (1986) *Hooligan.* London Weekend Television [VHS video].

Williams, J. *et al.* (1997) *FA Premier League fan surveys 1996–7: general sample report.* Leicester: Sir Norman Chester Centre for Football Research.

Williams, J. & Neatrour, S. (2002a) *The FA Premier League national fan survey 2001: summary report.* Leicester: Sir Norman Chester Centre for Football Research.

——— (2002b) *The FA Premier League national fan survey 2001: West Ham United supporters.* Leicester: Sir Norman Chester Centre for Football Research.

Willis, P. (1990) *Common culture: Symbolic work at play in the everyday cultures of the young.* Milton Keynes: Open University Press.

Young, M. & Willmott, P. (1957) *Family and kinship in East London.* Harmondsworth: Penguin.

——— (1960) *Family and class in a London suburb.* Harmondsworth: Penguin.

<www.hammernorth.demon.co.uk> accessed 15 July, 2004

<www.le.ac.uk/snccfr/resources/factsheets/fs3.html> accessed 15 July, 2004

HABITS OF A LIFETIME?
YOUTH, GENERATION AND LIFESTYLES

Peter Bramham

Leeds Metropolitan University

Introduction

This paper explores the concepts of age cohorts and youthfulness to provide an understanding of some aspects of current UK leisure lifestyles. Pearson (1983) has argued that sustained debates about young people and 'law and order' reflect tensions that exist and persist between generations. Each generation grows up in, experiences and makes sense of its own historical setting or context, shaped by distinctive economic, political, social and cultural formations. Yet each generation has periodically voiced identical fears about its young people. There is a recurring moral panic about youth that worries about their physical fitness, moral degeneration and a possible social breakdown of 'the British way of life'. Current media anxieties over childhood obesity, fast foods, eating disorders and unhealthy lifestyles are simply the latest chapter in this history of concern.

It is useful therefore to adopt some kind of historical perspective as outlined by the late Philip Abrams (1981). To understand present leisure lifestyles one needs to explore the changing collective experiences of generational cohorts and how these are expressed over a lifetime. This requires some Durkheimian analysis which focuses on the 'conscience collective', that social solidarity which crystallizes at distinctive historical episodes. Durkheim's work on deviance stresses the functions of social rules and rituals, the effervescence and celebration of shared experience and memories. Peer pressure and shared historical experience are crucial contexts

195

and resources for individuals growing up and growing old together, producing a distinctive 'spirit' for every age. Each generation inherits both material and cultural resources from the previous generation and in modernity each generation must endeavour to win some cultural space from its parents and from the past.

Hysterical sociology: moral panics, class and young people

Throughout the nineteenth and twentieth centuries, there have been recurrent waves of nostalgia breaking every thirty years or so, as older generations voice respectable concerns about the waywardness of next or new generations. Thinking about youth has historically been problem-centred and has subsequently focused on youth as a challenge for policy, demanding adequate education, management and control. Class relations were central to Pearson's overview, as middle-class media, especially newspapers, created myths about social cohesion and law and order in past communities and past times, whilst roundly denouncing working-class youth as 'hooligans'. Particular fear and despair has always centred on the urban street life of young men and their presence in gangs — especially in relation to violence, drug abuse and criminality. Girls have been defined as presenting less of a problem in relation to law and order. Troubles with girls have historically been less visible, confined to the private rather than the public sphere; for example, moral panics have related to teenage pregnancies and eating disorders.

This Marxist account of youth relations found its clearest expression in work of the Centre for Contemporary Cultural Studies at Birmingham University, under the aegis of Stuart Hall in the 1970s. A plethora of authors sought to make sense of what Bernice Martin (1981) termed the 'expressive' cultural revolution of the 1960s and the spectacular subcultural styles of mods, rockers and hippies in both the UK and USA. Brake (1980, p84) has argued that such research suggests a partial and distorted view of youth, a celebration of masculinity and one to be found primarily within the white English working class. This concentration reflects not only the biographies of male white researchers in the 1970s but the central Marxian 'problematic' of class structuration and working class resistance to middle-class cultural hegemony.

The doyen of the CCCS, Phil Cohen, (1972) argued that youth subcultural styles were not only based in material class conditions but were a reaction and response to parental cultural styles as well as dominant ideologies. Ostentatiously grounded in leisure, youth subcultures provided 'magical solutions' to the problems and contradictions of growing up in 1960s class-divided society. These solutions were class based, mediated by distinctive commodities, mass entertainment and popular culture. The precise focus of subcultural concern varied with lifestyle, sexual relations, political radicalism, drug use, deviance and criminality. Brake (1980) identified three main strands in 1960s youth culture — the bohemian, the delinquent and the political. The subsequent racialisation of inner city 'problem youth' was fully explored and theorised in Hall *et al.*'s (1978) definitive work on amplification of black street crime in *Policing the Crisis: Mugging, the state and law and order*. This ground-breaking work synthesised discourses about moral panics, labelling perspectives on deviance and demonisation, with an empirical case study of media, policing and criminal court outcomes. In the late 1970s Stuart Hall was interested in the politics of ideology, the legitimation crisis in the state and the emergence of 'authoritarian populism', which was to frame the political agenda of the New Right in the UK during the 1980s and 1990s.

Not all were convinced that class relations were central to understanding youth and the experience of adolescence. Class has been problematised further by gender divisions and not least by race and ethnic identity. Other writers developed black cultural studies and radical feminist approaches to understanding youth within the CCCS [see CCCS (1982) *The Empire Strikes Back*].

Youth studies: learning to grow up

The problems of growing up and living under capitalism were best explored by Paul Willis in *Learning to Labour* (1977) which focused on white working-class 'lads' resistance to middle-class ideology of education and schooling, encoded and symbolised by 'the lobes'. The lads shared an 'anti-school' culture that rejected schooling, exuded masculinity and a local shop floor culture of aggression, sexism, solidarity and hard physical labour power. The lobes were pro-school, were located in higher GCSE streams, valued paper qualifications, careers advice and 'girls' paper work. The 1980s saw Willis drawn into local policy implications of youth unemployment and the 'new vocationalism'. He coined the phrase 'the frozen transitions of youth' to describe the social condition of youth unemployment in Wolverhampton. For Willis, the three major institutions of industrial Britain have lost their rationale and direction — family, school and work no longer functioned. These three structures that traditionally processed the life stages of children from 0 to 5 at home, from 5–16 at school and from 16 onwards at work, had collapsed.

With declining work opportunities, particularly for young people, the escalator carrying young people to work, to an adult wage and into consumer society, had simply broken down.

In a more positive vein, Willis (1990) articulated his ideas about the changing nature of youth and youth studies in *Common Culture* that revisited issues of human agency, culture, class and consumption. Willis' concept of 'grounded aesthetics' heralded a postmodern argument and twist in that commodities were now not so much functional objects but rather were of symbolic significance. Young people creatively used commodities, as documented in his earlier book about motor bikers (Willis, 1978). Applying Wittgenstein's dictum that meaning is use, young people had diluted and subverted capitalist commodities thereby producing their own symbolic universe — a much weaker form of class 'resistance' than earlier suggested by Hall and Jefferson (1976).

This symbolic creative capacity of younger generations to win cultural space from those older than themselves was the hallmark of Dick Hebdige's (1979) analysis of punk style, although his analysis was grounded in the 1970s rather than the 1960s. Spectacular subcultures fabricated a distinctive style of their own, a form of resistance via bricolage. Mods, Rockers, Hippies, Punks, all managed to knit together specific forms of language, music, dress sense, dance and place, together to constitute a meaningful whole, a distinctive style. Translated into Anthony Cohen's (1985) cultural anthropology they had created their own imagined 'symbolic community', mapped out by symbolic boundaries with insiders and outsiders. As Barker (2000: p. 169) puts it, "punk was not simply responding to the crisis of British decline manifested in joblessness, poverty and changing moral standards, but *dramatized* it". Such ambivalence about symbolic boundaries has been developed in Hebdige's later work, *Dancing in the Light* (1988). Teenagers want to be noticed but certainly not to be recognised nor supervised by a parental generation.

My generation: the who?

One of the central themes of this paper is to explore the historical context in which generational identities are forged. The generational cohort of post war 'baby boomers' became teenagers in the growing affluence and consumerism of the UK in 1960s. In sharp contrast, their parents' formative teenage years were spent in 1930s and 1940s, in times of austerity, deprivation and poverty. So the 1940s and 1950s adult generations had the political will to lay the institutional foundations of the welfare state for their children. Their social reformist legacy was funded both by social insurance and progressive taxation policies, which resulted in the expansion of educational opportunities, pensions and health care. If the 1940s generation were Aesop's proverbial ants, the 1960s generation embraced the grasshopper lifestyle. If we stretch the metaphor horribly, we shall see later, the grasshopper 1960s parents in their turn have produced a 1980s youth generation of butterflies, who have to survive the risks of a more precarious environment.

Much ink has been spilt about the 1960s, but most writers agree that the times were not so much revolutionary as assuredly radical — the emergence of student power, shifting sexual and racial power relations and not least, media and cultural revolutions around music and consumption. For the purposes of this paper, it is useful to highlight the concept of *liminality*. The 1960s witnessed a generation of youth that challenged and redrew cultural boundaries, which pushed cultural norms, rituals and rules to their limits.

Bernice Martin (1981) has explored the concept of liminality fully, by drawing on the cultural anthropology of Mary Douglas with her key concepts of grid and structure to understand the expressive cultural revolution of the 1960s. Transgression and subversion have been recurrent themes in Rojek's work (2000) on dark and deviant leisure. The iconoclastic rock group "The Who" expressed this aggressive invasive style in their lyrics, sound, live concerts and their films and rock operas of "Tommy" and "Quadrophenia". The individual trajectories of the real lives (and deaths) of the band members (Pete Townsend, Roger Daltrey, John Entwhistle and Keith Moon) need not detain us here.

Youth in the 1960s had the collective experience of shaping and being shaped by liminal processes in affluent times. Importantly this youth cohort has carried that existential propensity with them into later life. Traditional life stages and family cycles have been undermined by subversion and challenged by rejection. The 1960s generation became rebellious parents in the mid 1970s, restless middle-aged divorcees in the 1980s/90s and atavistic born-again pensioners at the turn of the millennium. Sustained by the feminist movement, many have set about challenging marriage, childcare, sexuality and gender roles. As one consequence, the constraints of 1950s respectable working class culture have been diluted. Flexibility in work patterns has changed the sexual division of labour. Most importantly, white working class culture had to come to terms with issues around race and ethnicity, embodied in what Sivanandan (1982) terms the 'reserve army of labour'.

In stark contrast to Pete Townsend's injunction 'hope I die before I get old', the 1960s cohort refused to grow up and age gracefully into middle and old age in the manner of their parents. They have carried their rebellious edge forward, their thirst and taste for liminality, their deconstruction of stereotypes as they sought to rewrite traditional boundaries of middle age and explore longevity, becoming that oxymoron, the young old. The central argument proposed here is the importance of experiential continuities in history and in generation. This position directly contrasts with that adopted by others. For example, "Merleau-Ponty (1964) *Sense and Non-Sense* argues that at different stages of our lives we are different persons that 'accidentally' inhabit the same body. Different selves get woven together retrospectively into a 'false' biographical unity" (quoted in Featherstone, 1995: p. 60).

Grasshoppers, ants and butterflies

The 1960s generation had grown up in affluence and was restless to explore new tastes, new tourist destinations, new consumption styles and later on, new patterns of early retirement. By the 1980s this generation of 1960s baby boomers rejected the fiscal disciplines of social reformism and its growing burden of the welfare state. Politically they opted for the New Right discourse of choice and consumerism and settled for a less expensive and less intrusive residual state. If they had grown up in a world of free dental, nursing and health care, fixed-salary, inflation-proof pensions and publicly funded comprehensive education, they were not prepared to make similar collective provision for the next generation. They had further benefited as property owners from rising house prices, and according to Hutton (1995), the top 40% of the population, were wealthy from the one-off windfall of 1980s privatizations. They had both the cultural and economic capital to be interested in post modernity and engage with 'new times' as they took on the internet, mobile phones, globalised TV, fads in diet and lifestyles, along with a restlessness for make-overs, changing places, and second holiday homes in the UK or abroad.

In the world of leisure and sports studies, figuration sociology makes much of the functional interdependence and growing democratization of social and cultural networks. Divisions of class, gender and race become more egalitarian and the distance between generations become less pronounced. Rather than 'dancing in the light', 1980s teenagers find themselves dancing in the shadows of their parents.[1] Forty and fifty year olds are now buying more music albums than teenagers and it is all down to the '50-quid man'. Equally, videos seem to be a waste of money whereas DVDs are perceived as investments[2]. Stated simply, middle-aged groups now have the material and cultural capital along with the demographic weight to be leisure trendsetters and market heavyweights. Their tastes in clothes, music, holidays etc. provide an important backdrop to the choices available for young people growing up in the 2000s. Traditional icons of youthful rebellion and style are now subverted and consumed by the middle-aged...take for example, Willis' favourite, powerful motorbikes; driving one of these now carries dangerous consequences in increasing road accidents for the elderly[3]. Gender and sexual stereotypes also face scrutiny. Critics are challenging the gay media press's preoccupation with male youth or advertising's disregard for older role models in placing products[4].

There is therefore some irony that the New Right found much fault with the permissive revolution of the 'swinging 1960s'. This 'grass/shopper' approach to recreation drugs and consumption undermines serious work, so valued by past generations of parents and grandparents. The humoristic assault on tradition, the subversive interest in liminality, in progressive education, in alternative lifestyles and sexual identities, in the deconstructing of British identity, in alternatives to the institution of marriage, whilst turning a blind eye to the changing nature of communities and to spiraling rates of crime...all are now blamed on the children of the sixties. Yet in the decades of adulthood and middle age, this same (now parent) generation has also presided over the election of three Conservative governments. These governments consistently supported New Right ideas of what Hall and Jacques term 'authoritarian populism' which set its face against expansion of public expenditure and welfare rights.

This more individualized "grasshopper"-like approach, of enjoying abundance of the present (provided essentially by the ant-like endeavour of their parents), together with a marked collective reluctance to invest long term in material infrastructure for next generations, has been highlighted most by environmentalist criticisms. Green thinking (whether of light or more radical dark hue) has pointed out that grasshopper lifestyles are generationally unsustainable. Whether it is a question of mobility, lifestyle, landscape or biodiversity, things should change and change both globally and locally. Yet there is no sign that the 1960s generation are prepared to abandon their cars, holiday homes, cheap mass tourism by airplane or consumerist lifestyles.

This hyperactive 1960s generation was simply not ready to settle down into existing conventional patterns of class, gender and not least race. Post-colonial patterns of immigration provided new and different historical challenges in the 1960s from those faced earlier in the nineteenth and twentieth century. All in all, the old institutional solutions conceived by past generations — the vision of self, life course, family and community, of work and of religion simply seemed no longer appropriate. Sexual revolution in contraception challenged gender power relations and feminism raised questions about patriarchical processes in public and private spheres. The next generation in some ways became less important. They were suspended or delayed or reduced by smaller family size, as the large demographic bulge of the baby boom chronologically grew older. But socially and culturally, as we have seen, this was resisted. In some ways the 1960s cohort were reluctant parents, in the sense that they put their demands for self-expression and identity alongside the needs of their children rather than subordinating themselves into traditional roles as parents. It was not so much that the next generation of children was the future, but that they as the parent generation were reluctant to be sidelined and felt they had a crucial role to play.

This reluctance of the 1960s generation to act their chronological age is pervasive. Sainsbury's Bank research (2003) discovered that old people, the "bus pass" generation, are in denial, as marketeers describe a new generation of 'OAP youth'. Their research findings documented that 55–64 year olds feel that they are only 40, whereas those over 60 feel they have a brain age of 46. To give some examples; 350,000 pensioners went whitewater rafting last year, grannies want to dress like their grandchildren and membership rates at gyms continue to expand. [5] It is the middle aged and elderly who have accepted the message about exercise and healthy lifestyles. This ageing population has resulted in the usual policy problem of young people being overshadowed by policy concerns of the old — who will look after us in our old age? Who will pay for our pensions? Who will pay for expanding respite and long-term residential care? Such tensions impose pressure on key institutions such as the NHS. What should NHS priorities be over the next decades as generational cohorts have different interests? Should the NHS prioritise spending on pediatric research into obesity, IVF treatments or diagnostic approaches to Alzheimer's disease?

Generation X: Thatcher's children

Youth studies would benefit from paying closer attention to age cohorts and historical contexts and processes. Conflicts between generations are reworked on different material and cultural battlegrounds, orchestrated by shifts in commercial investment, labour markets and public policies. The post-war generation of 'baby boomers' grew up as teenagers protected by the welfare state of the 1950s and 1960s, enjoyed full employment in middle age and have taken retirement on relatively generous state and occupational pension schemes. Their children, and particularly their grandchildren, will not share this collective provision. Indeed, the 1960s generation of 'grasshoppers' has spawned a 1980s generation of 'butterflies'. Writers have used a variety of terms to try to capture this generational shift... Thatcher's children, the X generation, the 'cool' generation and so on. But all labels fail to capture the plight of this next generation of young people who are growing up, to use Beck's term, in a' risk society'. Awaiting them is a general distrust of politics, public policy and collective solutions of the past. The only certainty is that life is growing more uncertain and unpredictable.

Researchers working in the Institute of Popular Culture at Manchester Metropolitan University have closely documented growing trends of individualism and consumerism in the 1990s. There is a tinge of nostalgia as Steve Redhead surveys the fabrication of 1980s rave culture in contrast to the expressive authenticity of 1960s sub-cultural styles. He and many others (see Justin O'Connor and Derek Wynne, 1996) argue that authenticity in youth cultures is less possible as cultural industries have permeated youth forms and are now crucial resources in, for example, the production of garage/house music. There is also a critique from Sarah Thornton and Jim McGuigan that resistance is everywhere and what one has now are markers of distinction and taste. Sarah Thornton's work stresses the centrality of the media in construction and classifications of tastes.

The butterfly generation growing up as teenagers in the 1980s and 1990s are depressed and mentally 'stressed out' about their lives (Bunting, 2004). Experts are keen to point to a thousand reasons for children and young people to be cheerless. They are simply self indulgent, left too much to their own devices, growing up in self-organizing cellular families, eating fast foods, left in front of their own TV, with no shared family meals and an absence of clear timetables and bedtimes. It therefore should be no surprise that as teenagers they live their lives solely in the present, as short-run hedonists. Recent surveys document young Britons having the highest rates for hard drinking and unprotected underage sex (Scott, 2004). When faced with self-funding in higher education and flexible credit arrangements, why plan and save for the future? What chance of lifelong careers and property ownership? Why then worry about deteriorating state support and disappearance of final salary occupational pension schemes, when so many are being encouraged to be warehoused in university student culture, in 24hr licensed cities, where active weekend lifestyles are essentially drinking to get drunk, and with young women just as eagerly embracing ever higher rates of smoking and binge drinking.

Conclusion

Postmodern analysis implies that individuals can choose to be youthful and engage in distinctive exercise regimes and make active leisure choices. This paper has argued that it is essential to take a generational perspective emphasizing the historical, material and cultural contexts of each generation and how such spaces and identities are negotiated and constructed between different generations. Postmodern analysis celebrates diversity of individual experience and choice in relation to work, family and leisure lifestyles. Such analysis demands that traditional collective experiences of class, gender and race in the UK can be deconstructed and hence more attention must be paid to the individual. Indeed, Giddens suggests that one major feature of post modernity is we are all forced to choose, whether it be work, intimate relationships, leisure, diet or exercise regimes. However, an equally rich tradition is to be found in using historical sociology and generational continuities of time.

Table 1 provides a starting point to think about the significance of age cohorts marching through history at different speeds and at different times.

Table 1   *Age Cohorts Throughout the Twentieth Century*

				ANTS		GRASS-HOPPERS		BUTTER-FLIES			
1910	1										
1920	10	1									
1930	20	10	1								
1935	25	15	5								
1940	30	20	10	1							
1945	35	25	15	5							
1950	40	30	20	10	1						
1955	45	35	25	15	5						
1960	50	40	30	20	10	1					
1965	55	45	35	25	15	5					
1970	60	50	40	30	20	10	1				
1975	65	55	45	35	25	15	5				
1980	70	60	50	40	30	20	10	1			
1985	75	65	55	45	35	25	15	5			
1990	80	70	60	50	40	30	20	10	1		
1995	85	75	65	55	45	35	25	15	5		
2000	90	80	70	60	50	40	30	20	10	1	
2005	95	85	75	65	55	45	35	25	15	5	

However, there is one final *caveat*, that is the need to acknowledge problems of aggregation and naïve stereotyping of generational cohorts. A similar debate has recently arisen about interpreting the North–South divide when interpreting broad changes in 1991–2001 UK Census data. The New Labour government's response to claims of high regional variations is to highlight differences within regions which are claimed to be more pronounced than inter-regional difference. Indeed, there are still important resilient continuities of class, gender and racial divisions, so inter-generational and intra-generational differences must not be neglected, as both constitute grist to historical processes and outcomes.

Notes

1   Or more likely dancing on the same dance floor, as 50 year clubbers rekindle their interest in the rave and dance scene by dancing through the night fuelled by recreational drugs.

2   See British Phonographic Industry sales in 2002: 12–19 yr. olds 16.4%; 40–49 yr. olds 19.1%; and 50–59 year olds 14.3%. Soon, half of albums will be bought by people who have passed their 40th birthday. See Tim de Lisle 'Melody Maker', *The Guardian* March 1, 2004.

3   See article on 'Born Again Bikers', *The Guardian/Observer* June 28, 2004.

4   See Sandra Smith 'Is beauty youth, and youth beauty?', *The Guardian*, March 31, 2004.

5   See Julia Finch, 'Saga shunners are sold on shorts and action breaks', *The Guardian*, October 29, 2003.

References

Abrams, P. (1981) *Historical sociology*. London: Open Books.

Barker, C. (2000) *Making sense of cultural studies. Central problems and critical debates*. London: Sage.

Bramham, P. (1989) 'Youth and leisure: Backs to the future?', in Kew, F. (ed) *Leisure: into the 1990s*. Papers in Applied and Community Studies, No. 4., Bradford & Ilkley Community College.

Brake, M. (1980) *The sociology of youth culture and youth subcultures. Sex and drugs and rock 'n' roll?* London: Routledge & Kegan Paul.

Bunting, M. (2004) 'Reasons to be cheerless', *Guardian*, March 1, 2004.

Centre for Contemporary Cultural Studies (1982) *The empire strikes back. Race and racism in 1970s Britain*. London: Hutchinson.

Cohen, A. E. (1985) *The symbolic construction of community*. London: Routledge.

Cohen, P. (1972) 'Subcultural change in a working class community', in Butterworth, E. and Weir, D. (1984) *A new sociology of modern Britain*. Glasgow: Fontana.

Featherstone, M. (1995) *Undoing culture*. London: Sage.

Freysinger, V. (1999) *'Lifespan and life course perspectives on leisure',* in Jackson, E.L. and Burton, Thomas, L. (eds) *Leisure studies: Prospects for the twenty-first century*. State College, Pennsylvania: Venture.

Hall, S. and Jefferson, T. (1976) *Resistance through rituals*. London: Hutchinson.

Hall, S., Critcher, C., Jefferson, T., Clarke, J. and Roberts, B. (1978) *Policing the crisis: Mugging, the state and law and order*. London: Macmillan.

Hebdige, D. (1979) *Subculture. The meaning of style*. London: Routledge.

———(1988) *Hiding in the light*. London: Comedia.

Hutton, W. (1995) *The state we are in*. London: Jonathan Cape.

O'Connor, J. and Wynne, D. (1996) *From the margins to the centre*. London: Avery Press.

Martin, B. (1981) *A sociology of contemporary cultural change*. Oxford: Blackwell.

Pearson, G. (1983) *Hooligan. A history of respectable fears*. London: Macmillan.

Rojek, C. (2000) *Leisure and culture*. London: Routledge.

Scott, K. 'Young Britons amongst worst for hard drinking and under-aged sex', *Guardian*, June 4, 2004.

Sivanandan, A. (1982) *A different hunger: Writings on a black resistance*. London: Pluto Press.

Willis, P. (1977) *Learning to labour. Why working class kids get working class jobs*. Farborough: Saxon House.

——— (1978) *Profane culture*. London: Routledge & Kegan Paul.

——— (1990) *Common culture*. Milton Keynes, Open University Press.

Leisure Studies Association

LSA Publications

LSA

An extensive list of publications on a wide range of leisure studies topics, produced by the Leisure Studies Association since the late 1970s, is available from LSA Publications.

Some recently published volumes are detailed on the following pages, and full information may be obtained on newer and forthcoming LSA volumes from:

LSA Publications, c/o M. McFee
email: mcfee@solutions-inc.co.uk
The Chelsea School, University of Brighton
Eastbourne BN20 7SP (UK)

Among other benefits, members of the Leisure Studies Association may purchase LSA Publications at preferential rates. Please contact LSA at the above address for information regarding membership of the Association, LSA Conferences, and LSA Newsletters.

ONLINE

Complete information about LSA Publications:

www.leisure-studies-association.info/LSAWEB/Publications.html

EVALUATING SPORT AND ACTIVE LEISURE FOR YOUNG PEOPLE

LSA Publication No. 88. ISBN: 0 906337 99 2 [2005] pp. 236+xviii
eds. Kevyn Hylton, Anne Flintoff and Jonathan Long

Contents

YOUTH SPORT AND ACTIVE LEISURE: THEORY, POLICY AND PARTICIPATION

LSA Publication No. 87. ISBN: 0 906337 98 4 [2005] pp. 185 + xii
eds. Anne Flintoff, Jonathan Long and Kevyn Hylton

Contents

LEISURE, SPACE AND VISUAL CULTURE: PRACTICES AND MEANINGS

LSA Publication No. 84. ISBN: 0 906337 95 X [2004] pp. 292+xxii eds. Cara Aitchison and Helen Pussard

Contents

LEISURE, MEDIA AND VISUAL CULTURE: REPRESENTATIONS AND CONTESTATIONS

**LSA Publication No. 83. ISBN: 0 906337 94 1 [2004] pp. 282
eds. Cara Aitchison and Helen Pussard**

Contents

SPORT, LEISURE AND SOCIAL INCLUSION

**LSA Publication No. 82. ISBN: 0 906337 933 [2003] pp. 296
ed. Adrian Ibbetseon, Beccy Watson and Maggie Ferguson**

Contents

ACCESS AND INCLUSION IN LEISURE AND TOURISM

**LSA Publication No. 81. ISBN: 0 906337 92 5 [2003] pp. 288
eds. Bob Snape, Edwin Thwaites, Christine Williams**

Contents

VOLUNTEERS IN SPORT

**LSA Publication No. 80. ISBN: 0 906337 91 7 [2003] pp. 107
ed. Geoff Nichols**

Contents

LEISURE CULTURES: INVESTIGATIONS IN SPORT, MEDIA AND TECHNOLOGY

LSA Publication No. 79. ISBN: 0 906337 90 9 [2003] pp. 221 + xii eds. Scott Fleming and Ian Jones

Contents

PARTNERSHIPS IN LEISURE: SPORT, TOURISM AND MANAGEMENT

**LSA Publication No. 78. ISBN: 0 906337 89 5 [2002] pp. 245 + iv
eds. Graham Berridge and Graham McFee**

Contents

LEISURE STUDIES:
TRENDS IN THEORY AND RESEARCH

**LSA Publication No. 77. ISBN: 0 906337 88 7 [2001] pp. 198 + iv
eds. Stan Parker and Lesley Lawrence**

Contents

SPORT TOURISM: PRINCIPLES AND PRACTICE

LSA Publication No. 76. ISBN: 0 906337 87 9 [2001] pp. 174 + xii eds. Sean Gammin and Joseph Kurtzman

Contents

VOLUNTEERING IN LEISURE: MARGINAL OR INCLUSIVE?

**LSA Publication No. 75. ISBN: 0 906337 86 0 [2001] pp. 158+xi
eds. Margaret Graham and Malcolm Foley**

Contents

LEISURE CULTURES, CONSUMPTION AND COMMODIFICATION

LSA Publication No. 74. ISBN: 0 906337 85 2 [2001] pp. 158+xi
ed. John Horne

Contents

LEISURE AND SOCIAL INCLUSION:
NEW CHALLENGES FOR POLICY AND PROVISION

LSA Publication No. 73. ISBN: 0 906337 84 4 [2001] pp. 204
eds. Gayle McPherson and Malcolm Reid

Contents

JUST LEISURE:
EQUITY, SOCIAL EXCLUSION AND IDENTITY

LSA Publication No 72. ISBN: 0 906337 83 6 [2000] pp. 195+xiv
Edited by Celia Brackenridge, David Howe and Fiona Jordan

Contents

JUST LEISURE:
POLICY, ETHICS & PROFESSIONALISM

LSA Publication No 71. ISBN: 0 906337 81 X [2000] pp. 257+xiv
Edited by Celia Brackenridge, David Howe and Fiona Jordan

Contents

WOMEN'S LEISURE EXPERIENCES: AGES, STAGES AND ROLES

LSA Publication No. 70. ISBN 0 906337 80 1 [2001]
Edited by Sharon Clough and Judy White

Contents

MASCULINITIES: LEISURE CULTURES, IDENTITIES AND CONSUMPTION

LSA Publication No. 69. ISBN: 0 906337 77 1 [2000] pp. 163

Edited by John Horne and Scott Fleming

Contents

GENDER ISSUES IN WORK AND LEISURE

LSA Publication No. 68.ISBN 0 906337 78 X
Edited by Jenny Anderson and Lesley Lawrence [pp. 173]

Contents

SPORT, LEISURE IDENTITIES AND GENDERED SPACES

LSA Publication No. 67. ISBN: 0 906337 79 8 [1999] pp. 196
Edited by Sheila Scraton and Becky Watson

Contents

HER OUTDOORS: RISK, CHALLENGE AND ADVENTURE IN GENDERED OPEN SPACES

LSA Publication No. 66 [1999] ISBN: 0 906337 76 3; pp. 131
Edited by Barbara Humberstone

Contents

POLICY AND PUBLICS

LSA Publication No. 65. ISBN: 0 906337 75 5 [1999] pp. 167

Edited by Peter Bramham and Wilf Murphy

Contents

CONSUMPTION AND PARTICIPATION: LEISURE, CULTURE AND COMMERCE

LSA Publication No. 64. ISBN: 0 906337 74 7 [2000]
Edited by Garry Whannel

Contents

GENDER, SPACE AND IDENTITY:
LEISURE, CULTURE AND COMMERCE

LSA Publication No. 63. ISBN: 0 906337 73 9 [1998] pp. 191
Edited by Cara Aitchison and Fiona Jordan

Contents

THE PRODUCTION AND CONSUMPTION OF SPORT CULTURES: LEISURE, CULTURE AND COMMERCE

LSA Publication No. 62. ISBN: 0 906337 72 0 [1998] pp. 178
Edited by Udo Merkel, Gill Lines, Ian McDonald

Contents

TOURISM AND VISITOR ATTRACTIONS: LEISURE, CULTURE AND COMMERCE

LSA Publication No 61. ISBN: 0 906337 71 2 [1998] pp. 211
Edited by Neil Ravenscroft, Deborah Philips and Marion Bennett

Contents

LEISURE PLANNING IN TRANSITORY SOCIETIES

LSA Publication No. 58. ISBN: 0 906337 70 4
Edited by Mike Collins; pp 218

Contents

LEISURE, TIME AND SPACE: MEANINGS AND VALUES IN PEOPLE'S LIVES

LSA Publication No. 57. ISBN: 0 906337 68 2 [1998] pp. 198 + IV
Edited by Sheila Scraton

Contents

LEISURE, TOURISM AND ENVIRONMENT (I)
SUSTAINABILITY AND ENVIRONMENTAL POLICIES

LSA Publication No. 50 Part I; ISBN 0 906337 64 X
Edited by Malcolm Foley, David McGillivray and Gayle McPherson (1999);

Contents

LEISURE, TOURISM AND ENVIRONMENT (II) PARTICIPATION, PERCEPTIONS AND PREFERENCES

LSA Publication No. 50 (Part II) ISBN: 0 906337 69 0; pp. 177+xii
Edited by Malcolm Foley, Matt Frew and Gayle McPherson

Contents

Editors' Introduction

LEISURE: MODERNITY, POSTMODERNITY AND LIFESTYLES

LSA Publications No. 48 (LEISURE IN DIFFERENT WORLDS Volume I)
Edited by Ian Henry (1994); ISBN: 0 906337   52 6, pp. 375+

Contents